Failing Students in Higher Education

SRHE and Open University Press Imprint
General Editor: Heather Eggins

Current titles include:

Catherine Bargh et al.: *University Leadership*
Ronald Barnett: *The Idea of Higher Education*
Ronald Barnett: *The Limits of Competence*
Ronald Barnett: *Higher Education*
Ronald Barnett: *Realizing the University in an age of supercomplexity*
Tony Becher and Paul R Trowler: *Academic Tribes and Territories (second edition)*
Neville Bennett et al.: *Skills Development in Higher Education and Employment*
John Biggs: *Teaching for Quality Learning at University*
David Boud et al. (eds): *Using Experience for Learning*
David Boud and Nicky Solomon (eds): *Work-based Learning*
Etienne Bourgeois et al.: *The Adult University*
Tom Bourner et al. (eds): *New Directions in Professional Higher Education*
John Brennan et al. (eds): *What Kind of University?*
Anne Brockbank and Ian McGill: *Facilitating Reflective Learning in Higher Education*
Stephen Brookfield and Stephen Preskill: *Discussion as a Way of Teaching*
Ann Brooks and Alison Mackinnon (eds): *Gender and the Restructured University*
Sally Brown and Angela Glasner (eds): *Assessment Matters in Higher Education*
John Cowan: *On Becoming an Innovative University Teacher*
Gerard Delanty: *Challenging Knowledge*
Chris Duke: *Managing the Learning University*
Andrew Hannan and Harold Silver: *Innovating in Higher Education*
Norman Jackson and Helen Lund (eds): *Benchmarking for Higher Education*
Merle Jacob and Tomas Hellström (eds): *The Future of Knowledge Production in the Academy*
Peter Knight and Paul Trowler: *Departmental Leadership in Higher Education*
Mary Lea and Barry Stierer (eds): *Student Writing in Higher Education*
Ian McNay (ed.): *Higher Education and its Communities*
Elaine Martin: *Changing Academic Work*
Moira Peelo and Terry Wareham (eds): *Failing Students in Higher Education*
Craig Prichard: *Making Managers in Universities and Colleges*
Michael Prosser and Keith Trigwell: *Understanding Learning and Teaching*
John Richardson: *Researching Student Learning*
Stephen Rowland: *The Enquiring University Teacher*
Maggi Savin-Baden: *Problem-based Learning in Higher Education*
Peter Scott (ed.): *The Globalization of Higher Education*
Peter Scott: *The Meanings of Mass Higher Education*
Anthony Smith and Frank Webster (eds): *The Postmodern University?*
Colin Symes and John McIntyre (eds): *Working Knowledge*
Peter G. Taylor: *Making Sense of Academic Life*
Susan Toohey: *Designing Courses for Higher Education*
Paul R. Trowler (ed.): *Higher Education Policy and Institutional Change*
Melanie Walker (ed.): *Reconstructing Professionalism in University Teaching*
David Warner and David Palfreyman (eds): *The State of UK Higher Education*
Diana Woodward and Karen Ross: *Managing Equal Opportunities in Higher Education*

Failing Students in Higher Education

Edited by
Moira Peelo and
Terry Wareham

The Society for Research into Higher Education
& Open University Press

Published by SRHE and
Open University Press
Celtic Court
22 Ballmoor
Buckingham
MK18 1XW

email: enquiries@openup.co.uk
world wide web: www.openup.co.uk

and
325 Chestnut Street
Philadelphia, PA 19106, USA

First Published 2002

A catalogue record of this book is available from the British Library

ISBN 0 335 20825 8 (pb) 0 335 20826 6 (hb)

Library of Congress Cataloging-in-Publication Data

Failing students in higher education / edited by Moira Peelo & Terry Wareham.
p. cm.
Includes bibliographical references and index.
ISBN 0-335-20826-6 – ISBN 0-335-20825-8 (pbk.)
1. College dropouts. 2. School failure. I. Peelo, Moira T.
II. Wareham, Terry.

LB2333.F35 2002
78.1′685–dc21 2001036113

Typeset by Graphicraft Limited, Hong Kong
Printed in Great Britain by St Edmundsbury Press, Bury St Edmunds, Suffolk

Contents

Part 3: Working with Students

Notes on Contributors

Margo Blythman is Teaching and Learning Coordinator at the London College of Printing at the London Institute, where she has responsibility for a range of quality-enhancement initiatives. Her interests include the development of student writing, student retention and the micropolitics of policy implementation.

Shirley Brown is a student counsellor working at Lancaster University. In her 28 years with the Counselling Service, she has gained a wealth of experience and insight into a whole range of issues which arise during students' time at university.

David Cannon is a research fellow at London Business School, where his research focuses on how individuals recover and learn from setback and failure. He has spent over 15 years studying the changing attitudes and behaviours of young people in Europe and North America.

Maggie Coats is a senior lecturer in the Faculty of Education and Language Studies at the Open University, where her current work involves both curriculum and staff development. Her main concern is to ensure that in an 'open' access university, all students know how to get the learning support they need.

Roderick Floud is Provost of London Guildhall University and President of Universities UK. An economic historian, he is a graduate and postgraduate of Oxford University and has taught at University College, London, Cambridge, Birkbeck and Stanford.

Karen Hinett is Education Development Officer at the UK Centre for Legal Education. She has responsibility for research, publications and events in learning and teaching in legal education. Her specialist area is assessment, which builds on research into student learning in higher education.

Mike Ollerton works at St Martin's College, Lancaster, and specializes in Mathematics Education and Continuing Professional Development. He teaches on several programmes, including undergraduate primary Qualified Teacher Status, postgraduate secondary mathematics and Masters (Education) modules.

Susan Orr is Teaching and Learning Coordinator at the London College of Fashion at the London Institute, where her responsibilities include study support, tutorial and student retention. Her current research interests are academic literacies, retention and lecturers' conceptions of study support.

Gareth Parry is Professor of Education at the University of Sheffield and co-editor of *Higher Education Quarterly*.

Moira Peelo is Study Consultant in the Higher Education Development Centre and Research Associate in the Department of Applied Social Science at Lancaster University. Her research interests are in aspects of student learning and marginality in education, crime and health.

Colin Rogers is Head of Department and Senior Lecturer in the Department of Educational Research at Lancaster University. His main research interest is in the area of student motivation and the impact of education upon this.

Jo Tait is a lecturer in Teaching and Learning in Higher Education in the Institute of Educational Technology at the Open University. As a researcher, she is interested in the challenges of managing appropriate academic development with part-time teachers in distributed networks.

Terry Wareham is Director of the Higher Education Development Centre at Lancaster University, and is responsible for staff, educational and organizational development within the institution. Her research interests are in the area of higher education teacher development.

Lesley Wareing is Head of the Student Registry at Lancaster University, and is responsible for providing administrative support for admissions, monitoring student progress, assessment, results and reviews and appeals. She is also responsible for supporting quality management activities across the institution.

Mantz Yorke is Professor of Higher Education at Liverpool John Moores University. His work is greatly influenced by a commitment to enhancing the quality of the student experience in higher education.

1

Setting the Scene

Moira Peelo

Introduction

By the late 1990s, I had become aware of changes in my learning support work that were hard to pinpoint; a sense of unease, an awareness of meeting a few, increasingly desperate, students. Some had met significant academic failure a number of times already. Talking to colleagues – asking for advice, thoughts and suggestions for reading – opened a seam of shared concerns. Staff expressed worries about how they should respond to failing students and those withdrawing or dropping out; and they expressed anger if their professional judgements about what constitutes successful work and standards seemed to be questioned. Indeed, some felt that their right to make these judgements was being eroded by competing policies and agencies in a world of guidelines and externally-decided standards.

One outcome was that, in July 1999, we held a symposium at Lancaster University called 'Failing Students in Higher Education'. There was no view at the time that 'failure' had become a more frequent occurrence, no expectation of widespread changes in patterns of success and failure behind the organization of the symposium. Instead, there was a wish to expand understanding and knowledge. This book has grown out of these early debates and takes them forward, representing an intent to integrate and explore a range of related – but often neglected – issues. Underpinning the structure of this book is the belief that academic life and learning has to be understood holistically, with an awareness of the social and political context alongside the cognitive and affective components of intellectual activity. One aim is to link research and experience, so that we can inform practice in universities. 'Practice', in this context, encompasses the variety of professional activities found in higher education, in addition to teaching students, designing courses, engaging in research and scholarship. These can include counselling, advising, learning support (such as study skills, study counselling, language teaching and library work), as well as administration and policy making. However, we will not provide yet another set of guidelines (although some authors here do, indeed, offer guidelines and suggestions for practice), but instead will unravel the complexity which surrounds what is, paradoxically, both a mundane and a highly-charged issue.

Failing is not a popular subject. Even though failing, in some shape or form, is an everyday occurrence, it remains a subject rarely discussed. This silence occurs as much in the world of education as in the world generally, even though many educational assessment procedures are intended to discriminate, separating those students deemed unsuccessful from the rest. Such silence is, I believe, mistaken. The subject of 'failing' is integral to education – as a social, political and institutional concern, as a pedagogic issue and, of equal importance, as a powerful individual experience in the lives of both staff and students.

To use the word 'failing' seems, superficially, to be a negative approach to education. Indeed, in universities this unpopular word has overtones of the taboo, with the suspicion that using the word itself invites failure. Yet integral to all discussions of standards and access is the practice of failing students. All competitive systems have losers. The practice of teaching and examining in universities includes the activity of finding some students wanting – it is a part of the job. But the title of this book, *Failing Students*, has been chosen to be deliberately ambiguous, to allow the many layers of meaning attached to the word 'failing' to be aired. Just as important as the idea of students failing, is the need to question whether or not the system itself is doing the best for its students or is, indeed, failing the students it is trying to educate.

Failing: unravelling layers of meaning

Every year, all over the UK, academic staff assess student work. Outright student failure is rare, although it does occur; more often students struggle over a long period of time with coursework assessment. Failure in universities, whether of staff or students, is a matter of discomfort and embarrassment and yet is seen as an essential demarcator of successful work. It is an integral part of institutional structures, yet is often experienced individually and in isolation. This means that every year university teachers, support staff and students struggle to come to terms with the issues involved, redesigning failure in the light of their specific circumstances. Hence, the apparently most straightforward meaning of 'failing students' refers to students who *fail to meet acceptable academic standards*, for whatever reason. Behind this, however, can lie a history of struggle and, perhaps, a lot of staff time and attention; individual staff can share with students a sense of disappointment and regret when all strategies explored or advised do not work. Of course, there are students who feel relieved when failure liberates them from further academic endeavour.

Another meaning is the sense in which *institutions are failing students*, that is, failing to provide for students in a variety of possible ways. So, for example, student performance can raise questions about university teaching – its traditions, methods and effectiveness. Not least are questions raised about the extent to which universities have changed their practices to meet the needs of diverse student populations. There is a wider interpretation of 'failing institutions' beyond teaching matters, which questions the support offered, their role as communities and the quality of the educational experience which students undergo.

In a system of mass higher education there are real problems surrounding *how students are failed*, that is the allocation of rights and responsibilities between staff, as well as between staff and students, and the procedural pitfalls which open up when trying to administer an open and fair system. Staff do feel a sense of responsibility if students with whom they have worked eventually fail and wonder if more could have been done. As the process and criteria for success and failure are increasingly called to account, so assessment procedures need to be transparent and bear close examination. Some staff sense that their professional judgement is undermined by outside criteria, for others there is a concern that there will be pressure to maintain pass rates due to external forces, such as achieving acceptable levels of students graduating.

Failing Students in Higher Education implies *the process and experience of being a student who is failing* in the higher education system. However correctly dealt with by the system, a student who is failing in a system which is built on academic success may well experience a sense of isolation and strangeness. Similarly, few students suddenly and unexpectedly fail academically – there is usually prior warning. For many *failing is not an event but a series of hesitations*, a combination of moments of failure. For others *experiencing failure is not about external criteria, but about falling below their own, personal standards.* Externally, everything may be fine and they may well be passing their courses successfully. But internally, the pressure and striving can be enormous. If something else goes wrong in life then the fragile structures which support such students through university assignments can crumble.

Non-completion of academic courses is sometimes construed by the world in general as failure on the part of students. However, one must ask whether or not withdrawal, drop-out or failure to complete courses *is a failure of the system or a successful personal choice?* Regardless of how much the education system may regret the loss of students, failure and non-completion can be seen, psychodynamically, as an important formative experience. As a part of the lifelong journey of personal development, failure needs to be understood and accepted with meanings beyond those of immediate grades or assessment procedures. The work of university staff – counsellors, advisers and learning support workers as well as lecturers – is not always to ensure that students complete their degrees. Their work is also about providing students with the chance to make constructive use of their educational experience, including those who fail to meet internal ambitions and standards or who fall below external assessment standards or decide to withdraw from a course before graduation.

Does it matter?

In reality, those who are successful in universities depend on failing students – this is one way in which we define success and show that standards are being maintained. It could be said that, for much of the twentieth century, a set of stringent access criteria barring entry to many has been a defining feature of British universities. Waste of human resources was built into the foundations of the system. Where few get in, can we afford to lose any? Where few get in, can we afford to discard so many?

Failure is an essential part of the long tradition in which academic performance is accepted as a reflection of ability; within this perspective ability is assumed to be in limited supply. Hence, from this stance, more places will be seen to equal worsening provision and a lowering of standards. Indeed, it is a view that has been heard often: throughout the 1950s when universities 'were swelled to overflowing by returning servicemen and the first beneficiaries of the 1944 Education Act' (Hennessy 1992: 321); when new universities were built in the 1960s; when the old Colleges of Advanced Technology metamorphosed into new universities; and, more recently, as polytechnics became universities. Hollis (1997: 310), in her biography of Jennie Lee (the Minister involved in setting up the Open University for Harold Wilson) tells us that some of these assumptions were at work then, with education mandarins concerned that 'less able' students would 'dilute' the traditional universities. Rather than 'less able' students, Lord Crowther (the first Vice-Chancellor of the Open University) saw the systemic roots of much individual academic failure:

> The existing system, for all its great expansion, misses and leaves aside a great unused reservoir of human talent and potential. Men and women drop out through failures in the system, through disadvantages of their environment, through mistakes of their own judgement, through sheer bad luck.
>
> (Quoted in Wilson 1971: 862)

This tension between allowing the widest possible access to universities and the need to maintain standards has been with us for years. Doubt remains over whether we believe ability to be in boundless or limited supply – illustrated every year by the confused responses to the announcement that the percentages of pupils passing A levels with high grades has increased. Is this an educational success story or evidence that standards have fallen?

For the first half of the twentieth century, a belief in the concept of intelligence as a measurable phenomenon sat alongside a growing wish to provide educational opportunity for the brightest – both for their own benefit and for the wider economic good of the nation. Selection on the basis of testing was selection *in* as well as selection *out*. The acceptance of a threefold division of levels of ability and intelligence, subsequently embedded in a tripartite system of grammar, technical and secondary modern schooling, ran through government reports for half a century (Hadow Report 1926;

Spens 1938; Norwood 1943). 'Selection in' meant grammar school attendance, with the possibility of access to university and to graduate employment, whereas 'selection out' limited children's future education and work prospects from a relatively early age. Serious objections were levelled at the amount of 'wastage' in the competition for the available grammar school places, especially as 'class chances' of children of equal ability could be markedly affected by demographic factors, notably year of birth or place of residence (Floud and Halsey 1957).

If access to university was designed for the few and ability had been judged to be present, then non-completion was seen as an individual failing. Wastage was usually identified as problematic and the mental, physical and adjustment problems possibly affecting students were discussed (see, for example, Ryle 1969; Peelo 1977); adjustment work assumed a latent interactionist model, and completion of a degree was usually seen as a mark of success and as beneficial for individuals. Who, after all, could reasonably refuse the opportunities on offer? But while 'selection in' was seen as an egalitarian matter, offering economic and educational opportunity to the bright working-class child (usually male), it could also lead to disturbing social upheaval for some individuals as their education led to loss of family closeness (Jackson and Marsden 1966: 177–8). The embourgeoisement which could accompany selection for a better education did not suit everyone.

There have been quite different ways of conceptualizing ability in the debates surrounding pedagogy and student learning, which extend how success and failure in education may be defined. The notion of ability as something which can be developed and be influenced by education and teaching was emphasized in the second half of the twentieth century. A need to understand adult learning as something more than individual ability alone resulted in seminal research concerning students' academic work (notable examples have been the studies by Becker et al. (1968), which explored student learning in context, and the student-centred research of Marton et al. (1984, 1997)). A concern to provide the conditions in which intellectual growth in adults can be fostered has informed much learning support work and innovative approaches to teaching in higher education (see, for example, Beard and Hartley 1984; Ramsden 1992; Cowan 1998). The notion of learning as a personal, developmental journey allowing limitless potential for growth in humans links a range of thinkers. Freire ([1972] 1996: 48) saw libertarian education as potentially liberating because it recognizes 'the ontological and historical vocation of becoming more fully human'; rather than making students fit the world, a problem-posing, enquiring pedagogy encourages critical awareness. Rogers (1983: 19) described real learning as involving the whole person in 'significant, meaningful, experiential learning' in a lifetime of self-discovery, self-direction and the journey towards 'self-actualization'. Mann (2001) has taken up the theme of alienation in students' experience of higher education. By exploring seven theoretical perspectives by which estrangement might be understood, she takes us beyond the 'surface' and 'strategic' categorizations of earlier student-centred work (summarized by Entwistle 1997: 19). Mann argues that estrangement can be dissolved by providing the appropriate conditions for learning of solidarity, welcome, safety, redistribution of power and, finally, criticality. In acknowledging the humanity of her students (rather than solely their intellects), Mann is arguing for ethical education practice, embodying justice as an educational value.

However, these debates were not in the forefront of government changes which hit universities in successive waves throughout the second half of the twentieth century. Progressive expansion was interspersed with economic retrenchment and periods of attempted consolidation in recruitment. Universities now sit uncomfortably on a cusp between acting as agents of social change by adopting strategies intended to make learning available to all and acting as what Hennessy (1992: 321) has called 'a cultural bank in which the riches of the past are stored for the scholars of the present' – with teaching based on 'innate ability' models of potential. Confusions in the system reflect the seesaw of competing pressures to move towards one end or the other, according to government initiatives. The progressive massification of higher education since the early 1980s has occurred alongside an era of extensive monitoring. The introduction of guidelines, benchmarks and comparability in standards has been intended to ensure, maintain and clarify standards. Yet such initiatives itemize the numerous ways in which staff and institutions can be seen to be failing as well as succeeding. Paradoxically, government concern with competition as a way of allocating money and spurring education staff to higher standards (such as the Research Assessment Exercise) invariably produces large numbers of losers, whatever the effort expended and standards achieved. Rather than a generalized idea that we may be letting down students in what we offer, change has allowed us to specify many more ways of failing, and the potential for institutional failure is now assumed, anticipated and detailed.

In the 1980s, degree-level study moved from being viewed as a benefit to the whole country, economically and socially, to being seen solely as a commodity for private consumption and so to be bought by private consumers. Hence, it was not difficult to take the step of making students pay 'tuition fees' and to take out loans for their upkeep at university. For many years, it has been accepted that most British students did their degrees within 3 years, unlike on the mainland of Europe. This 3-year through-put (or 4 years in Scotland) has shaped our view of success and failure in higher education. We must now ask if this is a reasonable expectation – on the grounds of student finances alone. A developmental model of learning would usually include some notion of failing as an inevitable accompaniment to eventual success in mastering skills and course content. Yet how do students cope when their work is given lower marks than they would like or if, finally, they leave university with no qualification at all – especially if they have been encouraged to view themselves as customers? How do staff cope with the educational and pedagogic issues of occasional, intermittent or complete failure if students' performance is viewed as the result of teachers' incompetence in delivering a service or a commodity? If education is a commodity to be bought and paid for, then how do staff justify the design of discriminatory examinations which expect a 'normal distribution curve' in student performance? Should they not, instead, be designing teaching methods to ensure reasonable access to the curriculum for all?

Gibbs (2001) has argued that as universities accept commodification, other aspects of education are lost – if the commodity is the credential which indicates ownership, the value of the process and experience of education is lost. Gibbs comments that 'all institutional education ought to carry the moral fabric of society in a way the economic market is not designed to do' (2001: 89). In so doing, he takes us away from higher education as a matter of private good alone, back to one which is seen to be of both public and private benefit. Furthermore, the Select Committee on Education and Employment (2001a) reporting on student retention restated the view that education is for the public good – important for national prosperity and central to the 'new economy'. Insisting on 'value for money' remains an important part of the higher education debate, but the reasons for it have been shifting subtly.

Failing, therefore, has been identified over time as problematic in terms of social and economic waste, as anti-egalitarian and discriminatory. Yet, in educational terms, failing can be part of a developmental process and a means of learning. Attempts to tackle social and economic waste have led to a much expanded system of higher education. Do teaching strategies designed for large numbers of students (many of whom might formerly have been wastefully 'selected out') allow the conditions for individuals to develop intellectually, to fail occasionally and to succeed by their own criteria as well as by external standards? While 'failing' or 'failure' is a part of everyday experience in universities, it hardly seems to matter in the education literature. There have been few attempts to understand 'failing' as an ever-present phenomenon within higher education. However, there has been a long history of research into important aspects of 'wastage', particularly retention, drop-out or mapping students' progress, especially in the context of US universities. Non-completing students need not have experienced academic failure, and students who fail academically do not always leave university prematurely. Non-completion, nonetheless, is usually seen as problematic for the student and as a failing on the part of the institution.

The US tradition of exploring 'retention' and student progression has taken on an increased importance in an age of high voluntary drop-out rates and declining enrolments in many US universities. In recent years, the debate has been dominated by Tinto (1993); indeed, Braxton (2000: 7) has commented that research 'on the departure puzzle stalled in the mid-1990s because of the near-paradigmatic stature of Tinto's theory'. Braxton's own collected work is an attempt to renew the debate by allowing other possible theoretical approaches and additional empirical exploration. Tinto's model avoids stereotyping non-completing students and places faculty staff and the quality of students' education experience firmly at the centre of the debate. Tinto (1993: 81) locates the roots of departure (which is more commonly 'voluntary withdrawal', although it can also be 'academic dismissal') in the intention and commitment of students on arrival; in their post-entry experience of adjustment, difficulty, congruence and isolation; and in the external influences of obligations and finances. Tinto (1993: 4) argues that as it is student integration into an academic community which promotes student persistence, retention per se should not be the aim of college initiatives, instead concern for 'the education of students, their social and intellectual growth' should guide action which will then inevitably lead to improved retention statistics. These academic communities allow for 'the very important role classroom experience plays in the process of student persistence' (Tinto 1993: 137).

Yorke (1999b: 118–19) has commented that Tinto has little to offer with regard to students' views on their environment, problems with health and, vitally, little detailed analysis of students' experiences of teaching and learning. Yorke's recent work on behalf of the Higher Education Funding Council for England (HEFCE) on non-completion is a retrospective study which builds on students' perceptions of their experience of leaving university early. Yorke (1999b: 53) reported that in his study, for full-time and sandwich students, the factors which were seen as influential could be summarized as:

- poor quality of experience
- inability to cope with course demands
- unhappy with social environment
- wrong choice of course
- financial need
- dissatisfaction with some part of university provision.

The Select Committee (2001a) report on student retention acknowledges the changes in staff–student ratios and recruitment patterns over 20 years, yet states that there have been only slight variations in non-completion rates (varying from 13 per cent in 1982/83 to 17–19 per cent between 1991/92 and 1997/98). The report recommends that some 'portability' of sub-degree level attainment would reduce the impact of non-completion on individual lives, and that numbers of students not completing degrees should be reduced (without lowering standards or limiting access while being careful to admit students who have some chance of attaining a degree). The Secretary of State for Education is quoted as recommending that 'pressure' must be brought to 'bear down' on those institutions 'whose performance falls significantly below their benchmark'. Presumably, 'pressure' will result in penalties for those institutions most needing support in achieving appropriate numbers of student graduations.

However, focusing only on retention or through-put, important though these are, misses out the debate on the quality of the educational experience for those who 'succeed' in completing degrees, and with it the whole discussion of the place of interim or occasional failure in the process of learning – especially for those students who ultimately succeed in gaining degrees. Yorke (1999b: 98) has commented that studies of non-completers cannot be the basis for designing future policy, as 'not to include a consideration of those students who did complete their studies' would necessarily produce a strangely imbalanced picture of education. Likewise, one cannot design the system from the point of view of those who fail completely. Rather than seeing 'failing' as a category of people, in this book we consider failing as a dimension of educational experience, with multiple meanings and many facets. In a competitive education system one needs to be aware of the dimension of failing and failure in everyday activity – to question its role and its uses, its costs and its benefits – but, most of all, to recognize its daily presence.

The structure of this book

The structure of this book reflects the view that academic life and learning should be approached holistically; that the social and political context in which teaching and learning takes place has to be understood, as well as the cognitive and affective aspects of intellectual activity. Hence the book is separated into three parts:

- Part 1 Policies and Patterns
- Part 2 Teachers and Learners
- Part 3 Working with Students.

The following chapters draw variously on original research and on practice experience. Failing is defined in different ways, with each author discussing responses to, and strategies about, success and failure which reflect a range of vantage points.

'Wastage' remains a relevant, albeit unpleasant, term when examining issues of public policy and patterns of completion, because it acts as an umbrella concept that covers many sub-divisions. It traditionally includes those students who withdraw from study, but may return to complete degrees months or even years later, in other institutions and on other courses. There are some students who take time out, but return to complete the same course at the same institution. There are also those who 'drop out' of education completely and indefinitely, and there are students who fail academically. In Chapter 2, Parry tracks notions of success and failure through key 'policy moments' from the 1960s to current government interest in student retention. He brings us up to date with how the HEFCE includes retention as part of its active strategy of widening participation and 'in securing this alignment in government policy for the sector'. Yorke, in Chapter 3, examines data on non-completion to understand better academic failure. He echoes Tinto in seeing a need for institutions 'to assume a general orientation towards the academic *and* pastoral support of its students' (pp 38–40, this volume), but comments that attention is 'diverted from enhancement by the need to satisfy external demands' to show that universities are compliant with what is currently asked of them.

A part of the 'wastage' debate questions the extent of institutions' responsibility for student non-completion. Blythman and Orr argue in Chapter 4 that student failure is an institutional responsibility and view 'drop-out as an indication of institutional failure'. Within this perspective, then, retention must be the result of whole-institution activity, with learning support and teaching strategies planned as 'joined-up policy'. If Blythman and Orr show us the importance of institutional micropolitics, Floud addresses current macropolitics (in Chapter 5). He explores the extent of non-completion and reminds us that while this represents failure, 'it is failure in the midst of success'. He divides non-completion into 'avoidable and predictable failure on the one hand and unavoidable and unpredictable failure on the other'. There must, he concludes, 'be an irreducible minimum of failure'; it follows, then, that retention strategies need to be focused on avoidable non-completion, and need to be shown to be effective.

Part 2 appears, at first, to focus definitions of 'failing' more narrowly by comparison with the 'wastage' debate. But, by focusing on academic performance, the complexity of failure opens up further and reveals layers of meaning which are relevant to staff and students alike. Cannon's research shows the differing perceptions people can hold of failure, concluding that students at risk must also require varying responses from staff. In Chapter 6, he presents learning about failing as an important part of education for the whole of life and argues that while early departure from courses may not be due to academic failure, non-completers 'will at least partly see themselves as failing in some aspect of the experience'. Being a member of staff in a university does not preclude being subject to assessment, especially of one's teaching. Wareham's research draws on staff experiences as trainee lecturers in higher education and, in Chapter 7, she asks if insights drawn from this can aid teachers' practice or inform our understanding of students' experiences of failing. Coats and Tait also discuss student failure as it emerged in research with staff, this time at the Open University. Thus, in Chapter 8, the data is drawn from the words of associate lecturers concerning 'vulnerable students' and 'unexpected failure' and from regional staff on managing 'failing students'. Running through this chapter is a case study that underlines how current failure can be recognized as a 'decision point' and, in time, become success.

In Chapter 9, Rogers distinguishes between terminal and interim failure, and argues that interim failure needs to be recognized as a normal part of learning and an integral part of ultimate success. He draws on motivation theory to explain the variations between people's responses to the experience of interim failure and, hence, their capacity to learn from it and 'bounce back'. Ollerton takes the idea of learning from failure one step further, by looking at the importance of course design, teaching methods, resourcing and modes of assessment as the means by which institutions can enable student learning. In Chapter 10, he uses the example of mathematics teaching to explain ways of responding to the range of different experiences and expectations students bring to their academic work.

Part 3 explores failing from the perspectives of counselling, learning support and administration, finishing with assessment itself. It considers both the individual experience of failing and the institutional practices which both bring about and manage failure. In Chapter 11, Brown explores students' experiences of failing from a counselling perspective and discusses the links between academic performance and the emotional lives of individuals. She explores the complex relationship between personal growth and study, offering a definition of education as an activity that involves the whole person. In Chapter 12, Wareham and Wareing set the administrator's experience in the context of changing cultures in higher education from transformational to 'new managerialism', within which performativity and outcomes are valued. Chapter 13 examines the experience of struggling students from a learning support perspective. Students who struggle with individual assignments do not necessarily fail or leave their degree courses prematurely; and Peelo examines the themes of time, change and challenge, and the social context in the lives of struggling students. Finally, in Chapter 14, Hinett draws on her own research as well as the literature to argue that assessment has an affective impact and that students need to learn the difference between ego and task in order to avoid academic failure limiting future efficacy. Hinett questions how universities can achieve asssessment procedures which engage and stimulate students.

Hinett reminds us that passing judgement 'is a status activity, it is associated with authority, arbitration, the ability to referee and to be an accepted expert', all of which can be threatened by newer methods of peer- and self-review. Contradictions and stresses can arise for many university staff around failing students. Ilott and Murphy (1999) have discussed the tensions which arise as a result of being an educator and a keeper of professional values where educational qualifications confer 'fit to practice' status. In medical and allied professions especially, the educationalist has a duty to subsequent patients and clients to learn to fail students where necessary. Similar tensions are felt by other academics, caught between maintaining standards and being educators who develop ways of easing access to complex and sophisticated curricula for a range of learners – some of whom will, in the end, fail to meet assessment criteria. Wankowski has commented that research into student learning is complex because it is 'a part of the entire dynamism of life':

> The whole process is continuous, historical and hierarchical, reflective as well as ongoing, constrained as well as goaded by the experiences of the past, drawn into a flight of hope as well as overshadowed by the restraining tyranny of future commitments.
>
> (Wankowski 1991: 60)

Hence, in this text, we provide space in which to examine 'failing' in its many facets, not least as part of the dynamic process of learning. Failing in higher education is an occasional event, a state of being or a final decision. It can be a highly charged, emotional event, but it is, nonetheless, an everyday occurrence which needs to be faced with all its contradictions and paradoxes. Understanding failure better can, perhaps, lead to a more creative acceptance of the experience of failing in higher education, allowing us to learn from it and, perhaps, to fear it a little less.

Part 1

Policies and Patterns

2

A Short History of Failure

Gareth Parry

Perhaps the most remarkable thing about the problem of student wastage in the UK is the recency with which it has been recognized as a problem at all.

(Mallenson 1972: 83)

Introduction

Once considered a private and individual matter, the failure of students to complete their studies and achieve their academic goals has become a public worry for British higher education and its funding and quality agencies. Equipped with funding strategies on participation and retention, performance indicators on non-continuation, and quality assessment reports on progression and achievement, the central authorities have demonstrated a new concern for student success and course completion. The sources and conditions for this contemporary interest, along with the ways that notions of failure have been presented and interpreted in public policy since the 1960s, are the main themes of this chapter.

To help trace continuities and discontinuities, five policy moments are sketched and illustrated. The first, centred on the Robbins Report and the adoption of a binary policy for higher education, is a reminder of the different salience and significance attached to student wastage in a dual system. The second and third phases, coinciding with radical reform policies aimed at bringing increased efficiency and competition to higher education, chart the evolution of drop-out and completion as performance indicators in the shift to a mass system. In a fourth policy episode, that occasioned by the Dearing inquiry, the silences and omissions surrounding completion are highlighted and the nature of this paradox examined. Finally, as evidence of the journey made from low to high policy, the insertion of retention at the heart of current government policy is reviewed. Although the advent of mass higher education provided the principal push for national policy making in this area, the pattern of policy activity over the whole of this period has been neither straightforward nor consistent.

Robbins and the binary function

Set up at a time when many believed that substantial expansion of higher education could not take place without significant erosion of academic standards, it was to be expected that the Robbins inquiry of 1961–63 would investigate course completion with the same thoroughness as other aspects of higher education. For 'reasons of conformity', the inquiry chose to adopt the term 'wastage', but not before signalling some misleading implications carried by the word: 'It is a comprehensive term, and must not be thought to imply that all who leave without success have derived no profit from the course' (Committee on Higher Education 1963, Appendix Two, Part IV: 125).

At this time, there were only about 300,000 students in British higher education, with just over one-third enrolled in the universities, nearly all full-time and with over 80 per cent holding at least three GCE A level passes in England and Wales (with an average wastage rate of 14 per cent). The wastage rate was lowest (at about 7 per cent) in the teacher training colleges, where another 55,000 students were enrolled on full-time courses of 2 years duration. On these courses, where the minimum demanded for entry was five GCE O level passes, some 60 per cent possessed at least one A level pass and over one-third had two passes or more. In further education, where the tradition hitherto had been that any young person could be admitted with the relevant minimum qualifications, wastage rates were – unsurprisingly – the highest of any sector. Among full-time students working for the Diploma in Technology the wastage rate was 37 per cent and among home students reading for external degrees the wastage rate was about 55 per cent. Even so, across all advanced further education courses, virtually all students had one or more passes at A level or its equivalent. In respect of first degree education, this was indeed a small and a highly selective system.

On the basis of this evidence, taken from surveys carried out by the University Grants Committee (UGC) and the Ministry of Education and from official statistics, Robbins drew different conclusions for each sector of higher education. For the universities, the inquiry was struck by the different attrition rates between different universities and between different faculties in the same university. Furthermore, wastage rates had remained nearly constant in faculties where entrance standards were known to have risen, suggesting that it was customary in some faculties to fail a regular percentage of students. In condemning this practice in one recommendation, the inquiry recommended in another that university departments keep their wastage rates 'under review'.

However, it was the view taken about wastage in the institutions of further education which, in retrospect, was to acquire some potency, given the subsequent creation of a binary system of higher education and the future roles assigned to local authority institutions. Robbins saw 'special merit' in the less stringent admission requirements applied in further education and argued forcefully that this tradition be 'preserved'. The higher wastage rates found in this sector therefore needed to be interpreted 'in a rather different light' and, in respect of full-time students, were not entirely comparable with those of the universities – they did not take into account success in other courses to which students in further education might transfer if they found their courses too exacting, and they masked considerable variations both between the institutions in a group much less homogeneous than the universities and between categories of students within institutions. In summary, the inquiry saw no reason why the present rates of failure and wastage should continue. As more experience was gained and academic standards among entrants rose, and with the introduction of pass as well as honours degree courses, the sure prospect was of steady improvement. Accordingly, the inquiry recommended that within further education a wider range of courses be introduced at degree level and that more attention be given to 'teaching methods'.

If not always explicit in the declared objectives of the binary policy (Ministry of Education 1966), the access and second-chance traditions of non-university education, including its function as an 'alternative route', were to feature importantly, if unevenly, in the history of the newly created polytechnics and other local authority colleges. As Robbins had understood and affirmed:

> . . . in other colleges whose doors remain open to all with the minimum requirements for any particular course, as we think they should, more wastage than among the highly selected students in universities is almost certain to occur, and should be accepted without disquiet.
>
> (Committee on Higher Education 1963: 193)

Arguably, one of the main reasons why, in the post-Robbins era, only occasional policy interest was shown in wastage was the often unspoken assumption that attrition and failure rates in non-university institutions were likely to be higher overall; but not markedly so and with an expectation that rates would begin to converge with those in the universities. In the local authority sector, Her Majesty's Inspectorate (HMI) inspected by right all aspects of the work of the polytechnics and colleges. Their reports on individual departments and the results of sector-wide subject surveys provided statistics and commentary on the success rates achieved by students, frequently linking these to entry standards and sometimes touching on wider debates about the predictive value of traditional qualifications. For example, the Department of Education and Science (1983) reported on a 4-year survey of a hundred degree courses, praising the sector for courses which developed the practical skills which employers required, but criticizing the teaching which had been found to be over-formal and unexciting. On rates of completion it stated:

> A combination of insufficiently developed selection procedures, together with the admission of students to undergraduate courses with distinctly

> modest (and occasionally less than relevant) academic qualifications, gives rise to an uneven pattern of students successfully completing the course for which they originally enrolled. Transfer from particular degree courses to HND courses does mean, however, that the numbers of students who leave public sector higher education without a qualification are small.
>
> (Department of Education and Science 1983: 7–8)

It continued:

> It is not necessary to enter the debate concerning the predictive value of A level grades in order to feel occasional doubts as to the validity of the present practice on some courses for all students – even those with A level grades of D or E – to embark on an honours course.
>
> (Department of Education and Science 1983: 8)

The tacit assumption that there was or should be a relationship ('correlation') between entry and exit performance was another reason for the intermittent policy interest in wastage, especially when inspectors were able to report authoritatively on a broad range of provision and communicate their advice directly to central government. Like the binary system, the Open University was perhaps another creation accommodating concerns, latent or otherwise, about levels and patterns of completion in an expanded system. As a self-contained enterprise, semi-detached from the rest of higher education and with a part-time and open-access mission, it was able to justify rates of enrolment, re-enrolment and attrition which were unlikely to be tolerated in other settings.

Interestingly, the one exception to this low level of policy interest was an inquiry into student progress conducted by the UGC (1968), which took the bold step of publishing success rates separately for each institution. This concerted attempt to establish the extent of student success and failure in degree courses was explained, somewhat briefly, in terms of the 'substantial investment of resources involved' and a proper appreciation of the 'distress' caused to young people. The survey showed much the same general pattern of student progress, both overall and by subject group, as had the surveys conducted for the Robbins inquiry. The UGC intended to repeat these surveys on a regular basis, yet it was to be another 30 years before completion rates for named universities were published again. How far this indicated an unwillingness on the part of institutions to expose themselves again to scrutiny was 'hard for an outsider to determine' (Fulton 1977).

Efficiency and the rise of performance indicators

During the 1980s and into the 1990s, as a result of radical reform measures introduced by successive Conservative governments, institutions came under increasing pressure to improve efficiency and demonstrate the effectiveness of their provision – in enrolling and graduating larger numbers of students; in teaching and supporting their learning at lower unit costs; and in maintaining and enhancing the quality of their courses. Among a number of the indicators advocated to assess performance and productivity were rates of undergraduate completion, especially when used in conjunction with other indicators such as entry qualifications.

Although technical problems limited the widespread use of wastage rates as an efficiency indicator, much of their importance lay in highlighting the difficulties and dangers of linking such indicators with the objectives of higher education (Cave, Hanney and Kogan 1991). This was well illustrated when a policy of retrenchment and restricted access pursued during most of the 1980s was suddenly reversed, triggering an explosive expansion of student numbers, before being abruptly halted in the middle of the 1990s under a policy of 'consolidation'. Within each of these phases, relationships of access and quality were the subject of vigorous debate, with traditional assumptions about entry and exit performance, and customary meanings of success and failure, being challenged by new student populations and new curriculum structures.

Elected into office with a mandate to curb government spending and exact better value for money from public services, one of the first acts of the Conservative government was to cut the grant to the universities, leading them to reduce the number of places they offered. This enabled the polytechnics to recruit many of the students denied entry to university courses and encouraged them to expand their numbers steadily, albeit at a lower unit of resource. In these circumstances, attempts by some of the polytechnics to stimulate demand and target recruitment from 'non-standard' students were viewed with less than approval, especially if too many mature students, with or without formal entry qualifications, were accepted onto degree courses:

> . . . institutions should not accept too high a proportion of mature students and/or students lacking the normal minimum entry qualifications for degree courses which are not specifically designed for them. Such students can be very able, but often lack the technical skills for studying needed for effective study at degree level. Different approaches are needed for different types of student. If too high a proportion of students is accepted for courses not designed for them, they may founder and staff may be tempted to lower standards.
>
> (Committee of Enquiry into the Academic Validation of Degree Courses in Public Sector Higher Education 1985: 71)

Unless institutions adopted suitable procedures for assessing and selecting applicants not holding the minimum qualifications normally required for entry, teachers would be:

> . . . presented with the difficult choice of failing a high proportion of their students outright or, even more damagingly in the long term,

> lowering the standard required of them and thereby eventually causing unjustified doubt to be cast on the quality of all degrees obtained at the institution.
>
> (Committee of Enquiry into the Academic Validation of Degree Courses in Public Sector Higher Education 1985: 71)

Anxieties about the pursuit of open entry policies were not sufficient, however, to prevent the government from accepting 'ability to benefit' as a principle for determining access to higher education. Nor were worries about drop-out or failure a major reason for the preliminary work it had conducted on rates of non-completion in the universities. Revealingly, the government was only moved to note that, because most wastage occurred in the first year of study, the expenditure implications were therefore limited (Department of Education and Science 1985).

All the same, in the 1987 White Paper, support was given for the use of non-completion rates as an indicator of the quality of teaching. Non-completion rates, the numbers and class distribution of degrees, and the first destination of graduates were some of the 'essential data' on performance which each institution was expected to publish so that its record could be evaluated 'by the funding agencies, governing bodies, students and employers' (Department of Education and Science 1987).

Following publication of the Jarratt Report (Committee of Vice-Chancellors and Principals 1985), the Committee of Vice-Chancellors and Principals and the UGC had established a Joint Working Group to outline a set of possible performance indicators for the sector. Rather than adopting a conventional measure of wastage and drop-out, in 1988 the Joint Working Group introduced an indicator of undergraduate success based on the time spent by students in acquiring a degree. At the postgraduate level, where submission rates had been used for many years by the research councils to determine the allocation of studentships, the Working Group proposed an equivalent measure for doctorates and other research degrees. Outside the universities, where public sector establishments had experience of the forms of evaluation employed by HMI and the Council for National Academic Awards, the new planning and funding body for this sector was asked to take the lead in promoting performance indicators in the institutions it funded.

If economy, efficiency and accountability were the overriding concerns of government, fundamental questions about educational purposes and processes were not easily displaced. The development of new entry routes into higher education, mainly but not exclusively in association with the polytechnics and colleges, revived arguments about the preparative and predictive value of A level grades and, more generally, about the selection, formation and development of students in higher education. These found an expression in discussions of the 'value added' achieved by students in undergraduate education, based on a comparison of entry qualifications and degree performance. In the attempt to define entry and exit measures for this purpose, and in the testing of different approaches to the calculation of value added, non-completion proved to be a problematic concept, both in itself (Barnett 1988) and in combination with degree classifications (Council for National Academic Awards and the Polytechnics and Colleges Funding Council 1990).

Expansion and the return of standards

In the event, many of these exercises were overtaken by a spectacular period of expansion, largely unplanned and seriously under-funded, which culminated in the abolition of the binary line, the construction of a formidable machinery for external quality assurance, and a financial crisis which occasioned a national inquiry into higher education, the first since Robbins. Not only were many more students of different ages and backgrounds enrolled in higher education, but in many institutions the modularization of the curriculum had brought about a significant shift in the way learning was experienced, managed and assessed. Numbers had increased much faster than projected in the 1987 White Paper and, after 8 years of market-led growth, the government brought an end to expansion in 1994 and imposed a policy of consolidation on what had become, in scale if not in its values, a mass system of higher education. By this point, the total number of higher education students in the UK had reached 1.7 million, the full-time participation rate for young people had doubled to approximately 30 per cent, and a majority of those studying for an undergraduate qualification were of mature age.

Consolidation was largely a consequence of mounting financial pressures but, around the same time, ministers also began to voice worries about academic standards, in particular whether degree standards were slipping. In its 1991 White Paper, the government had praised the polytechnics and colleges for leading the 'efficient expansion' which had followed their removal from local authority control and was satisfied that the quality of their education was being 'maintained and enhanced' (Department of Education and Science 1991). With no such equivalent body as HMI to report on the quality of teaching in the universities, and with demand and competition expected to increase following abolition of the binary line, the government introduced new regulatory arrangements for quality assurance in higher education – an apparatus unrivalled in the intensity of its monitoring and reporting of quality in higher education.

The quality audit of all institutions, together with support for the enhancement of quality, were made the responsibility of the Higher Education Quality Council (HEQC) and it was to this body that the government turned for advice on how broad comparability of standards might be achieved in a diverse system. In response, the HEQC, through its graduate standards programme, recommended increased clarity and explicitness in identifying the outcomes of programmes, the nature of awards, the conduct of assessment and the approach to threshold standards. These and other proposals were later taken up by the national inquiry into higher education and passed to a new organization, the Quality Assurance Agency for Higher Education, for implementation.

The quality assessment of teaching and learning became the responsibility of the funding councils, along with a brief to develop performance indicators ('including quantifiable outcomes') and monitor access policies ('and responses to changing student profiles') (DES 1991: 30). Part of the evidence to be made available by institutions for assessment in a particular subject was data on wastage and completion. Despite attention to this dimension, and after 3 years of quality assessment, the HEFCE could only refer to 'anecdotal evidence' in suggesting that, after the expansion of the early 1990s, an increasing number of undergraduates were not completing their courses (Higher Education Funding Council for England 1997). The funding council thought that there were three main factors responsible for this increase:

- greater financial hardship for students (especially following the introduction of top-up loans in 1991);
- a more diverse student population with different requirements of higher education; and
- 'reduced institutional support for students'.

These features had figured large in a study funded by the former Employment Department which looked at the attendance and withdrawal patterns of mature students in both further and higher education (McGivney 1996). Apart from confirming the 'chronic' lack of reliable data on the extent and nature of student withdrawals, the research emphasized the need for greater convergence between the different sectors in their definition of terms and their presentation of data. Similar issues had been encountered by the funding councils themselves when reviewing the role of further education in higher education and the patterns of participation and progression involved in cross-sector collaborative schemes. They re-emerged with the recent decision to locate a significant proportion of future expansion in sub-degree education provided by further education colleges. However, there were other findings which pointed to 'complacency' in the way that institutions were dealing with high levels of withdrawal on some of their courses:

> The evidence as a whole suggests that, although there are wide variations between institutions, non-completion rates in both further and higher education are increasing and are particularly high in some subject areas. However, *perceptions* of non-completion vary: some perceive them as unacceptable and others as reasonable. There is evidence, for example, of some complacency, especially in higher education, based on the belief that the reasons for withdrawal are often beyond the control of the institution.
>
> (McGivney 1996: 168, original emphasis)

Against a background of increased use of outcome-related funding in post-compulsory education and training, and an Audit Commission report (1993) critical of poor data collection on course completion in further education, the funding council (HEFCE) commissioned research in 1996 to provide 'more robust evidence' on the extent, nature and causes of undergraduate non-completion in England. Unlike the work on graduate standards, this research did not feature in the deliberations of the national inquiry, but was used by the HEFCE to inform the development of performance indicators on non-completion and has since received a wider circulation (Yorke 1999b).

Dearing and the learning society

In contrast to the dearth of data available to the Robbins review, the task facing the Dearing inquiry of 1996–97 (National Committee of Inquiry into Higher Education 1997a) was the analysis of a whole range of information relating to the participation and performance of students, including their rates and patterns of graduation. While the issue of funding and student support was always expected to be a major preoccupation, the brief discussion and cursory treatment of drop-out was surprising, especially in view of the high priority given in the inquiry report to the improvement of learning and teaching. Drawing on recent data from the Organization of Economic Co-operation and Development, the inquiry was reassured that completion rates remained high, contributing to 'one of the highest first degree graduation rates in the world' (NCIHE 1997a: 25). At the same time, estimates from the Department for Education and Employment suggested that, for the pre-1992 universities and the post-1992 universities in England, drop-out rates for full-time first degree students had not changed significantly from 1984/85 to 1994/95, with the level increasing from 15 per cent in the mid-1980s to between 17 and 18 per cent at the beginning of consolidation.

There were a number of reasons for this relative neglect. The committee pointed to the technical difficulties surrounding the measurement of non-completion rates, namely that only in recent years had statistical records sought to track individual students through the higher education system and, even with this capacity, the task would become increasingly difficult if more students adopted flexible patterns of study over a long period. The value of a good database to comprehend the initial and lifelong learning of young people and adults was the subject of a specific recommendation for further work on the use of a unique student record number. The introduction of 'progress files' to record student achievement and the development of 'programme specifications' to identify potential stopping-off points and intended learning outcomes were the nearest the inquiry came to making specific proposals on student progression and course completion.

A more understandable reason for this brevity was the large remit and short timescale given to the inquiry, which meant that some areas of investigation received considerably less scrutiny than others. In justification, it was noted that the pattern of participation was 'not a dominant theme' (NCIHE 1997a: 23) in the evidence and that many submissions 'identified the high completion rates in UK higher education as a strength' (NCIHE 1997a: 26). A number of submissions were concerned, however, that inadequate funding threatened these rates – it might have reduced the academic support and guidance provided, and forced full-time students to spend too much time in paid employment. Such pressures might harm the efficiency and quality of higher education, but these were matters of funding and student support, the area in which the inquiry chose to invest most of its effort.

Part of the explanation might also lie in the work already put in hand by the HEFCE, although this had not prevented the inquiry from joining forces with other funding council projects in order to extend the evidence base for its work (Parry 1999). Unlike the studies it jointly funded on the comparative cost structures of higher education institutions, the results of the research it commissioned on non-completion were to arrive too late to influence the thinking of the inquiry (Higher Education Funding Council for England 1997).

As a result, many of the key recommendations with major implications for retention and completion – on resuming growth, widening participation, supporting lifelong learning, assuring standards and charging students – were unable to be informed by research and evidence beyond that offered by a narrow range of statistical indicators. These were the standard measures and headline rates published annually by the government, which were based on full-time courses leading to the first degree, calculated as a weighted sum of the separate figures for the pre-1992 universities in the UK and the former polytechnics in England, and approximated for the latter because of 'significant limitations in the underlying data' (Department for Education and Employment and Office for Standards in Education 1997). It was not just that these measures reflected assumptions associated with an earlier age of higher education, but that their averaged and combined numbers made them a blunt instrument for understanding changing patterns of participation, progression and completion under mass conditions.

A recent commentary on the Dearing proposals (Watson and Taylor 1998: 37) signalled some caution about evidence based on 'crude cohort analyses' and regretted the absence of equivalent information about the progress of part-time students, where non-completion was 'certain to be significantly higher', measurement was particularly complex and 'very large numbers' were studying in discrete modules or courses rather than award-bearing programmes. 'Such studies as there are', on the other hand, confirmed how 'remarkably efficient' the British system had been in turning students into graduates and how, in their view, drop-out had 'worsened marginally if at all' during the years of rapid expansion. Even so, given the central role assigned to higher education in the creation of a learning society, the Dearing Report devoted considerably less attention to short-cycle and part-time study than might have been expected, including what little evidence was available on completion and non-completion in these modes (see, for example, Bourner et al. 1991; Smith and Saunders 1991; Tight 1991; Further Education Funding Council 1996).

Although there were no specific recommendations on wastage, a concern to maintain high completion rates was an important dimension in debates about student support and graduate contributions, with principles of equity as well as issues of quality and efficiency guiding a decision in favour of retaining the maintenance grant but requiring a private contribution to tuition fees backed by an income-contingent loan. In reviewing the evidence on student hardship, the committee acknowledged that, in some cases, financial worries were the sole or a major factor in students abandoning their studies. Yet it 'is always difficult to establish the real reasons for drop-out, and we note that there has been no significant rise in the overall drop-out rate in recent years' (NCIHE 1997a: 278).

In another core recommendation by the inquiry, that future growth should be concentrated initially on sub-degree higher education, one of the variety of reasons given for expanding the system at this level was the international evidence suggesting that mass higher education systems needed to be accompanied by intermediate qualifications to 'help reduce drop-out' (NCIHE 1997a: 100). Here, as elsewhere in the Report, statements about retention invited interrogation and analysis in depth, not least in support of those proposals which sought to encourage and enable all students 'to achieve beyond their expectations' (NCIHE 1997a: 7).

Retention and the widening of participation

By rejecting the funding option proposed by the National Committee of Inquiry into Higher Education, but endorsing each of its other main recommendations, the newly elected Labour government was forced to defend a policy on student funding which, its critics claimed, depressed demand, deterred access and threatened completion rates. Anxious not to debate funding matters ahead of a general election, both major parties had agreed to the setting up of the Dearing inquiry and asking it to report to a newly elected government. Once in power, the Labour administration accepted the principle of graduate contributions but, in choosing to convert all maintenance grants into loans (Department for Education and Employment 1997), it embarked on a scheme which was vulnerable to several of the pitfalls the inquiry had been keen to avoid.

Soon after this 'difficult' decision, constitutional reform and devolutionary politics in Scotland served to crystallize opposition to the scheme, resulting in the establishment of the Independent Committee of Inquiry into Student Finance (1999) and the subsequent adoption by the coalition Scottish Executive of an alternative student finance system based on a graduate endowment. In Wales, the coalition Welsh Assembly initiated its own review of higher education funding. In the House of Commons, the Education and Employment Select Committee chose to undertake, for the first time in 20 years, a wider inquiry into higher education, reporting on student access in the first part of its work (Select Committee on Education and Employment 2001b) and, not by accident, focusing on student retention in the next phase of the inquiry. For their part, the university vice-chancellors undertook their own review of higher education funding, selecting four options for detailed scrutiny, each with major implications for access, participation and completion (Universities UK 2001). Partly because of the recent nature of the funding changes and partly because, as Miller (1970: 6) recognized, wastage is 'a highly ramified problem', much of the contemporary debate has tended to run ahead of the available research evidence, some of which has only just begun to be published (Callender 2000).

Intersecting with these investigations, and the major impetus for an explicit policy focus on retention, has been the work of the funding bodies, led by the HEFCE. Its role has been an interesting one, not to say strongly self-determined and self-supported. In two key areas of activity – the introduction in 1999 of new funding arrangements to encourage institutions to widen participation and the publication in the same year of performance indicators for all publicly funded higher education establishments – the HEFCE was instrumental in projecting retention into the heart of government policy at the beginning of the new century.

In the case of widening participation, the HEFCE developed funding proposals in line with the Dearing recommendations but, importantly, coupled these with measures to improve retention:

> Our key aim is to increase recruitment and retention of students from under-represented groups, primarily through formula funding but also through a complementary special funding programme to support partnerships, innovation and development work.
>
> (Higher Education Funding Council for England 1999b: 1)

Furthermore:

> We recognize that extra support is needed to help institutions to make the additional provision needed to recruit and retain such students. Student retention is a particularly important issue: our research has reported greater levels of non-completion among students from disadvantaged backgrounds than among other students.
>
> (Higher Education Funding Council for England 1999b: 3)

This broadening of the participation strategy to incorporate retention alongside recruitment and representation was foreshadowed neither in the Dearing corpus nor in the Report of the Scottish Committee set up to advise the national inquiry (National Committee of Inquiry into Higher Education 1997b). Nor was it anticipated in the formal response of the government to both these reports (Department for Education and Employment 1997; Scottish Office 1998) and the funding announcements which followed.

Responsible for implementing and monitoring the widening participation proposals, the HEFCE was alert to 'potential problems and unintended consequences' (HEFCE 1998: 2), in particular the danger that wider participation might simply result in more students failing. Alongside the incentive and reward elements in the additional funds made available for students from disadvantaged backgrounds and for those with disabilities, funding was to support institutions in establishing and improving structures 'to help such students succeed' (HEFCE 1998: 3). To this end, institutions were expected to provide additional academic support and counselling, additional contact hours, special retention schemes (for example, mentoring), dedicated staff development, and additional support structures and facilities (such as child-care arrangements for mature students). These structures were to be set down in institutional participation strategies and targets identified for improving both retention and recruitment. Governing bodies were required to monitor institutional plans and progress, and the HEFCE would do the same through the performance indicators it had developed.

The publication of indicators and benchmarks for named institutions on the non-continuation and non-completion rates of their students was more controversial (Higher Education Funding Council for England 1999a). Guided by a steering group with membership from government departments, the funding councils, the statistics agency for higher education, and representatives of the institutions, the extended role and reach of the indicators were underlined, namely to enable institutions to monitor and compare their activities; to provide better information about the nature and performance of the sector as a whole; to influence policy developments; to contribute to public accountability; and to identify and disseminate good practice.

At the outset, the HEFCE insisted that the indicators be taken as a whole:

> Non-completion rates for an institution cannot be considered separately from the access indicators, and both should be viewed in the context of the institution's mission. The higher education sector is so diverse that no single measure can adequately describe an institution. However, these indicators are the first step along the road towards providing measures that will reflect this diversity.
>
> (Higher Education Funding Council for England 1999a: 1)

This was not how some in the media chose to present this data and, even where newspapers described and compared more than one set of indicators, their construction of league tables was guaranteed to draw criticism from those institutions with the lowest completion rates and whose students were largely 'non-traditional' in their backgrounds or qualifications. While the use of adjusted sector benchmarks made for more intelligent comparisons, by making allowance for the subject mix of the institution and the entry qualifications of its students, the non-completion rates were based on the same category of students as in government statistics – full-time students studying on first degree courses at establishments of higher education. Lacking a national student tracking system to provide a comprehensive picture of the movements and achievements of students, the HEFCE had to employ 'a method of projection' to produce a summary of the outcomes for a cohort of students. Concerns over data quality also meant that no information was provided about module completions, an important means of recognizing the achievement of students who might be 'intermitting' and so taking longer to complete their studies.

Whatever the merits or limits of the new indicators, their importance for the HEFCE lay in underpinning and justifying the inclusion of retention in its strategy for widening participation and, more powerfully, in securing this alignment in government policy for the sector. Four years into his term of office, and following publication by the HEFCE of its widening participation strategy and its related performance indicators, the Secretary of State made it clear to institutions that retention as well as recruitment was a key focus of government policy to widen access to higher education:

> Notwithstanding progress on recruitment, institutions should focus on retaining students, particularly those from disadvantaged backgrounds. Widening access to higher education must not lead to an increase in the number of people who fail to complete their courses. I therefore expect to see the Council bear down on the rate of 'drop-out'. The evidence shows there are unacceptable variations in the rate of 'drop-out' which appear to be linked more to the culture and workings of the institution than to the background or nature of the students recruited. It is therefore time for much more substantial work to be done on identifying best practice and bringing pressure to bear on those institutions whose performance falls significantly below their benchmark.
>
> (Secretary of State for Education and Employment 2000)

A request that the central authorities 'bear down' on rates of non-completion was a mark of the seriousness which the government gave to supporting and achieving success in undergraduate education, even if some of its other policies on higher education were seen to run counter to this goal.

3

Academic Failure: a Retrospective View from Non-completing Students

Mantz Yorke

Definitions, data and some caveats

Academic failure can be defined in a number of ways, including failure of assessments, failure to progress and failure to achieve one's potential. In this chapter, the definition has had to be relatively loose, since the opportunity has been taken to rework data that were collected for another purpose and were not tied tightly to a definition of academic failure.

The data used in this chapter derive from studies of non-completion conducted during 1996 and 1997, the first of which was funded by the Higher Education Funding Council for England (HEFCE), whereas the second was self-funded. Surveys were conducted of students from six varied higher education institutions in the north-west of England who had left their programmes of study prematurely during, or at the end of, the academic years 1994–95 and 1995–96. The data from these surveys were combined since the patterns of response were very similar, giving a total pool of 2151 full-time and sandwich[1] respondents and 328 part-time respondents, representing roughly 30 per cent and 20 per cent of the total of 'non-completers' respectively. Accounts of this research can be found in Yorke et al. (1997) and Yorke (1999b). This chapter deals primarily with the full-time and sandwich students because their database is considerably more extensive, but a smaller-scale treatment of the part-time respondents is also included.

The questionnaires that were used asked respondents to indicate which of some three dozen (36 provided items in the first survey and 39 in the second) possible influences had borne on their premature departure, and how strong these influences had been. Factor analysis of the responses from the full-time and sandwich respondents produced the six factors[2] shown in Table 3.1. 'Lack of academic progress' appeared in factor 2 for the full-time and sandwich respondents, and in factor 1 for the part-time respondents. However, it has been treated separately in this analysis since it is a criterion

Table 3.1 Factors from analysis of full-time and sandwich student responses

Factor	*Label*
1	Poor quality of the student experience
2	Inability to cope with the demands of the programme
3	Unhappiness with the social environment
4	Wrong choice of programme
5	Matters related to financial need
6	Dissatisfaction with aspects of institutional provision

Source: Yorke 1999b.

Table 3.2 Factors from analysis of part-time student responses

Factor	*Label*
1	Poor quality of the student experience
2	Pressure of work (academic and employment)
3	Unhappiness with the extra-institutional environment
4	Problems with relationships and finance
5	Dissatisfaction with aspects of institutional provision
6	Wrong choice of programme

Source: Yorke 1999b.

for distinction between the groups. A broadly similar factor structure[3] was found to summarize the responses for the part-time respondents (see Table 3.2).

One of the influences on non-completion was the failure to make adequate academic progress. Whilst this was an adequate category for the wide-ranging survey of non-completion, it is loose in definitional terms since it does not distinguish between formal failure (as represented, for example, by not reaching a pass grade in assessments at the end of a year or semester) and informal failure (where the student perceives that he or she is not going to make the grade, and consequently withdraws from the programme of study).

This definitional looseness is compounded by the time categories used in the non-completion research. In order not to have too many categories for respondents (some of whom could have withdrawn after more than 4 years), the chosen categories were 'during the first year', 'at the end of the first year or during the second', and so on. From the point of view of academic failure, these are obviously not ideal since the actual end of an academic year is a better point at which to index it.

The third caveat is that the data consist of post hoc self-reporting, which has the potential to be influenced by forgetfulness, self-serving distortion and the like. That said, a considerable number of respondents wrote comments on their questionnaires which elaborated on their survey responses. As far as can be judged, the vast majority of these 'rang true' and, thus, provided something of a testimony regarding the accuracy with which the optical mark reader 'bubbles' on the survey form had been filled in.

These caveats notwithstanding, a re-analysis of the non-completion data offered the prospect of some insight into academic failure.

Full-time and sandwich students

Data analysis

The database of full-time and sandwich 'non-completers' was dichotomized in terms of failure to make adequate academic progress and the absence of such failure. Since institutional records of actual failures were unreliable (one institution, implausibly, reported no academic failures at all), the first-level criterion for distinguishing between groups was respondents' self-reports regarding whether, on the one hand, insufficient academic progress had been a 'moderate' or a 'considerable' influence on their non-completion or whether, on the other hand, it had had little or no influence in this respect. As a shorthand (which, it is acknowledged, understates the complexity of the situation), the terms 'weak progress' and 'satisfactory progress' are used here to differentiate between the two groups of respondents. The respondents were further sub-divided as indicated in Figure 3.1.

Figure 3.1 Schema showing the sub-division of the 2151 full-time and sandwich 'non-completers'

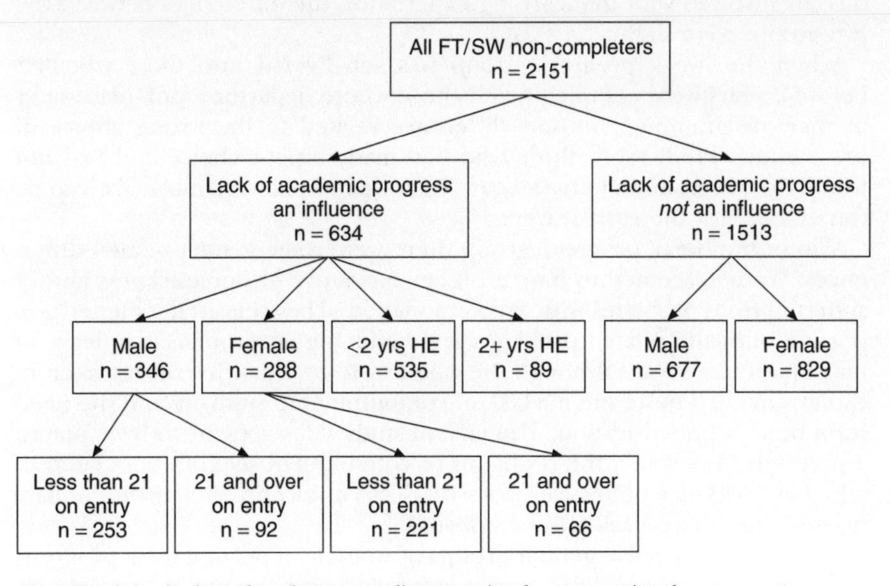

Note: Totals in the branches show some discrepancies due to occasional non-response to items; FT = full time; SW = sandwich; HE = higher education.

Table 3.3 Differences between the 'weak progress group' and the remainder of the full-time and sandwich students who left their studies prematurely

Factor	*Short label*	*Number of items per factor where the 'weak progress' group reported a higher level of difficulty*
1	Student experience	6 out of 7
2	Inability to cope	5 out of 5
3	Social environment	1 out of 5
4	Wrong choice	5 out of 5
5	Financial need	0 out of 6
6	Institutional provision	1 out of 5

Note: The criterion for noting a difference between groups was taken as 10 percentage points between the proportions citing the influence on withdrawal as having been moderate/considerable.

Findings

When those who fell into the category of 'weak progress' were compared with those for whom academic progress was not identified as a problem, differences (summarized in Table 3.3, and given in detail in Appendix 1) were clear, and not particularly surprising. The most noticeable differences are related to the choice of programme, the perceived quality of the learning experience and the capacity to cope with study. Where the factor was less directly involved with the learning experience, the differences between the two groups were slight.

When the 'weak progress' group was sub-divided into those who left before 2 years were completed and those whose departure took place later in their programme, the only difference related to the wrong choice of programme. Predictably, those who had made a poor choice and had not found the programme to have been as they expected were more likely to be found amongst the early leavers.

Within the 'weak progress' group there were some gender-related differences. Women seemed to have a higher incidence of homesickness and of suffering from problems with accommodation. They reported a higher proportion of health-related problems and had a higher propensity to leave to take up employment (although the causality is unclear). In contrast men in this group cited more often a lack of commitment to studying and the need for a break from education. The lack of study skills appears to have played a part here. For some, the problems of commitment seem to be related to a higher incidence of involvement with drugs or alcohol, but again the data do not allow the causality to be inferred.

Within the respective gender groups of students reporting weak progress, there were some marked differences when age was dichotomized as 'younger than 21 on entry' and 'aged 21 or more on entry'. The progressive division

Table 3.4 Differences between older and younger 'weak progress' students, differentiated by gender

Factor	*Short label*	*Number of items per factor for which there were differences between older and younger students*	
		Female students	*Male students*
1	Student experience	0 out of 7	0 out of 7
2	Inability to cope	0 out of 5	1 out of 5 (older students having more difficulty)
3	Social environment	5 out of 5 (younger students having more difficulty)	0 out of 5
4	Wrong choice	5 out of 5 (younger students having more difficulty)	4 out of 5 (younger students having more difficulty)
5	Financial need	4 out of 6 (older students having more difficulty)	3 out of 6 (older students having more difficulty)
6	Institutional provision	0 out of 5	0 out of 5

of the respondents produced some fairly small sub-groups, and so the caution attached to the interpretation of the data has to be increased.

As would be expected, the older female students were less likely than their younger peers to cite matters related to wrong choice of field of study. 'Mature' entrants tend to have taken time over a decision that is often buttressed by their experience of life outside the educational system. Basically, they know what they want to do. On the evidence of this study, however, these students more frequently run into difficulty with finance and family (as can be seen in Table 3.4 and Appendix 1). It is perhaps no surprise to find that roughly one-third of respondents in this sub-group left higher education for employment.[4]

The male students showed the same general differences regarding the wrong choice of field of study and finance and family issues (although the needs of dependants figured less strongly). Nearly half of the older men cited study-related stress as having influenced their departure, in contrast to only one-third of their younger peers. The older men cited health problems with twice the frequency of the younger men.

Part-time students

The number of part-time respondents (328) is very roughly an order of magnitude smaller than that of the full-time and sandwich students, and

Table 3.5 Differences between part-time students who had made weak progress and those whose progress had been satisfactory

Factor	*Short label*	*Number of items per factor for which the 'weak progress' group had a higher degree of difficulty*
1	The student experience	8 out of 9
2	Pressure of work	6 out of 7
3	Dislike of environment outside the institution	1 out of 4
4	Personal problems	1 out of 6 (also 1 item for which the 'satisfactory progress' group had more problems)
5	Institutional provision	1 out of 4
6	Wrong choice	2 out of 3

therefore allows only the rudimentary analysis that is summarized in Table 3.5 and given in more detail in Appendix 2. Particular caution has to be exercised in interpreting the data since there were only 25 respondents who fell into the 'weak progress' group.

The differences are concentrated in three of the six factors which plausibly have a conceptual interrelationship, even if this is not statistical[5] – the pressures associated with employment (the dominant influence on withdrawal for part-time students) and academic workload, commitment to the programme and the quality of the learning experience. Weak progress is associated with perceived difficulty in these three general areas. If the demands of employment are placed to one side, the remaining issues all relate to the process of studying. A number of the individual item differences are sufficiently large for credibility, even though the number of 'weak progress' students is low. There is little evidence of differences in respect of the other three factors, but it is worth noting that both sub-groups tended to have problems with personal matters outside the higher education institution (see the breakdown of factor 4 in Appendix 1).

Dealing with the problem

Causes and some possible cures

The extensive literature on non-completion (the bulk of which has emanated from the United States, where offices of institutional research routinely survey students and alumni) and the research reported here point to the following broad conclusions.

Withdrawal or failure is more probable when:

- students have chosen 'the wrong programme';
- students lack commitment and/or interest;
- students' expectations are not met;
- students come from a working-class background;
- students are 'mature' entrants;
- students enter with low academic qualifications;
- the quality of teaching is poor;
- the academic culture is unsupportive (even hostile) to learning;
- students experience financial difficulty; and
- demands of other commitments supervene.

Disregarding adventitious causes such as accident or illness, there are three main groups of risk factors. The first relates to choice of programme and commitment, the second to background demographics and the third to aspects of being a student (although this can be sub-divided into matters over which the institution has control and those over which it does not).

If a student has made a poor choice, the options are to grit their teeth and carry on to the end, to switch to a different programme, or to leave higher education until they are ready for a second attempt. The research reported here was undertaken prior to the 1997 change of government in the UK, which led to the introduction of fee charging and to an increase in the need for students to take out loans. Now students in the UK, like their counterparts in the United States and Australia, have to work out the financial implications of entering higher education prior to committing themselves. By late 2000, there was no evidence available of the impact on non-completion of changes in the funding of students.[6] However, the changes can be anticipated to point in two opposing directions: on one hand, better decision making prior to entry leading to a reduction in non-completion and, on the other, sharper rises in student indebtedness leading to an increase.

The need for some intending students to improve their choice making led the Universities and Colleges Admissions Service (UCAS) to commission a report, based on the research of Yorke and his colleagues, aimed at advisers and the students themselves (Yorke 1999a). This report acknowledges the wide range of information that students really need in order to make a well-informed choice of programme in higher education.[7] There is a need to obtain information not only about the programme itself, but also about matters beyond it, such as the kind of area in which the student might find him or herself living. Contextual issues such as these bear on non-completion in general, and in some cases bear on the more precise issue of academic failure.

Similarly, the demographic variables which comprise the second group of risk factors bear on non-completion, and will, to some extent, bear on academic failure. The performance indicators that were published for higher education institutions (Higher Education Funding Council for England 1999c) show, on further analysis, that a combination of social class and maturity on entry is a very strong predictor of non-completion (Yorke 2001).

It is well understood – although less easy to demonstrate, because of the variety of ways in which students nowadays enter higher education – that social class and maturity are inversely correlated with qualifications at entry. In other words, there is a nexus of demographic conditions that points towards the higher levels of non-completion that are found in the less prestigious institutions.

The third group of risk factors relates to 'being a student'. There is little an institution can do about other demands on a student's time or about his or her financial position.[8] However, an institution has the power to create and run curricula that maximize the potential for student learning. The extensive qualitative research undertaken by Seymour and Hewitt (1997) into retention in, and departure from, science, mathematics and engineering courses in the United States shows just how inimical to student learning an academic climate can be. One of the causes was found to be the dominance of research over teaching – an issue which readers from countries other than the UK and the United States will probably recognize. The requirement for institutions in the UK to produce learning and teaching strategies (Higher Education Funding Council for England 1999b) has begun to restore balance to the relationship between teaching and research, and has aligned with thinking that seeks to find ways of creating more of a synergy between teaching and research (see, for example, Brew 1999a; Donovan 2000; Yorke 2000).

Coming down from the level of general policy, some students who responded to the surveys pointed to poor organization of their programme and to various aspects of the quality of teaching as being influential on their departure from the institution. In recent years, the pressures of rising student numbers and reducing state funding have increased, with the consequence that the opportunity for staff–student interchange has declined. Higher education is becoming more impersonal. Lectures are given to larger groups, the size of seminar and tutorial groups has increased, there is greater use of part-time staff and graduate teaching assistants, and so on.

In addition, the move towards modularity has had some effects. In some institutions it has made it more difficult for a student to identify with an academic 'home'. A study at Seattle Community College has shown the improvement that can happen when study units are grouped in a coherent manner (Tinto 1997). Modularization has led to semester-end (rather than year-end) assessments. The consequence has been a reduction in the amount of formative assessment being given to students – and formative assessment is a critically important part of the learning process.

The decrease in staff–student interchange of various kinds has particular implications for students who enter higher education relatively unattuned to the demands of study at this level. Whilst many who enter from school on the basis of their performances at A level can cope with the academic demands,[9] those who enter via other routes may take rather longer to 'get up to speed' regarding academic study. The need to perform for summative assessments at the end of the first semester is a particular pressure on those who are acclimatizing.

Preparedness for, and acclimatization to, the first year in higher education are important (see, for example, the student perspective captured in Chapter 3 of Mentkowski and Associates 2000; the survey data collected by McInnis et al. 1995; Yorke 1999b). Roughly two-thirds of premature departures take place in, or at the end of, the first year of full-time study in the UK. Anecdotal evidence from a number of institutions indicates that early poor performance can be a powerful disincentive to continuation, with students feeling that perhaps they were not cut out for higher education after all – although the main problems are acculturation and acclimatization to studying. Having recognized the deleterious consequences of early summative assessment and that the first year of full-time study is typically only a kind of qualifying year for an honours degree, some institutions are removing from their assessment regulations the requirement that students pass summative assessments at the end of the first semester. This should allow students more of an opportunity to build confidence and to come to terms with academic study, and ought to allow more of the vital formative assessment to take place.

There is, however, a broader issue to be addressed. Developments in communications technology are providing increasing opportunities to learn from materials delivered electronically. This kind of resource will become more significant in higher education, and has the potential for remedying sub-optimal use of that expensive resource, academics' time. For example, much lecturing is routine transmission of information which, as Bligh (1998) makes clear, is not particularly effective. A radical reappraisal of teaching and learning is needed across higher education, such that lecturers' contact time becomes, to the fullest extent possible, 'quality time' as far as student learning is concerned.[10] One could anticipate that, as a result, the incidence of academic failure would be mitigated. This would not only be of obvious benefit to the students, but would also benefit institutions (not least because it would help them to keep their funding streams up).

Firefighting

When things are going wrong, to whom do students turn? In the non-completion research, students were asked to whom within the institution they turned for help. The full-time and sandwich respondents differed from the part-time respondents (see Table 3.6).

For all modes of study, members of the academic staff were most often approached by students for advice. Part-time students, however, made less use of personal tutors – perhaps because not all courses made this sort of provision available. They also made much less use of support staff in a variety of institutional roles. This is likely to have been because support staff tend to be present during the day time and not for 'twilight' and evening courses. It is impossible to say, from the evidence available, whether the presence of support staff in the evenings would have made any difference

Table 3.6 Differences between full-time/sandwich students and part-time students in their sources of advice when considering leaving higher education

Source of institutional advice	*FT/SW students (N = 2151)*	*PT students (N = 328)*
	%	%
Personal tutor	40.4	16.8
Lecturer	25.5	20.1
Other students	14.3	6.1
Careers officer	14.2	1.2
Counsellor	8.6	0.9
Welfare officer	4.8	1.8
Student Union	4.2	0.3
Religious figure	0.7	0.0
Hall warden	0.1	n/a
Other (unspecified)	–	4.0

Note: FT = full time; SW = sandwich; PT = part time.
Source: Data from Yorke 1999b.

to student non-completion. An institutional commitment to the quality of the student experience would see the development of staff–student 'quality time' (noted earlier) as offering the opportunity for student support as a by-product of the teaching process. It might also, in a period in which the full-time/part-time distinction is eroding, see a greater commitment of support resource outside the 9am to 5pm time-band.[11]

Principles for institutional action

Academic failure has a multitude of causes. An institution has the power to influence some of these. However, to exert influence systematically, the institution has to assume a general orientation towards the academic *and* pastoral support of its students, since their effects are likely to be synergic. This orientation can be expressed in a number of principles which have been influenced by Tinto (1993), who has written about retention with considerable thought.

The principles for institutional action aimed at minimizing academic failure are to:

- have an institution-wide policy commitment to students' development;
- have in place structures and processes consistent with this policy;
- ensure that new students enter with, or have the opportunity to acquire, the skills needed for academic success;
- run programmes in which the emphasis is on maximizing students' development;

- acknowledge through practice that support for students' academic development needs to be augmented by support for their personal development; and
- see retention as an integral part of educational policy and practice, and not as a freestanding initiative.

In the UK, non-completion has become a political issue. Press coverage of the HEFCE (1999b) performance indicators demonstrates the point.[12] In some newspapers, non-completion has been treated as synonymous with academic failure, and the more right-wing press has taken the opportunity to suggest that some students ought not to be in higher education at all. The evidence from the higher education system indicates that such a reaction is simplistic. Non-completion and academic failure are the outcomes of complex interactions between background variables and institutional conditions.

Whereas a higher education institution cannot do much about students' background circumstances, it is probable that there is more academic failure in UK higher education than there should be. There appears to be scope in institutions for improving the ways in which they support students' learning – and hence for reducing the incidence of academic failure. In the end, this comes down to an orientation towards the enhancement of the quality of the student experience. A problem for institutions is that their attention is being diverted from enhancement by the need to satisfy external demands to demonstrate that their existing provision complies with expectations. The 'gurus' who write on quality – and tomorrow's students – would want to see something better.

Notes

1. Sandwich students spend a substantial part of their programme (typically a full year) on an employment-related placement. As a consequence, their programmes of study are correspondingly extended compared with full-time programmes.
2. In order, the factors accounted for the following percentages of the total variance: factor 1, 19.6 per cent; factor 2, 8.0 per cent; factor 3, 6.6 per cent; factor 4, 5.9 per cent; factor 5, 4.6 per cent; and factor 6, 3.7 per cent. The percentage of variance explained is to some extent a methodological artefact, and should not be confused with the salience of the factor. For example, wrong choice of field of study and financial problems appeared in the top three individual influences on non-completion.
3. The percentage of the variance explained by each factor was: factor 1, 17.3 per cent; factor 2, 8.1 per cent; factor 3, 7.3 per cent; factor 4, 5.6 per cent; factor 5, 4.9 per cent; and factor 6, 4.6 per cent. The caveat in note 2 regarding salience applies.
4. This comment applies only in respect of 1995–96 leavers, since the item was not put to those who left during the previous academic year.
5. The factors are statistically uncorrelated.
6. There does seem to have been an impact on applications to enter higher education, particularly amongst potential mature entrants.

7. The widely published 'league tables' of institutions are an inadequate source of information about what it is really like to study subject X in institution Y.
8. Institutions do have so-called 'access funds', the purpose of which is to mitigate hardship, but the amounts of money in them are relatively small.
9. The demands on them in terms of organizing their lives when they live away from home are a different, but not inconsiderable, issue.
10. Stephenson and Yorke (1998) propose a 'capability envelope' in which an ongoing tutorial activity runs alongside the academic component of the curriculum. This would be consistent with the notion of 'quality time' in respect of staff–student contact.
11. The institutional costs involved would almost certainly have to be offset by savings elsewhere. Multiple institutional sites add to the problem.
12. See Yorke (2001).

Appendix 3.1
Full-time and sandwich students: influences on leaving higher education

Factor	Item, in brief	All Satis. prog. (N = 1513)	All Weak prog. (N = 634)	All Satis. prog. <2yrs (N = 1253)	All Satis. prog. 2+ yrs (N = 225)	All Weak prog. <2yrs (N = 535)	All Weak prog. 2+ yrs (N = 89)	Satis. prog. Female (N = 829)	Satis. prog. Male (N = 677)	Weak prog. Female (N = 288)	Weak prog. Male (N = 346)	Weak prog. Female age <21 (N = 221)	Weak prog. Female age 21+ (N = 66)	Weak prog. Male age <21 (N = 253)	Weak prog. Male age 21+ (N = 92)
1	Quality of teaching	17	37	17	20	37	37	17	18	38	36	39	32	36	37
1	Lack of academic support outside timetable	18	38	18	20	38	40	19	17	37	38	37	38	38	39
1	Programme organization	20	43	20	21	44	42	20	20	38	47	37	42	47	50
1	Way programme was taught did not suit	23	49	24	16	51	43	22	24	47	51	46	50	52	49
1	Lack of staff support	19	36	19	20	36	37	20	17	37	35	37	38	35	36
1	Class size	12	27	12	8	27	26	11	12	27	27	26	29	26	28
1	Timetabling difficulties	9	16	9	4	16	17	8	9	16	16	14	23	15	22
2	Stress related to the programme	16	37	15	21	35	48	18	15	38	36	38	41	33	45
2	Difficulty of programme	13	39	13	11	39	42	12	15	35	43	35	33	41	48
2	Heavy workload	12	29	12	16	27	37	13	12	28	30	25	36	30	29
2	Lack of study skills	10	34	10	7	34	34	8	11	27	40	27	27	38	43
2	Lack of support from students	12	22	12	10	21	27	14	19	26	19	26	26	15	29

Appendix 3.1 (*cont'd*)

Factor	*Item, in brief*	*All Satis. prog.* (*N* = 1513)	*All Weak prog.* (*N* = 634)	*All Satis. prog. <2yrs* (*N* = 1253)	*All Satis. prog. 2+ yrs* (*N* = 225)	*All Weak prog. <2yrs* (*N* = 535)	*All Weak prog. 2+ yrs* (*N* = 89)	*Satis. prog. Female* (*N* = 829)	*Satis. prog. Male* (*N* = 677)	*Weak prog. Female* (*N* = 288)	*Weak prog. Male* (*N* = 346)	*Weak prog. Female age <21* (*N* = 221)	*Weak prog. Female age 21+* (*N* = 66)	*Weak prog. Male age <21* (*N* = 253)	*Weak prog. Male age 21+* (*N* = 92)
3	Dislike of city/town	13	19	14	7	20	15	14	13	22	18	24	12	20	11
3	Homesickness	10	12	12	3	13	7	13	7	18	8	21	5	9	4
3	Fear of crime	8	14	8	8	14	13	7	9	14	14	17	3	15	13
3	Difficulty in making friends	8	12	8	4	13	10	8	7	15	10	17	9	9	13
3	Accommodation problems	11	33	12	6	34	28	10	12	41	26	44	30	27	25
4	Chose wrong field of study	33	54	35	19	57	40	34	30	53	55	58	38	61	40
4	Lack of relevance of programme	17	35	19	9	38	19	16	19	32	37	35	24	39	32
4	Lack of commitment	30	56	31	24	56	57	26	35	44	66	48	29	73	49
4	Programme not as expected	29	55	31	16	60	30	30	28	52	57	55	44	61	45
4	Needed a break from education	25	35	25	25	33	43	24	27	30	40	33	20	43	33
5	Financial problems	36	40	36	34	38	48	31	42	35	44	32	48	40	57
5	Demands of employment	13	19	12	15	18	22	11	16	18	19	16	23	17	27
5	Lack of support from family	11	15	11	7	15	13	12	9	17	13	15	26	10	22
5	Needs of dependants	17	13	16	19	13	11	19	14	15	10	11	29	8	16

5	Travel problems	15	16	16	9	15	13	16	12	17	15	14	24	13	21
5	Emotional difficulties with others	22	27	22	21	26	29	24	19	31	23	29	36	21	28
6	Institutional library facilities	6	13	6	8	13	12	6	7	13	13	13	12	14	12
6	Institutional computing facilities	7	15	7	5	15	16	6	8	14	16	14	14	15	20
6	Institutional provision of specialist equipment	4	14	5	2	14	17	4	5	14	15	12	18	16	10
6	Institutional social facilities	7	14	8	4	15	8	7	8	13	15	14	9	15	14
6	Institution not as expected	15	27	17	6	29	16	17	12	26	28	28	21	30	23
None	Health problems	23	23	21	31	20	39	25	21	29	19	27	35	15	28
None	Drug/alcohol problems	5	10	5	6	10	10	3	8	5	15	5	5	15	15
None	Bereavement of someone close*	5	7	5	8	4	13	6	5	10	3	11	6	3	0
None	Pregnancy of self or partner*	6	4	5	10	1	20	9	1	4	3	4	6	4	0
None	Left to take employment*	10	13	8	17	12	7	8	14	16	6	11	31	4	11

Notes: Factors noted are those on which the highest loading was obtained.
Lack of academic progress would have appeared in factor 2.
* indicates an untypically low N since item appeared only on 1995–96 questionnaire.
Weak programme implies moderate/considerable influence of lack of academic progress on leaving; satisfactory programme implies little or no influence.
Age refers to age on entry to the programme; <2yrs and 2+ yrs refer to the time after enrolment when the student left.
All figures are percentages.

Appendix 3.2
Part-time students: influences on leaving higher education

Factor	*Item, in brief*	*All Satis. prog. (N = 303)*	*All Weak prog. (N = 25)*
1	Lack of academic support outside timetable	18	48
1	Lack of staff support	16	32
1	Programme organization	20	40
1	Quality of teaching	18	28
1	Way programme was taught did not suit	17	40
1	Class size	13	28
1	Lack of support from students	4	12
1	Programme not as expected	13	32
1	Institution not as expected	6	20
2	Heavy workload	24	40
2	Demands of employment	50	72
2	Stress related to the programme	15	40
2	Timetabling difficulties	20	36
2	Difficulty of programme	8	32
2	Needed a break from education	9	12
2	Travel problems	12	24
3	Dislike of city/town	1	4
3	Homesickness	0	4
3	Fear of crime	1	8
3	Accommodation problems	1	12
4	Lack of support from family	11	24
4	Emotional difficulties with others	12	20
4	Needs of dependants	27	16
4	Financial problems	23	20
4	Difficulty in making friends	2	4
4	Health problems	17	16
5	Institutional social facilities	3	0
5	Institutional computing facilities	6	20
5	Institutional provision of specialist equipment	2	8
5	Institutional library facilities	10	16
6	Chose wrong field of study	7	12
6	Lack of relevance of programme	6	28
6	Lack of commitment	13	36
None	Lack of study skills	3	44
None	Drug/alcohol problems	1	0
None	Bereavement of someone close*	5	
None	Pregnancy of self or partner*	7	
None	Left to take employment*	8	

Notes: Factors noted are those on which the highest loading was obtained.
Lack of academic progress would have appeared in Factor 1.
* indicates an untypically low N since item appeared only on 1995–96 questionnaire.
Numbers of Weak programme students are too low for comparison.
Weak programme implies moderate/considerable influence of lack of academic progress on leaving; Satisfactory programme implies no or little influence.
All figures are percentages.

4

A Joined-up Policy Approach to Student Support

Margo Blythman and Susan Orr

Introduction

Higher education does not exist in isolation. It is not isolated from the previous experience, lives and values of its students, or its teachers. It does not exist in isolation from the social and political ideologies and pressures of the world in which it is located. Equally, it is not isolated from the systems, values, culture and pressures of other sectors of the education system. There is a web of relationships, which are dialectical. In this chapter we aim to show how our experience of further education and our knowledge of its recent history have helped us develop a broad approach to the issue of student failure in higher education. We recognize student failure as an institutional responsibility and examine drop-out as an indication of institutional failure. Additionally, we argue that an understanding of micropolitics, developed both through experience and knowledge of the relevant literature, has also contributed to a strategy which begins to approach joined-up thinking. We illustrate this with our current work to reduce student failure in our own higher education institution.

We both worked through the mid-1990s at an inner London further education college (Kingsway), which was at that time in the forefront of many such developments. As a result of incorporation, other colleges of further education were sliding into a forced obsession with finance, property, management information systems and legal matters, but Kingsway, under the then principal, managed to stay as a crucible for innovative educational development with a central focus on supporting student learning. We grappled with retention and worked on a variety of strategies with a particular emphasis on additional support for individual students, strong tutorial systems and listening to the student voice through systematic student feedback.

Our philosophy

We recognize that students arrive in higher education with different approaches to learning and different life experiences. Our model of student support to enhance retention has wide parameters, is influenced by values of equity and social justice and an understanding of the concept of cultural capital (Bourdieu 1997). This concept contributes to our understanding of unequal educational achievement among different social classes through differential class access to this form of capital. We agree with Bourdieu's point that cultural capital can have relatively disguised modes of acquisition so that it may be unrecognizable as capital and instead be seen as a legitimate competence.

Our aim is to foster a deep approach to learning (Entwistle 1988) through helpful feedback, clear objectives, clear expectations and good explanations (Ramsden 1991; Trigwell and Prosser 1991). We see academic support for students as an important part of a college's strategy to maximize student achievement and, therefore, equip all students better for successful achievement and progression within the education system and beyond.

The concepts of student potentiality and educatability are central to our institutional strategy to reduce failure rates. We have a non-categorical view of students which rejects a model of students as rigidly defined categories (Harris and Thorp 1999). In education there are contested discourses employed to describe student success and its inverse, student failure. These discourses trace to particular conceptions of the student that are critical to the failure debate. Whilst we do not seek to oversimplify, we argue that lecturers' discourse about student achievement often traces to conceptions of the student that relate either to student ability or student potential. The former conception has its roots in a Burtian view (Burt 1961). Burt argued that 'no grindstone can make a good blade out of a bad metal' (1961: 9) and that no teaching can transform a 'weak' student into an 'able' student. At first appearance, Burt's ideas sound dated and irrelevant, but within the school sector Skidmore's (1999) study of the discourses used by teachers to describe pupil attainment, particularly in relation to students with special needs, found evidence that two opposing discourses exist. In the first discourse all pupils are seen as possessing the potential to learn which is 'open-ended, unbounded and without predetermined limits' (1999: 21). In the second discourse pupils are viewed as having fixed levels of cognitive ability that are 'bounded and circumscribed' (1999: 22). In earlier work in higher education (Orr and Blythman 2000), we identified that some lecturers essentialize the student and categorize a predetermined group of 'weak students'; it is the student who succeeds or fails. When lecturers seek to externalize and individualize failure, an ability conception is implied.

In 1997 the Kennedy Report, produced by the first government-funded widening participation committee, argued that 'equity dictates that all should have the opportunity to succeed' (Further Education Funding Council 1997: 15). The Report sets out clearly the parameters of widening participation with the emphasis on success and progression, rather than on access to education per se. Kennedy suggests that it is the institution's responsibility to ensure that students access the educational opportunities that unlock their potential. Once a model of student potential is adopted, educational institutions (whether school, further education or higher education) need to look at failure as an institutional concern. This understanding is not yet as clear in higher education national policy. The four government strands to widening participation focus exclusively on entry (Department for Education and Employment 2000a).

The further education agenda

The higher education sector has not traditionally looked to further education as a source of inspiration, but the two sectors are interrelated. In this section we look at the priorities and political agendas in further education and argue that higher education has much to learn from its further education counterpart. As academics moving from further education to higher education, we experience a sense of echo and resonance. Not only do increasing numbers of further education students progress into higher education, many educational priorities are making the same transition.

It is a truism to say that further education has no elitist past. It has always catered for those who want a second chance. Many colleges of further education are descendants of technical colleges established to educate the working classes. One of our former further education offices used to be a mock laundry room, where working-class Victorian girls were taught how to be maids. This history means that the shared ethos of further education is not built on elitism. Selection has never been a central part of the further education admissions system. The assumption is that there will be such a wide variety of courses available that there will be something to suit all students' needs. It may seem strange to define further education by what it is not, but it is important to do so in order to counterpoise further education practice and ideology against those groups within higher education which have viewed the widening participation agenda as a lowering of standards. Widening participation is at the core of further education, it is not an add-on, nor does it threaten traditional ideas about standards in the way that it has in some parts of higher education.

In the mid- to late 1980s, the government drive to increase post-16 staying-on rates led to the massification of further education several years before higher education went through the same process and widening participation was explicitly on the agenda. Colleges undergoing inspection were specifically asked how they met the needs of the local community and resources were focused on compact schemes with local schools that sought to broaden the mix of an already diverse student population. These initiatives were deemed to be successful because student recruitment rose, and in London particularly, ethnic minority groups were recruited in larger numbers.

It was in the early 1990s that two separate documents emerged that were to challenge further education seriously. These reports forced the further education community to address drop-out and failure, thus fore-shadowing the issues that the higher education community are engaging with this decade. The first report, from the Audit Commission and OFSTED (1993), showed that over one-third of all further education students did not finish the course for which they enrolled. This was a figure that surprised the further education community. On some courses drop-out rates were calculated to be as high as 80 per cent. This militated against the drive to expand; if one-third of all students were never going to complete, it problematized further expansion until the retention and achievement rates of those already enrolled improved. There was a need to address the 'revolving door syndrome', whereby students were recruited to courses in ever-increasing numbers but ended up back in the community without a qualification. Further education had to address the fact that massification is not the same thing as widening participation. True participation is only realized when the new students attracted to education succeed and leave with qualifications that do justice to their potential. As Kennedy (FEFC 1997: 3) states, 'attracting and keeping those for whom learning is a daunting experience is hard work and financially unrewarding. The effort and resources required to support such students on courses receives insufficient recognition in the current funding system'. The Report also commented on the paucity of further education student tracking systems, which made full analysis of drop-out patterns impossible.

Drawing directly on the findings of the Report, the Further Education Funding Council (1994) produced its funding methodology for the newly incorporated sector. This document radically changed the way that further education was funded. In future, all funding was to be tracked to individual students. Payment was made to the institution at three points in the year for every student. This was at entry, on course and on achievement, but more significantly the on-course element was also divided into three audit points and only became payable if the student was still on course. Thus, non-completion had severe financial penalties. This, combined with pre-existing concerns about equality of opportunity, ensured that retention was high on the further education agenda.

It was within this context that Paul Martinez (1995, 1996, 1997) started to research drop-out in further education. In *Student Retention in Further and Adult Education* (1995) he challenged prevailing ideas (Roberts and Webb 1980) about the inevitability of drop-out. Martinez identified that students were more likely to give personal reasons for drop-out if they were asked by a lecturer that was known to them. If an independent researcher asked the same question, students felt freer to explain their drop-out in terms of aspects of the college experience that they found unsatisfactory. Thus, information collected previously by colleges had over-emphasized personal 'within student' reasons for drop-out. Martinez interviewed retained students as well as students who dropped out. Within his sample, students who dropped out were not financially poorer than retained students (Martinez 1995). In fact, more students experienced financial hardship in the retained group than in the group that dropped out. In addition, a larger percentage of retained students had personal problems. However, Kenwright (1996) found that, while students who stay and students who leave are equally likely to depend financially on part-time jobs, those who leave are more likely to report an inability to manage on their income. This study did not establish whether or not their incomes were actually lower. Later research by Martinez and Munday (1998) pointed to the interrelatedness of factors that lead to drop-out. Martinez' research challenged lecturers' tendency to individualize drop-out by supporting the idea that retention rates could be improved through college-based initiatives (Martinez 1997). His research meant that the locus of responsibility moved from student to college. Fitzcharles surveyed a number of published and unpublished studies of student retention in further education and concluded that 'student retention and drop-out appear to be significantly influenced by the experience of study and learning and colleges can adopt strategies which improve retention rates' (2001: 25).

Much of this will be familiar to colleagues working in the higher education sector today. The main difference is that further education has had a focus on retention coming from a longer history of addressing the needs of a diverse group of learners. The so-called 'new types of learners' in higher education are, in fact, the traditional learners in further education. If we look at how further education addressed retention and widening participation over the 1990s, we find a testing ground for initiatives that are currently being developed in higher education. For this reason alone, a closer inspection of the further education experience is justified.

A higher education institutional approach

Having worked together in further education, by chance we both came to work at the London Institute in 1997, one of us at the London College of Fashion and the other at the London College of Printing. We found a very different situation. Although 40 per cent of the students at the London Institute were on further education programmes, its funding base, management systems, management priorities and organizational culture were firmly located within a higher education ethos. Particularly important was that, as a higher education institution, it was not subject to the same financial penalties as a college of further education for student drop-out. For this reason in particular, little attention had been paid to issues of student retention. However, 1997 was a year of political change and institutional managers in higher education who were alert to the external environment began to see student drop-out as a significant issue both financially and in terms of government expectations. Therefore, we entered a situation in which institutional managers were open to the development of strategies to improve retention.

We began our work by trying to establish reasons why students dropped out. A telephone survey of students was carried out by a neutral facilitator at the London College of Printing in 1997. The group investigated were the students who had left during the year from a range of part-time courses. We placed a lot of emphasis on the stories the students had to tell since we come from an epistemological position that assumes that knowledge of the world varies for different sections who are positioned differently in relation to power. There are multiple realities which need to be captured and compared in order to bring meaning to a social situation. These realities must be captured through the voices of the social actors being able to 'name the world' (Freire 1996). Their stories told of the pattern familiar from the further education literature of a complex combination of factors. These included the failure of the course to meet students' expectations, partly due to apparently over-enthusiastic marketing and a range of personal factors, including changes in job situation, significant illness and changes in personal relationships. There were also examples of where the students felt that their learning experience had been less than satisfactory and that this had contributed to their early departure.

We realized that, from an early stage, we needed to influence academic staff attitudes. We had a developing understanding of the theory and importance of micropolitics from our own professional experience and from the research literature on schools, especially analyses of micropolitics (Gronn 1986; Ball 1991; Ball and Rowe 1991; Blase 1991; Hargreaves 1994), work on teachers' lives and careers (Ball and Goodson 1985; Becker 1995) and critiques of the school improvement movement (Bascia and Hargreaves 2000). We understand micropolitics to mean the interplay within organizations of the status and power of various groups based on their material interests and values to achieve their preferred outcomes (Gronn 1986; Ball 1991; Blase 1991). In essence, retention must be located within the domain of interest of academic staff. Our experience in further education had taught us that initial responses are often to locate all responsibility with the students. It is comfortable to see the world as one where students leave for personal or financial reasons and other factors external to the institution. We would not seek to deny these reasons, but we wanted to encourage staff to see that there was also an institutional contribution to improving retention. We knew the further education research showed that students left for a complex combination of reasons and that their experience of a supportive learning environment could encourage them to persevere even in the face of considerable individual difficulty (Kenwright 1996). Therefore, we wanted academic staff to appreciate the importance of retention. Again, our experience from further education was that, in recent years, college managers had appealed to staff by highlighting the financial penalties on the institution for drop-out and that this loss of income was a threat to lecturer employment. Our view was that staff had received this with a certain cynicism, suspecting that management values were primarily financial. In our experience, it was more effective to recognize that most academic staff operate from a value position of concern about their students and would respond more positively when improving retention was presented as avoiding students leaving with a sense of failure.

We work on the principles of developing a culture of retention improvement, which is founded on the professional values of the academic staff, and then allowing staff space to identify strategies which they think will work best in their particular context. We also recognize that many academic staff suffer from innovation fatigue, irritation at being blamed for success or failure of various initiatives and a sense of powerlessness over the implementation of both national and institutional policy (Bascia and Hargreaves 2000). Therefore, we focused our staff development effort on supporting small practical projects which academic staff felt would make a difference to retention in their particular situation. At the London College of Printing, we combined Martinez' (1997) collection of strategies to improve retention in further education colleges with the methodology developed by Graham Gibbs at the Oxford Brookes Centre for Staff Development. The model is that each participant chooses a strategy from the collection which they feel would be appropriate for their situation and explains it to the rest of the group. This led to the development in both colleges of various groups of academic staff running small retention projects which were essentially action research. Our experience is that this approach is much more effective than the set staff development presentation. There are clear parallels between what we know about deep and surface learning for students and what we should do in staff development.

Various approaches emerged. At the London College of Fashion, the groups were course teams whose projects included improved tracking of student progress, redesigning aspects of the curriculum, identifying and supporting 'at risk' students, using exit interviews to identify retention issues and forming firmer links with study support. At the London College of Printing, the projects were carried out by the tutorial co-ordinators. These included monitoring the tutorial records of students who drop out to see if, in retrospect, the possibility of dropping out could have been spotted earlier, and a survey of students who considered dropping out but stayed. The aim was to identify factors affecting their decision. We have continued this model of small-scale projects and they now include prioritizing particular courses for additional tutorial monitoring and support, the development of case-study training materials situated firmly within a particular course or programme and the piloting of student–student mentoring.

We recognize both structure and agency as having significant importance in understanding and, therefore, changing the social world. These act in a dialectical relationship (Giddens 1979). This meant that as we worked with the key 'agents', we also needed to tackle structural issues. Martinez (1997), having challenged a 'within student' model of drop-out, went on to research the efficacy of strategies used to increase retention. The majority of successful strategies fall into one of five categories. First, there are best fit initiatives. These refer to work done to ensure that there is a good match between student and course at entry by improving pre-entry information. Second, there are supporting activities such as the development of learning support strategies, study support, language support and curriculum enrichment programmes. Third, there is financial support which looks to the extension of the use of bursary schemes aimed at reducing the financial hardship experienced by some students. Fourth, colleges used connective activities to build the connection between the college and the student via mentoring schemes and enhanced tutorial packages. Finally, transformational strategies were introduced to raise student expectation and self-belief through the development of careers and progression activities.

At the London College of Printing we prioritized improving student induction. Our knowledge of further education literature and practice told us the importance of ensuring that students settled in at the beginning of the course (Hayes 1996 quoted in Fitzcharles 2001). Our own data confirmed the national pattern, whereby most students leave in the first half of the first year. From our further education experience, we brought a three-part model of induction which foregrounds induction into the college with an emphasis on support services, induction into the group focusing on the encouragement of informal networks and friendship groups among students, and induction into the curriculum focusing on course requirements and expectations. We supported staff through an induction handbook with checklists for planning and outlining good practice. This handbook was produced by an open group, including interested partners such as course directors, student services, study support and the Student Union, an example of our principle of trying to give voice to different groups with different access to power.

A parallel development was the focus on study support at both colleges. Research in further education (Basic Skills Agency 1997) indicated that students who accessed study support had lower drop-out rates. By study support, we mean an offer to students of one-to-one or small group support with the aim of maximizing their opportunity to succeed. We use a broad model of study support, since it is influenced by our philosophy outlined above of a commitment to equity and social justice by maximizing opportunity for all students. Study support therefore offers help with many aspects of learning, including situated (discipline-specific) study skills, understanding disciplinary cultures, reading, research skills, time management, analysis, writing development and help with progression. It also offers support to students with a specific difficulty, such as dyslexia, those who have English as a second language and those with a disability. It is open to all students from further education to postgraduate level and students can self refer or be referred by a lecturer, another support service or a friend. We arrived at the London Institute just as study support was emerging, used our experience in further education to gain recognition for its importance and built a rapidly developing and successful service. It was important to develop this service on the principles of maximizing student potential and encouraging independent learning that we have outlined above. Therefore, we do not see the students who come to study support as a fixed group of weaker students, but a diverse and ever-changing group. A student may come with an essay that has been identified by a member of staff as having weaknesses, but equally a student may use study support to increase their chance of getting very high grades.

As we recognize different conceptions of learning, we have built teams of tutors in study support who work across various paradigms, including English for academic purposes, academic literacies and dyslexia models. Study support has an academic focus which is linked firmly to the curriculum. Our view is that the starting point must be the students' curriculum rather than the students' personal circumstances, although of course we recognize that they may be related and would not deny or ignore the importance of personal factors for some students. We aim to ensure that study support is high profile and not associated with 'having problems'. Fundamental to our approach is a belief that students do not fit into pre-set categories. International students may speak English as a first language, home students may be bilingual and students have degrees of dyslexia (Orr 2000). We counter the 'standards are always falling' notion of literacy in further education and higher education. Thus, we avoid the use of pejorative, moralistic language when articulating students' needs (Lillis 1997; Creme and Lea 1999; Turner 1999). We also wish to use the various strategies of student support to influence curriculum, assessment organization and delivery so that these are clear, explicit and equitable, thus enabling learning for all students. Therefore, we link structural issues back to the culture of academic staff.

Study support is, of course, for the few rather than the many. The majority of students do not come to study support, therefore an institutional strategy to build good support to improve retention must develop structures that reach all students. Consequently, it became a priority to improve and enhance the tutorial systems, by which we mean group and individual academic guidance given to students by academic staff with a focus on improving student learning. Evidence from student feedback and course monitoring suggested that the quality of tutoring was variable across both colleges. We set out to improve both access to and quality of this provision. We used the open group model outlined above to develop a tutorial policy which then formed part of a handbook for tutors. As in the induction handbook, we developed frameworks, models of good practice and useful checklists rather than a rigid model imposed from above. We also realized the importance of support for tutors and monitoring the student experience, so our second step was to argue for tutorial co-ordinators in each school. This was a model we had developed successfully in further education and our belief was that it was key in any strengthening of the tutorial system. As this was part of our retention strategy, we were able to argue for the time for the resource of a member of the academic staff in each school to take on this role. Their role includes monitoring the student experience, providing tutors with support and information, and identifying and helping to deliver staff development opportunities in order to enhance tutoring skills. This has given us a network of staff who are located within the schools, who work closely with the study support team and student services and provide collaborative development of staff skills and an infrastructure of support for the whole retention project. Thus, all the strategies come together.

Continuous improvement

We are committed to a culture of continuous improvement, while recognizing the demands this makes on staff and current critiques of the concept (Morley 2000). Our commitment comes from our inability to find a viable alternative within the current political, social and economic climate. As part of continuous improvement, we evaluate our strategies to seek further improvement. Our methodology is qualitative and is based on 'thick description' (Geertz 1973) and 'the reflective practitioner' (Schön 1987). Our model of evaluation is:

> . . . a form of self-reflective enquiry undertaken by participants in social (including educational) situations in order to improve the rationality and justice of (a) their own social and educational practices, (b) their understanding of these practices, and (c) the situations in which these practices are carried out.
>
> (Kemmis 1993: 177)

We aim to illuminate a complex situation rather than offer causal explanations by claiming 'success' for any particular intervention or combination of interventions. We understand the importance of local structures and cultures and do not regard initiatives as automatically transportable to other situations (Oakes et al. 2000). Our model of validity comes from the reflexivity of the researchers, our openness to critical peer judgement (Phillips 1993) and the use made by others of our insights (Nias 1993).

Within this paradigm, we use a number of ways to build the picture, including the extent to which study support is used by students, student feedback questionnaires and focus groups to identify levels of student satisfaction, staff team analysis of the result of their interventions and participant evaluation of all staff development activities. This gives us considerable information, but our priority is to feed back local information to academic staff to enable individual and team reflection. We also take advantage of any opportunities to access external evaluation and pay attention not only to the grades in subject review, consistently 4s in Student Support and Guidance, but any issues raised in that process.

Conclusion

In this chapter we have argued for joined-up thinking from a range of perspectives. First, higher education has a lot to learn from the earlier and more intense experience of further education in addressing issues of student retention. Second, retention strategy at the institutional level must ensure the coming together of all relevant structural and cultural elements of the picture. Finally, success depends both on local factors and on an understanding of micropolitics. There is a wealth of experience to be learned from research literature on this from the schools sector. This leads to any institutional policy being mediated through the interests and values of individuals and teams.

5

Policy Implications of Student Non-completion: Government, Funding Councils and Universities[1]

Roderick Floud

Introduction: failure in the midst of success

Discussing failure is a rather gloomy activity; it is important therefore to remember immediately that it is failure in the midst of success. During the 1990s, the British university system achieved more than most people thought possible. It has collectively expanded the proportion of young people going to university from around 20 per cent to about 32 per cent. It has given opportunities to hundreds of thousands of mature students, redressing the inequities and inequalities of access which applied to past generations. More than half of its students are women. Britain's ethnic minorities are now over-represented as a whole in higher education in comparison with their share of the population (Higher Education Funding Council for England 1996; Modood and Acland 1998), although some individual groups still need assistance. It has become much better at catering for the needs of disabled students and has recognized the need to help students with their study skills.

All these successes have not come by default. London Guildhall University, for example, has worked for nearly 15 years to encourage members of its local Bangladeshi population to come into higher education; over 500 now study at the University, compared with fewer than 10 about a decade ago. Great efforts have been put into the development of study skills programmes for a wide range of students. The University's dyslexia support unit works with hundreds of students. Almost all universities can tell similar stories of effort crowned by success.

One of the many aspects of this success is that Britain has created a mass higher education system that still manages to achieve higher completion rates than most other systems in the world and, as a result, has one of the highest proportions of people graduating. It also produces graduates who have excellent employment and career prospects. Although the government expresses worries about graduate unemployment, the fact that graduates have average rates of unemployment of about 5.5 per cent only 6 months after graduation (and only about 2 per cent after 2 years) seems to need little excuse. Moreover, graduates still command substantially higher salaries throughout their working lives.

It is in many ways paradoxical that this increasing success of the British university system has been accompanied by ever more strident expressions of dissatisfaction and calls for more and more public accountability. Of course, the very success of the system in expanding so much and so rapidly means that there are more people to be dissatisfied and that more public money is at risk. The sheer size of the system breeds enquiry into whether failure, whenever it occurs, is a systemic problem rather than the product of individual difficulty. It is arguable also that the introduction of the payment of tuition fees by full-time students has stimulated more complaints about failure, on the grounds that students have not received the service for which they have paid.

Nevertheless, for whatever reason, there is public and ministerial concern about whether there is avoidable failure, with causes that can be laid at the door of universities. On 29 November 2000, for example, the Secretary of State sent his annual letter to the Higher Education Funding Council for England (HEFCE). Paragraph 11 reads:

> Notwithstanding progress on recruitment, institutions should focus on retaining students, particularly those from disadvantaged backgrounds. Widening access to higher education must not lead to an increase in the number of students who fail to complete their courses. I therefore expect to see the Council bear down on the rate of 'drop-out.' The evidence shows there are unacceptable variations in the rate of 'drop-out' which appear to be linked more to the culture and workings of the institution than to the background or nature of the students recruited. It is therefore time for much more substantial work to be done on identifying best practice and bringing pressure to bear on those institutions whose performance falls significantly below their benchmark. I want to see within the next few months a report on a programme of work and action plan developed by the Council in conjunction with institutions.

Essentially, David Blunkett's concern is that public money is being wasted if some students fail to achieve what the HEFCE now calls 'learning outcomes'. In addition, there is genuine anxiety about the human costs of what is perceived to be an increasing amount of failure. Such concern also lies behind the growth of quality assurance mechanisms. It helped to stimulate the call by the Dearing Committee for the formation of the Institute for Learning and Teaching.

Even more fundamentally, these concerns have led some to question what they see as the provider domination of higher education, in which universities are given grants essentially to do with as they wish and are governed and managed mainly by academics. The recent post-16 review, altering the whole structure of education and training outside the universities, is instructive here (Department for Education and Employment 1999). The system based on this review, that of the Learning and Skills Council (LSC) which began operations in April 2001, is business dominated. It has an explicit mission to serve the needs of business and the economy; there is no element of local democratic accountability and words such as 'academic freedom' are nowhere to be found in the review document or the relevant legislation. The structure of funding is to be radically simplified; in what direction is not yet clear, but the concept of output-based funding is certainly being discussed. For those who know their educational history, this is what was known in the late nineteenth century as payment by results. Universities are not directly part of the new structure, although they receive funding from the LSC, but its lessons and the thinking behind it cannot be ignored.

Further fuel to the fire is being added with the increasing sophistication of management statistics in higher education as a whole. From 2002 onwards, it will be possible to examine the time spent on, and thus the costs of, teaching year by year in each university. This possibility arises from the Research Transparency Exercise (introduced by the universities at the behest of HM Treasury), designed to provide reassurance on the use of public funding for research. Although such use of the data is not currently envisaged, it will not require much ingenuity to match the data on teaching inputs to the numbers of graduates, or failed students, in order to produce statistics on cost per graduate or failed student. It will then be easy to calculate the relative costs of producing a graduate between institutions. The outcome is very difficult to predict.

So what can the university system do to respond to these pressures? First, it must accept that they are matters of legitimate public concern – universities receive very substantial public funds and the government is entitled to ask what they do with them. Second, it must welcome the fact that the current government accepts that widening participation is expensive and that it has increased support for access and hardship funds, partly at least to avoid increasing levels of failure due to financial pressures; again, universities need to show that this funding is well used (Department for Education and Employment 2000a). Finally, and fundamentally, universities must understand why failure occurs and what might be done about it.

On the basis of this survey of current activity, this chapter first considers the extent of non-completion in British higher education. This is followed by a discussion of the causes of non-completion. Finally, the chapter suggests policy responses by individuals, universities and government.

Defining the questions: the extent of non-completion

What is the current evidence about student failure? It is important to discuss failure in terms of non-completion, a much wider and larger problem than academic failure in the sense of people who fail exams and are excluded. This latter group is very small indeed; it is probably more difficult to fail British university exams than it is to get a first class degree. The pioneering study by Mantz Yorke and his colleagues identified (from HESA statistics) 170 failures in the strict sense within the six universities studied (Yorke et al. 1997: 9).[2] These universities had at least 60,000 students in total and, therefore, perhaps 20,000 in each undergraduate year. On this basis, 170 failures is a failure rate of approximately 0.75 per cent. Academic failure of this kind is very distressing, but it is much less serious for the system as a whole than non-completion in the broader sense. Indeed, it is arguable that proper quality control requires, or at least makes it likely, that some people will fail.

Non-completion (where the term is used in the sense of those who commence a university course but, for whatever reason, do not attain a qualification of any kind) is a larger and more serious problem, although still one affecting only a small minority of students. The study by Yorke and his colleagues suggested that in 1994–95 withdrawal rates from 'all but a small number of atypical institutions' averaged at least 5 per cent per annum according to HESA statistics, but that the true figure was probably closer to 10 per cent per annum (Yorke et al. 1997: ii).[3]

There is no doubt that patterns of study are now much more varied and flexible than when all but the exceptional undergraduate completed his or her course in 3 years of full-time study. Students switch from full-time to part-time study, take breaks from study, move from one course to another within a single institution and also move from one institution to another, possibly after a break from study. Such flexibility poses great problems for the estimation of rates of non-completion, since an individual recorded as a failure at one university may some years later become a success at another. The effect will be that each university will over-estimate its non-completion rates, being ignorant of what actually happens to the student in question. It is for this reason that the HEFCE is now attempting to track individual students and publish statistics of overall non-completion. Unfortunately, such an effort takes time, and certainty cannot be achieved until the tracking is complete, which may well be 5 or 6 years after the first entry of a student.

In October 2000, however, the HEFCE published its second annual *Performance Indicators in Higher Education in the UK*, covering 1997–98 and 1998–99. This publication contains interesting information concerning patterns of student retention; in particular, data are given for 'non-continuation following year of entry' and 'projected learning outcomes and efficiencies'. The former are based on actual experience of a cohort of students, while the latter are 'extrapolations, or projections, of current patterns' (Higher Education Funding Council for England 2000: 90).

The data show that, for full-time first degree entrants in all UK higher education institutions, 88 per cent qualify or continue (normally into the second year) at the same institution, 3 per cent transfer to another institution and 9 per cent are not to be found in UK higher education. There is a large difference between young entrants, 8 per cent of whom are not in UK higher education, and mature students, where non-continuation is 15 per cent. Within these overall figures, there are substantial differences between institutions, the largest figure for non-continuation being 29 per cent and the smallest 1 per cent (Higher Education Funding Council for England 2000: 56–63, Table 3a).

In interpreting differences between institutions in these statistics it is important to take account of the differing characteristics of entrants. The HEFCE does this through the calculation of 'benchmarks', which allow for 'the subject mix of the institution, the qualifications on entry of its students, and the age on entry of its students if the indicator covers all ages' (Higher Education Funding Council for England 2000: 17). The benchmark calculated on this basis is 'the value that the whole UK sector would have had if it had the same subject and entry qualification (and age) profile as the institution' (Higher Education Funding Council of England 2000: 17). Another way of describing it is as the average value (although not calculated as a simple arithmetic mean) found among institutions which have similar student profiles. Thus, it enables one to compare like with like and to identify institutions which have higher or lower non-continuation rates than that average.[4]

The HEFCE data show that 13 out of 127 English institutions, 7 out of 19 Scottish institutions and 1 out of 13 Welsh institutions had non-continuation rates which were significantly different (in a statistical sense) from their benchmarks. Of these, 7 English and 2 Scottish institutions had rates significantly worse than their benchmarks.[5] These 9 institutions together accounted for 6.5 per cent of entrants to British higher education in 1997/98.

The statistics for overall learning outcomes are necessarily more complex and more speculative, since the students concerned have not actually completed their courses or exhausted the time during which they might have been expected to complete either at their original or another institution. However, for what they are worth, the data show that in the UK as a whole it is expected that 17 per cent of students will not achieve an award, with the figures ranging from 1 per cent to 38 per cent.[6] A total of 43 English, 4 Scottish, 3 Welsh and 1 Northern Irish institutions had predicted figures for 'neither award nor transfer' which were significantly different from their benchmarks. Of these, 15 English, 3 Scottish and 2 Welsh institutions were significantly worse than expected.[7] It is noticeable that, of those 20 institutions, 12 are also shown in another table to be significantly better than their benchmarks in recruiting from either or both of state schools and colleges or from social classes IIIM, IV and V. It is worth repeating that the benchmarks *do not* take account of those characteristics of the students.

These statistics clearly show that there is a wide range of experience and that individual institutions need to examine their own practice to see whether there are ways in which non-completion rates can be improved. At first sight, the overall non-completion rates shown are very similar to those identified by Mantz Yorke, at between 5 per cent and 10 per cent per annum. If this is really so, it is encouraging that the further widening of participation which has taken place since Yorke's study (1997) of 1994–95, and the introduction of fees and changes to student support arrangements, have not led to substantially increased drop-out rates. However, figures from the Department for Education and Employment (compiled on a different basis) do show a gradual increase in non-completion from 14 per cent for 1983/84 entrants to 18–19 per cent for 1995/96 entrants (www.dfes.gov.uk). In addition, all these statistics pre-date the changes to fees and student support introduced since 1997.

What are the costs of this level of non-completion? Without the benefit of the HEFCE data, but taking as many as possible of the relevant factors into account, Yorke and his colleagues calculated the most likely cost of non-completion to the public purse to be £91 million (in 1994 prices) with an upper-bound estimate of £178 million. While these are large absolute sums, they represented 3 per cent and 5.8 per cent respectively of public expenditure on higher education in the year in question. The HEFCE has not published similar estimates based on recent data, but in principle they could be calculated. However, if, as suggested above, the HEFCE performance indicators do not suggest that drop-out has increased substantially, then it may be that these proportions still hold, at least approximately. The cost to the public purse may even be lower, because of the reduction in public expenditure on student maintenance and the introduction of the student contribution to tuition fees.

The HEFCE performance indicators do suggest, however, that even students who do ultimately complete may be taking longer to do so. The HEFCE has calculated a so-called 'efficiency' index, which compares the actual average time to complete a qualification with the expected average time to complete. In broad terms, this shows, as one might expect, that the average time to complete is greater for institutions which admit students with poorer qualifications from disadvantaged backgrounds.

The interesting policy question is whether this matters. Many universities with such students would argue that what is important to them is the ultimate achievement, not the time it has taken. Indeed, many modular schemes are explicitly designed to enable students to progress at different rates, perhaps to take account of financial or family circumstances. If this was not possible, many of these disadvantaged students might never enter university, or might soon drop out. On the other hand, the longer the period of full-time study, the greater the cost to the state (through the grant to institutions) and the student (in fees and maintenance). It is a policy question as to whether these additional costs are justified if they reduce drop-out and aid ultimate completion. In other words, the acceptance of a longer average time to complete may be a penalty worth paying to avoid even larger non-completion rates.

The essential questions remain: whether, and if so by what means, these rates of non-completion can be significantly reduced. This is the challenge set by David Blunkett to the HEFCE and the institutions which it funds, as a preliminary to reducing non-completion in individual institutions and in the system as a whole. However, it must be remembered that the performance indicators show that most of the variation in non-completion rates can be explained (at least in statistical terms) by variation in the characteristics of student recruits. Bearing down on individual institutions which are performing less well than their benchmarks, to repeat David Blunkett's instructions to the HEFCE, is unlikely therefore to make very much difference either to the overall national rate or to the rates experienced by groups of institutions. The problem appears to be almost entirely a systemic one, rather than something that can be attributed to the faults of individual universities and colleges.

Understanding and partitioning failure: the causes of non-completion

Before we can devise policies to avoid or mitigate failure, we first need to understand it. Traditionally, this effort at understanding has proceeded from the individual problem – a student seems in danger of failing, therefore he or she is counselled or assisted in some way. In times when the university was seen to be *in loco parentis*, great efforts were made by tutors or by student advice services to prevent failure or non-completion. Even when students were demonstrably unhappy at university, to the extent of threatened or actual self-harm, it was regarded as all-important that they should be kept on their course. For them to leave was a failure, not only for them but also for the college or university.

Such an approach is analogous to the medical model of disease. According to this model, doctors are presented with people who are ill. Doctors and medical researchers set out to devise methods to treat the symptoms, alleviate distress and, if possible, cure the patient. Continued ill-health or death is a sign of failure. Treatments are improved by trial and error or by research which concentrates on those who are ill and on devising new methods, through drug therapies, surgery or otherwise, to cure them. As the numbers who are ill increase, or as knowledge of how to cure them is enhanced, more and more resources are directed to therapy and care.

Current treatment of failing students is very similar to the medical model. Counsellors, student advisors and individual lecturers try to help those who are in danger of failing, devising new structures and methods, learning from experience and generalizing from particular cases. A further similarity is that knowledge of the problem is built up from the individual to the general. Thus, Yorke's study for the HEFCE surveyed 1478 full-time and sandwich students and asked them to specify their reasons for withdrawal (Yorke et al. 1997: 9). Their replies showed that three main factors underlay withdrawal – financial problems, inability to cope with the demands of the programme and dissatisfaction with the institutional experience. This confirms the experience of many student counsellors and others who have tried to cope with or prevent failure.

What it does not do, except tangentially, is to enable universities to design policies which will reduce or eliminate non-completion. Most students have financial problems, but only a few withdraw from their courses. Many, no doubt, find difficulty with their academic work or are dissatisfied with the institutions at which they are studying, but again only a small proportion drop out. Unless there are common factors which produce non-completion, which the university or someone else can identify, there is little that it or anyone else can do to 'design out' the problem.

Identifying such common factors requires an approach which is fundamentally different from that of the medical model. The method is, by contrast, that of the epidemiologist or specialist in public health. Such disciplines seek to measure the prevalence of disease, to understand its underlying causes, to predict when it may break out and to try to devise strategies to prevent it. They establish the risk of a particular group of people falling ill, as an aid to diagnosing what the causes and correlates of the disease may be. It is important to note that the epidemiologist is concerned essentially with groups of people, not with individuals, and with establishing how likely it is that a certain proportion of those groups will fall ill, not with predicting which individuals within those groups will do so.

In following the epidemiological, rather than medical, model of failure, an initial step is conceptually to partition failure into avoidable and predictable failure on the one hand and unavoidable and unpredictable failure on the other. These categories are not clear-cut, but one can exemplify. Into the category of unavoidable and unpredictable failures can be put life events which are wholly unrelated to the fact that a student is at university, such as accident, bereavement or the need to care for a sick relative. It is essentially impossible for anyone to predict that such an event will occur to a given student or to avoid the consequences if the event does occur. Pastoral care can be offered, but its success in helping the student to complete the course is again unpredictable.

Some fraction of non-completion arising from simple academic failure is also unavoidable, although its prevalence may be predictable. It is not the primary function of academics to be gatekeepers, failing a specified number of students so as to show that standards are being upheld. Yet quality control does imply that some students will fail because they have not done enough work or, brutally, because they are not clever enough. Some of those students will have possessed good entrance qualifications and were expected by all who knew them to be likely to succeed; they did not, but no-one knows why.

Therefore, there must logically be an irreducible minimum of failure, which no conceivable policies could affect. No-one knows what proportion this irreducible minimum forms of total non-completion. Health problems, for example, were indicated as having a moderate or considerable influence on withdrawal by 23 per cent of those surveyed by Yorke and his colleagues (Yorke et al. 1997: 10). Some of these withdrawals must have been caused by illness which was linked to the university or the course, while others would have occurred even if the student had not been at university. It can be hazarded, but it is a pure guess, that at least 20 per cent of non-completion is neither avoidable nor predictable.[8]

Logically, however, some other proportion, and probably the majority of non-completion, must be both avoidable and predictable, and it is with this group of failure that policy has to be concerned. Ideally, universities need first to know which categories of students are most likely to fail, as only when they have this knowledge can they devise policies to deal with the problems which lead to failure. In other words, they need to know the risk factors so that they can calculate the risks of failure and concentrate attention on the groups most at risk.

To do this effectively would require a new type of research study, to identify which groups of students are more likely to fail. We need to know the risk that someone recruited in clearing, or a student aged over 25, or a student of history, or someone from a public school, or a student of physics, will fail. It is important to note that such conclusions cannot be drawn logically from study only of those who *have* failed. Mantz Yorke concluded, for example, that those who withdrew from the pre-1992 universities were more likely to cite grounds such as 'wrong field of study, lack of commitment, lack of study skills and programme difficulty' than those who withdrew from post-1992 universities. However, this does not imply that students at old universities were more likely to suffer from such problems than students at new universities. What we need to know is not the likelihood that a withdrawing student will have suffered such problems, but the likelihood that such problems will cause a student (from a group with particular characteristics) to withdraw.[9]

At the national and institutional level, the HEFCE's current research into learning outcomes will provide some indicative data.[10] However, such analysis will need to be supplemented by work at subject level within institutions. There is a need to calculate and seek to explain differences in outcomes, department by department and even course by course. This has been done at London Guildhall University for first-year courses, despite the fact that it can be threatening for individual lecturers, as a guide to the courses to which additional teaching resources should be allocated or where the programme should be redesigned.

Such procedures are, or should be, an important part of quality control. Ideally, the chances of a student securing a particular class of degree should not be affected by his or her choice of optional unit within a course. Therefore, quality control implies that departments should examine the chances of failure unit by unit. If one unit differs markedly from the others, remedial action must be taken. Extra teaching or tutorial assistance might be appropriate, or a redesign of the syllabus or, possibly, attention to the units which have preceded the 'problem unit' in the student's programme.

Once the risks of failure are known – course by course, institution by institution or type of student by type of student – the next step is to calculate the costs of reducing failure. Many universities are now taking action to help students in difficulties. At London Guildhall, for example, there is an expanded Learning Development Unit and a Dyslexia Centre. Peer support systems have been introduced, and many courses now incorporate study skills modules. Consequently, there are plenty of data on which to work, plenty of costs with which to contrast the costs of failure. None of this will be wholly accurate, because human beings are unpredictable, but it should be indicative, a guide to action. It is, in fact, the analogue of 'evidence-based medicine' which is increasingly guiding the work of doctors and the National Health Service.

It is possible, of course, that the causes of student failure are so diverse, or that such a high proportion fall into the category of 'unavoidable and unpredictable', that the avoidable and predictable risks turn out to be very small. In that case, universities and the government might be able to stop worrying and instead accept the existing levels of failure as an unavoidable overhead. Indeed, it is arguable that if, as Yorke and his colleagues suggest, the most likely cost of non-completion is as little as 3 per cent of public expenditure on higher education, this may be a tolerable level of overhead cost, particularly as that figure must include the cost of some failures which are both unavoidable and unpredictable.

Identifying risk factors does itself carry some risk. There is the danger that the identification of risk attached to particular groups of students will lead some universities to try to avoid problems by refusing to take students from groups with those characteristics. It would be like GPs clearing all the old age pensioners off their lists. This is a serious danger, particularly when some academics consider that the expansion of higher education has already gone too far and that ill-qualified students are being admitted to inappropriate courses.[11] However, it is a danger that cannot be avoided if we are to devise strategies to overcome the difficulties which students face. It must be clear that the danger would become much greater if the funding councils, or government, were to penalize institutions with a relatively high level of non-completion.

Is the demand for more enquiry, for the calculation of risk factors, for 'evidence-based' policies merely the traditional academic response to any problem, namely that 'more research is needed'? Not at all. It is, instead, the response of a Vice-Chancellor dealing with the allocation of scarce resources and wishing to have some rational basis for making decisions. Similarly, at the level of government or funding council, it is sensible that decisions and priorities should be set rationally.

Lessons and challenges: the policy response

The present level of non-completion presents challenges for individuals, institutions, funding councils and the government. Each needs to design an appropriate response.

There is a challenge for those whose job it is to deal with students in need. Most universities have an increasing number of counselling and student advisory staff, often responding to student requests for help with finance, study problems and pastoral needs. The corollary of the evidence-based approach at the national or institutional level is that such staff must consider how they can demonstrate that their efforts are producing worthwhile results. The work gives us all a warm feeling, but we need to show that it is really cost-effective.

At the institutional level, the challenge is to balance the costs of preventing failure against all the other costs of providing education for the considerable majority of students who do not fail. This is a complex equation. One example of the complexity is that, in strict economic terms and while current funding methods prevail, universities do not lose much financially from failure, provided (and it is a significant proviso) that they can recruit sufficient students each year to compensate for those who withdraw.[12] Universities are funded to provide education for a given number of students each year, not to secure them a qualification at the end. It could be argued therefore that, aside from the possible effect on their reputation and hence on their ability to attract new students, universities could tolerate high failure rates. In practice, however, universities are made up of human beings who are not so callous. Moreover, few universities wish to have the reputation of being indifferent to the fate of their students.

At the level of the government or funding council, the first challenge is to calculate the true costs of unavoidable failure. If, as Yorke calculated, the total cost of avoidable and unavoidable failure is 3 per cent of overall expenditure, it is conceivable that the cost of avoidable failure is as little as 1–2 per cent. While even such a sum is worth saving, the challenge will be to devise mechanisms which encourage universities to minimize failure without doing harm in other directions. This does require confronting the issue of diversity. In recent years, the funding councils have celebrated the diversity of the higher education system, but their policy has been to equalize funding by subject group across all institutions. Thus, to the extent that there are avoidable and predictable causes of failure, perhaps related to the social class or ethnicity of students, the funding councils have taken very little explicit notice of them in their funding decisions. If increased drop-out is very largely the result of policies to widen participation, and if minimizing drop-out is regarded as the principal policy priority, then it is likely that funding systems will have to change. It might be argued, for example, that more funding should be directed to support the teaching and learning of the least well-qualified students, who are most likely to drop out.

In England, the only exception to level funding has been the 'widening participation funding', based on geodemographic profiles. Universities have received funding based on the number of students from neighbourhood types identified through postcode areas as being socially or economically disadvantaged. They have also received premia for part-time and mature students. These initiatives, although a welcome and overdue recognition of diversity, are almost certainly too small in financial terms to reflect the additional costs involved for institutions in recruiting and retaining such students. The HEFCE needs to have the courage of its convictions and direct much larger sums than at present to the institutions which have proved that they are doing the job which the HEFCE wants done.

Government and funding councils should be particularly wary, by contrast, of seeking to use the funding system to penalize universities which appear to have high levels of non-completion. While such a course of action would be superficially attractive, it would be an incentive to universities to discriminate against social groups which were thought to have a high risk of failure. To the extent that these groups are those from socially or economically deprived backgrounds, this would run counter to other government policies to encourage access from such groups. Such a policy of penalizing failure would also be difficult to square with a commitment to quality control, which demands that universities should have no financial incentive to lower the standards of their degrees. As educational policy-makers found over 100 years ago, payment by results has unintended consequences. Above all, it is in the nature of higher education that students gradually take responsibility for their own learning; this is a process that cannot be risk-free.

Universities, the government and funding councils can unite in supporting the core activities of universities. It needs to be emphasized again that the evidence available at the moment suggests that only a relatively small proportion of students fail. This implies that the most successful policy should not try to stop students failing, but should instead help them to succeed. This may appear to be a tautology, but it is nevertheless true.

Looking at failure in this way implies first and foremost that all universities need to take seriously their teaching functions and the support for learning that they give. It is a depressing fact that there are still many university teachers and managers who deride the concept of university teaching as a profession whose skills can be, and must be, learnt. The Institute for Learning and Teaching has a long road to travel.

The government, funding councils and universities must also accept the modern student as he or she is. A recent survey in part of London Guildhall University revealed that 85 per cent of students have jobs during term-time and that the hours worked range from 5 to 22.[13] For this reason, 80 per cent of universities now provide an employment service for their students. It is a fact of modern university life – as it was not even 20 years ago – that students have jobs, live at home, are married with children, need to pay the mortgage and want lives outside student halls of residence. They want choice in what they study and the ability to change their minds, to have the relative freedom of modular structures and continuous assessment. All this leads to students taking longer to complete their courses and being at greater risk of failure. Yet it is the reality of modern student life. Universities will maximize success and minimize failure only if they recognize that reality and devise policies which will work with it.

Notes

1. I am grateful to the editors, to the participants at the Lancaster conference and to John Thompson and Bahram Bekhradnia of the Higher Education Funding Council for England for their comments on earlier drafts. All errors of fact or interpretation remain mine.
2. It is likely that this figure is an underestimate, particularly since only about 30 per cent of leavers have a recorded reason for leaving in the HESA returns. It is also likely that some students leave, or are encouraged to leave, in anticipation of academic failure. However, the fact remains that recorded failures are small.
3. The study also suggested that 56 per cent of those students who withdrew during or at the end of the academic year 1994–95 had returned to study by the autumn of 1996 and that a further 18 per cent still planned to do so. Many of these students were taking a break from study and, under the regulations of degree schemes, could take up their courses again after the break, possibly at another institution. However, more recent studies by HEFCE (see below) suggest that the levels of return to study or transfer are substantially lower than estimated by Yorke et al.
4. This explanation of benchmarks has been lengthy, because they have often been misunderstood. An average cannot be a target, because some must be above and some below an average figure, and it is therefore a serious logical mistake to see benchmarks as targets. It is legitimate, however, to enquire into the reasons why an institution's figure is significantly (in a statistical or other sense) different from its benchmark. It is also important to note that the benchmarks do not make allowance for other factors that may be relevant, such as the ethnicity of entrants.
5. The institutions were Bretton Hall, the University of Central Lancashire, the University of East London, the University of Luton, the University of North London, the School of Oriental and African Studies, Thames Valley University, Glasgow Caledonian University and the University of Paisley. Statistical significance was evaluated at the 5 per cent level.
6. See HEFCE (2000: 13, Table 6). The average of institutional non-completion rates is 16 per cent.
7. The institutions were Anglia Polytechnic University, Bolton Institute of Higher Education, the University of Central England, the University of Central Lancashire, the University of Derby, the University of East London, the University of Greenwich, the University of Huddersfield, the University of London (Senate House), London Guildhall University, the University of Luton, UMIST, the School of Oriental and African Studies, the University of Sunderland, the University of Wolverhampton, Glasgow Caledonian University, Napier University, the University of Paisley, the University of Glamorgan and North East Wales Institute.
8. There are reasons for thinking that the figure of 20 per cent may be much too small. For example, non-completion rates in Britain are already much lower than those in other comparable countries – from the Organization of Economic Co-operation and Development data show Germany as having non-completion rates of 28 per cent, the United States 37 per cent, France 45 per cent and Italy 66 per cent. It is difficult to see how overall British non-completion rates can be greatly improved when they are already the best in the world (with the possible exception of Japan's) and this implies that more than 20 per cent of British

non-completion may be unavoidable. However, that there is a logical division between avoidable and unavoidable non-completion is clearly correct.

9. It is to be hoped that a study of graduate non-completers, to be conducted by the Institute of Employment Research at the University of Warwick on behalf of the Department of Education and Employment, does not fall into the logical trap of inferring reasons for non-completion from study of those who have not completed. It is, however, welcome that the study intends to track the subsequent history of non-completers, although only for a short period. This may help to explore the question of the consequences of non-completion, which is a neglected subject.
10. It is very welcome that the HEFCE has embarked on a major project to examine risk or propensity factors in student outcomes. However, there is a danger that current political pressure on this issue will lead to decisions being taken before such factors have been elucidated.
11. Professor Graham Zellick, Vice-Chancellor of the University of London, was quoted in *The Sunday Telegraph* of 2 August 1999 as believing that: 'You've got people of moderate academic ability doing questionable academic courses culminating in degrees, leaving university, as they arrive, with inadequate literacy and numeracy.' Professor Zellick is said to have argued that the percentage of 18- to 21-year-olds entering higher education should be reduced from 32 per cent to a figure in the 20 per cent range, in particular by cutting the numbers entering academic courses. Instead, these students should be encouraged to pursue job-related training in the former polytechnics. These remarks were reported before the introduction of foundation degrees; these are intended to raise the standing of vocational qualifications, an ambition supported by Professor Zellick.
12. However, a student who fails to complete a year of study is not counted for the purposes of funding council grant to his or her institution.
13. DFEE (2000b: Table 4.5) shows that average term-time working was 11 hours per week for full-time students. Between 1995/96 and 1998/99, hours worked in paid employment by students from social classes IV and V rose by 15 per cent to a total of 181 hours. This contrasted with an average of 126 hours worked by students from social classes I and II, which had risen by 9 per cent.

Part 2

Teachers and Learners

6

Learning to Fail: Learning to Recover

David Cannon

Can you remember sitting in school thinking 'Oh, please, please don't pick me' as the teacher scanned the class looking for a likely victim to answer the question? Try to recall the rising anxiety as his eyes came to rest upon you – the confused panic at not knowing the answer, of not even understanding the question. Relive the embarrassing struggle to say something, anything, intelligent and the humiliating laughter of classmates reacting to your desperate reply.

The search for the right answer

For many young people, school can feel like a cruel game of 'Get the right answer'. To win the game, one must deliver the required number of right answers. Those who do are rewarded with praise, elevated status and financial support. Those who do not are either ignored or made the target of patronizing special attention aimed at fixing their obvious shortcomings. For many of the losers it is difficult to determine which of these is the worst punishment.

In his landmark book *How Children Fail* (1974), John Holt (a teacher) was the first to draw our attention to the sad consequences of this competitive game of 'Get the right answer'. Describing young children pressured into faking understanding, he depicts the classroom as the place where we learn to pretend to know, where we learn how to appear knowledgeable. My work in the business community over the last 15 years shows this to be an enduring behavioural lesson.

Form over content

As a schoolboy, I failed the subject of French language. This was a bit of a shock and meant that I had to retake the course during summer holidays in order to have sufficient credits for university. While my friends sunbathed on the beach, I practised tenses in a stuffy classroom convinced that the hallowed halls of university would be worth the extra effort. Naively, I pictured college life as a dreamy world in which one sat about speculating on various theories, dabbling in creative thinking and generally playing around with really big ideas. I was keen on history and English and signed up to study these favourites in my initial year. With sadness, I dropped both of them the following year. Similarly, friends who had been besotted by biology or energetic about engineering found themselves switching into other subject areas – their enthusiasms had turned out not to be their forte. Like myself, they too learned the lesson that one does not win the university game by having the right answer, but by answering in the right way.

This shift from the importance of the right answer to the right way of answering is best illustrated by the story of the Oxford student who responds to a long-winded exam question with a few brief lines. His terse answer states that any person truly knowledgeable about the subject could see that the question as constructed is flawed and irrelevant, thus not warranting an answer. Indeed, it would be wrong to answer a question so wrongly put. According to the urban myth, the tutor assigns the young man top marks because his response shows superior insight and real intellectual courage. Whether true or not, the point of this tale is that getting on well in higher education is partly about learning content and partly about mastering form. Those of us who continued on and now struggle to publish in academic journals know this exceedingly well.

The importance of appearing clever

The key to success in higher education is to convince others that you are clever and intelligent. If you fail to do so, tutors and peers alike will come to see you as not belonging in higher education and you will be relegated to the margins. Once marginalized, students either give up and withdraw or practise behaviours that further enhance their marginalized status, eventually resulting in them being asked to leave.

Thus, the people most at risk of failing in higher education are those who come to believe that they cannot, by real deeds or trickery, convince their fellow community members that they have sufficient mental capital. Such a self-perception can develop slowly over time or be triggered by a single critical incident which leads the individual to believe that they do not have the required mental horsepower. When this perception takes hold, it sets off a crisis in self-confidence fuelling the growing inner belief that they do not belong in the programme or in the institution. This often proves to be a self-fulfilling prophecy.

A matter of confidence

Statistics collected in the UK during the 1990s show females entering university with higher marks than their male cohorts. However, it is the men who end up with the most firsts. The reason given for this surprising turnaround is that men have more confidence than women, which makes them more likely to take risks when answering exam questions. Appearing clever or bright has a great deal to do with confidence. Even amongst students who score the highest marks on assignments and exams, confidence (or lack of it) still plays a key role. We have all read shocking stories about a top student taking their life because they were unable to meet the outrageous standards they set for themselves. Feeling like impostors, these brilliant young people lose whatever shred of confidence they have, often becoming overwhelmed with guilt at having let others down, such as parents or tutors.

The critical question is how do students in higher education come to lose their confidence? Are some students at greater risk of losing self-confidence than others? What can be done to enhance student confidence and sense of belonging? To tackle these questions, we must first examine the origins of failure, or more accurately, the origin of people's concepts of failure. By understanding what failure means to an individual, one learns how that person perceives themselves as failing. It is this self-perception, which can differ considerably from the perception of others, that erodes confidence; and it is this self-perception that points the way to the most appropriate path to recovery.

Where do our concepts of failure come from?

We learn them from others. Newborn infants come into the world having no concept of failure or of success. Unlike adults, they do not fear failure. On the contrary, they experiment with strategies in play, learning equally from those things that work and those that do not work (De Gues 1988). This learning by experiment continues into primary school. However, as pointed out earlier, it does not take long for children to pick up the message that the world puts value on 'right answers' and that wrong answers and failed strategies are for the most part socially unacceptable.

Individual perceptions of what constitutes a success and a failure begin with our early experiences of punishment. Although some children are punished more than others (physically, through verbal criticism, or by withdrawal of attention and love), all children experience varying degrees of penalty when demonstrating certain behaviours. The emotional sting of failure comes from its link with the sense of shame and guilt we learned to associate with being a 'bad' or 'naughty' child. Hence, common setbacks experienced as students, such as failing to get a good grade on an essay, can sometimes call our whole self-worth into question.

Given that different people have been taught different punishment lessons, it is important to appreciate that an individual's concept of what it is to 'do badly' may not be the same as that held by others. For some students failing to give the teacher the right answer in class is a humiliating event remembered long afterwards. For others, it is of less importance and is forgotten by the next day. They may be more upset about not being invited to be part of a project or study group, interpreting this exclusion as failing to fit in. The fact that individuals have unique childhood reward and punishment experiences means that each of us has our own concept or internal definition of what constitutes a personal failure. Those failures which prove most salient to a person are those which fit into their internal definitions of what it is to fail. They are also the ones they remember.

What kinds of failures do people remember?

As part of my ongoing research on failure, I conducted a study in which 61 individuals were asked to talk at length about past failures and setbacks. Two samples of people were interviewed – individuals from diverse walks of life including business people, artists, students, athletes and trainee accountants who had recently failed a professional examination. Each person participated in a 2-hour semi-structured interview, in which they related several experiences of past failure and later completed a battery of assessment instruments.

A content analysis was conducted on the total collection of 90 failure stories. These narratives resulted in a rich and varied collection of remembered failures including: making a career choice which did not work out; failing to secure a leading role in an opera; crash landing a jet aircraft; failing an important exam; being unable to win the admiration of a potential lover; and the break-up of a long-term business partnership.

Whilst some of these personal setbacks appeared more significant than others, with few exceptions, each experience was described by participants as a painful event which on recall continued to arouse feelings of anger and sadness. What the study found proved consistent with prior research in the field of memory. Events which are highly charged with emotion tend to be well remembered (Robinson 1980; Pillemer et al. 1986), especially if they bring 'durability of the self' into question (Brown and Kulik 1977). Participants from both samples told lengthy stories containing precise details, such as times, days of the week and what people had said. When asked to describe events in the days preceding or following the negative experience most participants could remember very little.

Isn't it better to forget about failures rather than dwell on them?

Failures, like other anxiety-raising experiences, are simply difficult to delete from memory, so advising people to 'forget about it' may not always be helpful. Although the brain acts to protect our sanity by suppressing deeply shocking events involving violence and abuse (Kilhstrom 1995), many negative events such as failing an exam, giving a poor classroom presentation or not being picked to be part of a project group do not fall into this extreme category. Whilst we may claim to forget about 'things gone wrong', it is more likely that we avoid thinking about these painful experiences (Lazarus 1983). On those occasions when one does have time to reflect, such as during a train journey, whilst on holiday or in a counselling session, the suppressed ghosts of failure past can leap into mind rather unexpectedly.

Are there patterns in the failures people remember?

The data from my study shows that people tend to remember failure experiences for which they are highly self-critical. In other words, the setbacks we seem least able to forget are the ones for which we blame ourselves. Out of the collection of 90 stories, only 2 stories were found to have low levels of self-critical comment. Whilst participants' narratives confirmed the multi-textured nature of individual self-criticism, an analysis of the findings revealed the following three patterns.

1. Wrong thinking, wrong doing

This form of self-criticism takes the form of blaming oneself for doing something wrong due to faulty thinking: 'I acted wrongly because I thought about it wrongly.' People who tend to interpret their role in a failure in this manner typically focus on the quality of their actions and the thinking behind them. They appear to believe (perhaps unconsciously) that there is a right answer to everything and that it can be found through careful or 'right' thinking.

Wrong thinking was described by subjects in the research as 'not enough thinking', 'not thinking about it in the right way' and 'thinking which results in wrong actions'. Many business people, scientists and faculty members in higher education are inclined to favour this form of criticism, for themselves and for others. Bergner (1995) describes people with extreme versions of this pattern as mental perfectionists. It is probable that students who take their own lives because they feel they are not brilliant enough suffer from such perfectionist tendencies.

2. Being caught off-guard

This type of self-criticism takes the form of blaming oneself for not being aware of or for misreading the true nature of the situation surrounding a failure event: 'I should have known. I was naive and caught off guard by something that I ought to have been able to see.' People who criticize themselves in this manner focus on their lack of understanding of the context in which the failure took place. Underlying this response appears to be the assumption that it is possible to possess perfect information, to be 'all knowing' and that once one is aware of 'what is going on' then the 'right' answer or appropriate behaviour becomes self-evident.

Students who favour this type of self-criticism frequently blame themselves for not knowing (guessing) beforehand what was in an examination. Unlike individuals who fret about wrong thinking, people who favour this form of self-criticism rarely express concern about the quality of thinking underlying their behaviour, since the situation dictates the required action.

3. Because of who I am

Individuals invoking this type of self-criticism focus on themselves in a holistic manner and not just on their vigilance or thought and action processes. Here, the underlying assumption appears to be the belief that things go wrong in a situation because of one's standards, beliefs, personality or idealized way of seeing the world. Stories from individuals who favour this pattern contain self-critical language, such as 'I am undisciplined', 'I am idealistic', 'I am immature' and 'I am too emotional', expressing a degree of global self-censure. The implication is that failure can be avoided by modifying or adopting new standards, expectations, values – in a sense becoming someone else by changing or transforming oneself.

People who think this way fear not fitting into real-world situations because of 'the way I am'. Thus, most failures are portrayed as 'fit-failures', such people regularly seeing themselves as misfits in one situation or another. For a few students assuming the role of misfit can actually boost self-confidence. However, for most students feeling that they do not fit in has negative consequences for both performance and retention.

Although people use a mix of self-criticisms when reacting to failure, there is always a favourite form. These three types of interpretive bias identified by my study can be thought of as either constructs (Kelly 1955), cognitive schema (Fisk and Taylor 1984) or anchoring heuristics (Tversky and Kahneman 1981). They are learned responses probably rooted in early concepts of shame and guilt, and it is reasonable to hypothesize possible links with personality. Results from the NEO-PI-R Big 5 personality inventory (Costa and McCrae 1991) point to emotionality, sometimes labelled neuroticism, as the personality dimension which best correlates with failure response patterns. In my research, the highest levels of emotionality were found amongst individuals evoking the 'because of who I am' response, the lowest were found amongst those employing the 'wrong thinking, wrong doing' pattern.

What are the implications of this for failure in higher education?

Not everyone leaves higher education because they experience a setback or series of setbacks. In some cases pull factors, either on their own or in combination with the push factor of perceived failure, cause an individual to withdraw. For example, a person may be tempted away from college by an attractive job, a love affair or a unique opportunity to travel abroad. However, the majority of people who withdraw from their programme once underway will at least partly perceive themselves as failing at some aspect of the experience. Real or imagined, the consequences of this perceived lack of success remain the same – voluntary withdrawal or a downward spiral of absence and underperformance which ends in the individual being asked to go.

The research outlined earlier shows people holding different perceptions of failure. If this is true, then it follows that students at risk in higher education demonstrate distinct patterns of failure behaviour. Each of these behavioural patterns is likely to require a somewhat different remedy in terms of counselling, assistance and support. The following patterns are given as examples to illustrate this point and are not meant to be an all-inclusive list. There are no doubt other behavioural variations in at-risk populations.

The mental perfectionist

In their own view, mental perfectionists are never mentally good enough and, therefore, condemn themselves to perceived academic failure. No number of top grades or evidence of academic progress can stop them from constantly criticizing themselves for being less than brilliant. For these individuals, one wrong answer erases a thousand right answers. Constantly worrying about being wrong, of thinking wrongly, mental perfectionists punish themselves brutally for not making the absolutely right comment or analysis in class, on assignments and in exams. Although occasionally perceived as arrogant, their bragging is mostly aimed at convincing themselves. Of course, this never really works. The warm glow from success or positive feedback is always a fleeting experience. For a few moments they feel like a god, but shortly afterwards the reoccurring need to mentally prove themselves returns.

Mental perfectionism is the dark side of the 'wrong thinking, wrong doing' failure interpretation. Present in varying degrees, this type of inner self-punishment is hard to detect and especially troublesome for individuals with excellent grades. Whilst top students can appear to be enjoying their academic success, underneath the surface they may be constantly criticizing themselves. Astonishingly, some bright students even sabotage their own performance to reinforce their self-concept of being stupid and unworthy, eventually dropping out to save further embarrassing parents, professors and former teachers.

As one might expect, telling a mental perfectionist that they are doing fine and should not worry serves no purpose. These behaviours are deeply ingrained, and very difficult to unlearn. However, a counsellor can help a student identify their perfectionism, thus making it possible for them to manage the impact of this cognitive bias. The real danger with mental perfectionism is being unable to detect it before it is too late. While some at-risk students such as those demonstrating anti-social behaviour and those with failing grades are more easily identified, one needs to be vigilant to spot this particular problem early on.

The surprised newcomer

'If I had only known college would be like this.' 'I should have realised this before I came.' 'This is so different than I thought.' One expects a student coming into higher education to be surprised by various dimensions of their new experience – classes, tutorials, assignments, peers, the faculty and even accommodation. Unless their parents happen to work at an institution of higher learning, it is equivalent to moving to a foreign country. As others settle in, some students may continue to display 'I had no idea . . .' behaviour well into their programme. These individuals appear constantly surprised by aspects of higher education (such as what is required, and the reactions of faculty and peers), often in a negative way.

Less worried about getting all the right answers, they tend to criticize themselves for not being able to figure out the system (even when there is no way they could have). This feeling can prove a particular problem for mature students who may use their frequent disorientation as evidence that they do not belong in higher education. People from disadvantaged socio-economic backgrounds or from families where few (if any) family members attended higher education are most at risk. Nervous and unsure whether they belong at college, their constant self-criticism about not being able to read the situation can impact peers, faculty, and even counsellors, who may eventually send back subtle signals that they agree.

Once identified, compensation can be made for this exaggerated reaction. Given that higher education is all about opening doors to new experiences, not knowing how everything will turn out is part and parcel of the adventure. For people with the strong need to figure out the system and predict people's behaviour, college offers the opportunity for real personal development. This is a chance for them to become more relaxed. However, counsellors and the faculty ought to watch out for new students with high structure needs, especially if they are mature students. If they feel lost for too long, it will undermine their self-confidence. These are the people who desperately need the course outlines, the timetables and the expectations laid out to the letter. Giving in to their obsession for predictability is not the answer, however, small gestures towards helping them overcome their anxiety about the unknown can have a big impact.

Lessons can be learned here from the corporate world, where some businesses make an effort to familiarize incoming talent by giving them organizational previews in the form of tours, day visits, social events and short-term placements. People returning to higher education after working for a while might like to try out being a student for a few days before they accept a place. Other vehicles used by organizations to help satisfy people with a strong 'need to know' include user-friendly web sites, information centres and mentor programmes, whereby a newcomer is provided with an experienced 'buddy' to help them to get their bearings. Higher education institutions that offer ways for potential and existing students to get to know them better are certain to boost the confidence of those who do not like being surprised.

The misfit

When you interview an actress about why she failed an audition for a play, she will tell you that her style, the way she acts, the way she moves or the way she looks did not fit in with the sort of play that was being produced. In other words, she may say 'I failed (at getting the part) because of who I am.' Some students, especially those with a creative or entrepreneurial bent, leave higher education programmes because they do not see themselves as fitting in. This can be a good thing, given that people occasionally pick the wrong course, degree or institution. De-selecting oneself out of a course becomes a problem when it is done prematurely. People who favour the 'because of who I am' self-critical bias may react to their immediate feelings of being a misfit and drop out of a programme before giving it a decent try.

Much of higher education promotes diversity at least in thinking and, unlike in some employment, personal uniqueness is appreciated if not encouraged. However, if students find themselves in a community that accentuates differences, this can trigger immediate alienation and shake self-confidence (for example, a foreign student, someone from a state school surrounded by others from public schools, someone from southern England surrounded by northern students, or someone without much money surrounded by students with lots of money). People who tend to define themselves in terms of their personal style, values or roots almost always see themselves as part of a minority. As a result, they have the choice of becoming an outlaw or a special star. The latter leads to superior academic performance and completion whilst the former often results in antisocial behaviour and eventual failure. Outlaws by definition do not succeed in the conventional sense. Faculty members are especially well placed to help self-perceived misfits to overcome their initial integration problems. By showing visible recognition for a person's unique point of view or way of doing things in the tutorial, lecture theatre or studio, a teacher can lead a student to the realization that they have a role as a special minority contributor. Once they see the opportunity to stand out from the majority in a positive way, the misfit often makes the most of it (sometimes to the extreme).

Personality factors

Personality mediates and forms the foundation of the learned behaviours described in this chapter. Two personality factors stand out as particularly salient from the research – the dimensions of conscientiousness/dutifulness and emotionality.

People who measure high on the conscientiousness/dutifulness (and self-discipline) scale study and revise without much reliance on self-motivation. Many have deeply established patterns of doing homework and preparing for exams that they follow as a matter of course (for example, every evening between 6 and 8pm). Individuals who have low levels of these personality traits can study just as hard, but they will need to motivate themselves to do so.

Aroused emotion can destroy self-motivation. This means people strong on emotionality and weak on conscientiousness are in double trouble. Emotions set off by problems such as the break-up of a relationship or trouble at home can erode motivation to study, and because these individuals lack the habitual behaviour of the highly conscientious the required work or preparation does not get done. On a positive note, those higher on emotionality are also less vulnerable to burnout. They will stop when the stress starts to hurt. Less emotional people are less aware of how stressed they really are and may press on until they physically collapse.

Harder for some, easier for others

In this chapter I have argued that the challenges of higher education prove to be a more difficult experience for some people than for others, and that students experience difficulty in rather different ways. Those at greatest psychological risk are men and women obsessed with proving how brilliant they are and people who for one reason or another feel like misfits. Less at risk but still in the danger zone are individuals for whom everything is a constant surprise. Add low levels of conscientiousness and high levels of emotionality to any of these three self-critical patterns and you end up with cause for real concern. Of course, these factors (and others not included here, such as passion for the subject, personal goals and social background) overlap. Careful vigilance is required to diagnose accurately the nature of the problem given that students, young and old, are surprisingly cunning in masking the true state of their mental, emotional and physical health.

I hope that I have not discouraged those readers who presently teach, counsel and administer students by further complicating the picture. As in parenthood, there are many ways one can go wrong. However, if you get the important things right, a lot of the other problems sort themselves out. My research into the origins of failure along with my observations made over the years on what leads to continuing failure in student populations shape my final prescription.

- First, those who serve higher education must do all they can to boost the self-confidence of students. This means being able to detect fading confidence and to understand the causes undermining it. Whilst some individuals believe deep down that they are not bright enough, others feel frightened by the unknown or continue to question whether they fit it. Each of these, and other confidence-destroying belief systems need to be tackled in different ways, employing different tactics.
- Second, students must be encouraged to feel that they have something special to contribute. As success in higher education is mostly about answering in the right way, individuals need to learn how to shape this form to highlight rather than diminish their unique contribution. Just as many of us use Windows on our computers, we all have the opportunity to customize the established format. In higher education faculty members are key players in helping students find their own voice in the intellectual choir. Discovering this voice facilitates mental independence, which ensures participation and prevents dangerous isolation.
- Finally, institutions and those who run them need to take an active role in helping students feel they belong. Ways must be found to broaden and increase the number of paths students can take in order to truly feel a part of the community they are joining. Due to location or specialization, some institutions of higher education will not have a diverse population. However, it is essential to promote and celebrate diversity in thinking and expression, regardless of the demographic composition of the student population. Institutions of higher learning ought to be places where people can learn from themselves, and more importantly from others.

Learning how to learn from failure

Of course, it is not all the responsibility of the college or university. Each student has an active role to play in ensuring their own success in higher education. Helping students to manage and learn from setbacks improves their chances of attaining that success, given failure's ability to teach important lessons. The essential first step is jettisoning the notion of failure as rare, something that happens to an unfortunate minority of people. This commonly held illusion keeps each of us from coming to terms with failures – public and private. As a result, we may not learn how to recover and move on; and, of equal importance, we may not learn how to help others to recover and move on.

In business and higher education alike, sustained success depends partly upon having the right answers and right ways of answering, but mostly about moving forward, in terms of taking action and acquiring knowledge. Individuals in both domains need to find ways through and around obstacles that slow their progress along the chosen path, making course corrections when required. They also need to know how to pick themselves up and keep going should they take a fall. Educating students to become more mentally resilient has obvious benefits – saving money and time, enriching learning and avoiding unnecessary pain. However, it also necessitates an understanding of how different individuals respond in different ways to life's experiences. Personal failure, as a uniquely difficult experience, underscores the point that learning how to learn means learning in your own way.

The educational organizations and businesses we design today will be the places in which our very own children will live out their lives tomorrow. In shaping the world in which we hope the ones we love will succeed, it is important to consider the way they are, not just the way we would like them to be.

7

Failing Teachers, Failing Students: Learning about Failure from a Teaching Development Programme

Terry Wareham

Introduction

Imagine the following typical scene in a university. It is the beginning of a 3-hour workshop session. The students have been sent material in advance to read and they have an outline of the programme for the session. The course handbook gives them lots of detail about the course – the rationale behind it, how it fits in with other courses in the institution, what prerequisites there are. It gives them the intended learning outcomes and the outline timetable, an annotated reading list and the support mechanisms provided, such as mentors, on-line tutorials and so on. The students arrive for the session. Some come into the room chirpy and ready to get stuck in; others slide in, avoiding the tutor's gaze, and try to slip discreetly into the farthest corner of the room. Some of the students have actively signed up for this course; others are obliged to do it. Still more are doing it for entirely instrumental reasons – they want the qualification. As the time for the start of the workshop comes and goes, there are still only half of the expected students there. Most of the remainder turn up one by one over the first half hour. Some do not arrive at all. The tutor asks about the reading, mentioning that they will be doing work on these texts later in the session. There is some cynical laughter – they have been too busy, the material did not arrive, one or two just plain forgot. Those who have done the reading look annoyed at the others.

Does this sound familiar? However, this cameo does not describe a workshop for undergraduates, it is the beginning of a session on a certificate course in learning and teaching in higher education for university staff and postgraduate student teaching assistants. The significance of the resonances between academics learning to teach and the experiences of their own students is the focus of this chapter.

I have been involved with running courses for teachers in higher education for over 10 years and have been fascinated by the ways in which academic colleagues in particular respond to being on such a programme. What strikes me with such force is the similarity between some of the apparent experiences of staff on courses of this kind and the experiences of 'normal' undergraduate and postgraduate students. By examining the perceptions of some of these teacher/students and analysing various issues surrounding being a student in the institution in which one is also employed, I want to consider what staff's own experience of potential or actual failure is and how this experience might provide insights which can inform their own practice with their students – in particular their practice in relation to underachieving or failing students.

This chapter draws on data from a number of sources, including in-depth interviews with participants and contributors to the programme; an open-ended questionnaire sent to all staff participants; comments made by tutors about assessed work; and field-notes of conversations with tutors, participants and those with management responsibilities for the quality of learning and teaching within the institution. These data are used to illustrate a discussion of the significance of notions of success and failure for those who provide and participate in teaching development programmes of this kind and what these insights might offer to help in our understanding of students' experiences. The first section provides a brief background to the development of these programmes in the UK.

The training of higher education teachers

For centuries, no-one gave any particular thought to how university teachers acquired their knowledge and understanding of teaching. It was assumed, for example, that a distinguished physicist or historian would have the intelligence and innate ability to teach students. Simply being in proximity to great minds would mean that students would learn and be inspired. There was certainly no suggestion that lecturers should receive any training for doing this part of their job and, for the most part, they would build their practice on what they had experienced as undergraduates and postgraduates. If students could not benefit from their teaching, however good or bad this might be, then they had no business being at university. The notion of *reading* for a degree implied that the onus was on the student to study the discipline with some guidance from a tutor, not that the tutor would be responsible for *teaching* the student.

This attitude to teaching in universities sat alongside a state of affairs where a small proportion of the population went to university, where those who did probably came from families whose members had also been to university (possibly even the same Oxford or Cambridge college) and who probably had the cultural background and cultural capital needed to succeed whether or not they were taught well. With the growth of universities in the early 1960s in the UK, a growth which accelerated hugely in the 1990s, to the current situation where nearly one-third of the age cohort now attends university, it has been argued that the university system has moved from being an 'elite' to a 'mass' system (Trow 1972). One of the results of this is that many so-called 'non-traditional' students, perhaps with less understanding of and preparation for university, are now in the system. The phrase 'reading for a degree' has all but disappeared and in its place the notion of being taught – and being taught effectively – has gained ascendancy.

With this huge expansion in numbers of students in universities has come a concern about the growing cost of maintaining such participation rates. Thus, systems have been established to monitor quality, so that the general public and other 'stakeholders' can feel satisfied that their money is being spent properly (Randall 1997). As part of this monitoring, there has developed a concern about the quality of teaching. Whilst there is no evidence that teaching was poor – indeed, the UK has an enviable reputation in the rest of the world for the quality of its degrees – there is a concern that university teachers are out of line with virtually every other professional field:

> Imagine a world in which our children are taught by untrained teachers, or in which we are treated by doctors and nurses who have received only some ad hoc on-the-job training. Imagine if we had to live in houses which were built by architects without professional accreditation.
>
> Pretty horrific, isn't it? So why is it then that teaching, particularly in higher education, is treated with so little respect in some quarters?
>
> (Sporing 2001: 5)

In 1992 the Standing Conference on Educational Development – now the Staff and Educational Development Association (SEDA) – put in place a scheme to accredit the programmes emerging to train and develop higher education teachers, mostly in the polytechnics. The numbers of programmes, both accredited and non-accredited, grew steadily (Ecclestone 1995). However, these developments were generally prompted by local demand, either from institutions requiring or expecting probationary staff to undertake training or from individuals within the institutions. By 1996 the Association of University Teachers had become concerned by the vulnerability of its members to the charge of being unqualified for a substantial part of their work and raised the issue in a discussion paper (1996). It was then taken up by the Dearing Committee in its report in 1997 (National Committee of Inquiry into Higher Education 1997a). The bandwagon of training and accreditation was now rolling with a vengeance. The Institute for Learning and Teaching was created in 1999 as a direct result of the Dearing recommendations, to raise the profile and status of teaching in higher education, and this body took over the responsibility of providing national level accreditation from SEDA. Funding from the Higher Education Funding Council for England for the implementation of institutional learning, teaching and assessment strategies has allowed an even greater expansion of programmes for higher education teachers, as the plethora of job advertisements for programme leaders and tutors since its introduction will testify.

Higher education teachers as students

A new generation of academic staff is finding itself on courses, mostly at masters level, on the theory and practice of teaching in higher education. This is a curious situation – being a student on a course in an institution in which you are also a teacher, the course having been through the same validation process as your own courses, and being subject to the same assessment processes as your students.

Unlike many institutions, at Lancaster the teaching certificate programme for staff and teaching assistants is voluntary. Whilst the completion of the programme can be used as evidence in cases for probation or promotion, there is no formal requirement for anyone to attend, although there *is* a requirement for those new to teaching to undertake *some* form of appropriate training. Having said that, many departments are strongly encouraging new staff to join the programme. Thus its participants include those who are undertaking the programme for its intrinsic interest and value; those who see it as a means to certain ends, such as promotion or other career development prospects; and those who have been more or less forced to join it by peer or head of department pressure:

> Joining the programme was a 'strong suggestion' made during the interview for my current academic post.
>
> I view the . . . programme as a desirable qualification that provides formal recognition of my teaching activities at Lancaster.
>
> I like teaching, would like to do it as well as possible, and wish to take advantage of any programme that helps me do that.
>
> A genuine interest and desire.

These motivations for being on the programme[1] – pressure from other stakeholders, desire for a particular, legitimizing qualification and out of intrinsic interest respectively – could map quite easily onto the motivations of undergraduate, postgraduate and continuing professional development students.

Staff as students

The opening story indicated many behaviours which might be typical of any students in universities. It is my experience that being on a course and being *taught* and *assessed* by people who are, in effect, peers brings out certain behaviours in staff. Suddenly the tables are turned. However much the course leaders may negotiate the content and structure of the programme, the participants may still experience a sense of loss of power, they feel they are being dropped into a disciplinary environment which is alien to them (as one participant said, 'I don't want to become an educational researcher'), with a discourse which they do not share. Even though they may be intrinsically motivated to do the programme, some participants feel that they should not have to fit into a systematic programme with rules and requirements which are not of their making. The programme participant quoted above spent many weeks resisting the first assignment for the course, as the following extract from the reflective log shows:

> Major scepticism over report . . . What has it got to do with teaching? How does it make me a better teacher? The ability to write does not equate to good teaching, although I accept the ability to reflect may equate to good teaching. The ability to express (in writing) personal experiences is different to reflecting and changing *in practice.*

Ivanic's work on writer identity (1998) picks up on a possible reason for the discomfort of this participant:

> Writing is an act of identity in which people align themselves with socio-culturally shaped possibilities for self-hood, playing their part in reproducing or challenging dominant practices and discourses, and the values, beliefs and interests which they embody.
>
> (Ivanic 1998: 32)

Attempts by the course tutors to improve and develop the course in the light of feedback have also had negative as well as positive responses. One objection from a programme participant was that there was: 'A problem with the goalposts being a little unclear and moving for a while.' In extreme cases, some may revert to the behaviours of the school classroom – trying to disrupt sessions in a deliberate manner, using inappropriate language in an apparent attempt to shock, and so on, although this is relatively rare.

Perceptions of failure

Student failure

Before considering the impact of the course on staff thinking, I will look at how the questionnaire respondents perceived their students' failure. The questionnaires revealed a range of views – both as it related to students and to themselves. For their students, they interpreted failure as:

> Getting less than 40 per cent.
>
> Not realizing their full potential at university.
>
> Failure seems to me to be a personal belief; I have taught many students who, although capable, do not believe they are capable of the work.
>
> The most obvious meaning of failure is when a student fails to achieve the pass mark for a module, or indeed fails to gain a degree at all.
>
> However, very bright students who achieve poor marks have 'failed' to live up to their potential. For that matter 'average' students may be

trying, and failing, to meet expectations of, for example, parents.

> In my case some fail because they are too good at being uncritical speakers of corporate lingo without much thought. But in the institution's terms or society's or their own they are brilliant successes.

The majority of views appear to assume that the goal of their students is intrinsic success – achieving one's potential, having appropriate self-belief or living up to the standards of others. This perhaps reflects their own success orientation. The last quotation, however, raises some difficult issues in relation to conflicting values. In this case, those of the academic relate to the achievement of a critical perspective on language and social structures compared to those of the student and the institution which centre on achieving good grades and, ultimately, a good degree. Given these conflicting positions, it is quite possible that a student can both succeed and fail at the same time, depending on which perspective one adopts. The rhetoric of traditional university values is that students will increasingly become independent, critical thinkers as they go through their degree course. In reality, there are constraining conventions which allow only very specific forms of originality of thought. Working towards a degree or other university qualification can be a convergent activity – trying to find the right language, structures and procedures to fit the disciplinary paradigm – rather than a divergent process leading above and beyond what one is taught. A recent discussion in a colleague's second year undergraduate seminar about the value of being independent and creative in one's studies indicated that students felt that this was penalized, and that the activity they were engaged in as they went through their degree programme was about learning the rules of the game and becoming strategically cue-conscious. The greatest rewards went to those who had 'sussed out' the system and could work it to their advantage.

Higher education teachers failing as students

Let us turn now to the perceptions the course members had about themselves. The notion of failing the course has exercised the teaching certificate course team from the outset. One course contributor stated 'People are earning their living by the thing they're being tested on. How do you deal with failure?' The logical extension of having a course for people to develop certain skills as they simultaneously deploy them in the work context is that if they should fail (or not complete the programme) they should have their employment terminated. In reality, of course, this is unthinkable, but for practising higher education teachers to have a sense of failure about such a course can lead to powerful reactions of anger, rejection of the values behind the course and perhaps even rejection of the principle of qualification for an essential and important part of the job of university academic. In effect, it changes their relationship with the employing institution.

Some respondents to the questionnaire had quite different conceptions of failure as it related to themselves than they did about their students' failure. The focus of the failure was frequently not upon themselves, but on the programme itself:

> . . . being a waste of my time and effort . . . Participating . . . has to justify itself in terms of perceived benefit, over the time and effort taken.
>
> Failure would represent a failure to benefit from the course and a lack of sense of achievement or a failure to recognize improvements in my teaching activities.

Although other responses had resonances with 'standard' students:

> Depends if I tried hard and failed (in which case a serious blow to the esteem) or if because too busy elsewhere, then my choice and . . . ok.
>
> Basically, to attend everything and then not pass.
>
> Since it implies having done a lot of other things, simply getting the piece of paper at the end would do me fine.

Some implications of failing as a student

Clearly, failure in terms of not achieving an appropriate grade is intrinsically related to what is assessed. Without assessment, there would be no such thing as failure in this sense. For the undergraduate seminar group mentioned earlier, what they perceive to be assessed is the ability to write what lecturers think they should write, and not necessarily what appear as assessment criteria. In their example, creativity only has value if it is a very specific form of creativity. For some of the participants on the teaching certificate programme, what is assessed (namely written submissions) is misaligned with what they feel they should be learning from the programme:

> what has frustrated me is that I haven't been able to just walk away and go 'Oh, I'm not cut out for that' without negating in some way my validity as a teacher. There is some overtone . . . that if I was going to be a half decent teacher I would take tasks like writing and researching for [the certificate programme] in my stride – but I just couldn't do it.

Of course, learning in the area of professional knowledge and development is in many ways quite different from the kinds of learning being undertaken by undergraduate and postgraduate students on academic courses (although there is a clear parallel with courses which provide entry to a profession or continuing professional development programmes). One of the problems encountered by this first group is that their learning is disembodied from application in the 'real world' to a very large extent. It is 'just in case' rather than 'just in time' learning. This renders the process of assessment even more arbitrary in relation to its connection with failure.

Types of knowledge

One area which may provide a key to understanding student failure is the consideration of the forms of knowledge which are being taught (and learned) in universities. Blackler (1995) offers a formulation of five 'images' of knowledge in organizations: embrained, embodied, encultured, embedded and encoded. It is appropriate to apply this analysis of knowledge in organizations to the context of students learning in higher education since they are clearly engaged not just in learning facts and theories about a particular discipline, but in learning about a whole discourse, both disciplinary discourses and discourses of higher education or, to go back to the undergraduate seminar students, the 'rules of the game'.

At the overt level, much knowledge in higher education is embrained knowledge, that is high-status propositional knowledge which is publicly available. This is the kind of knowledge demonstrated by students in essays and seminar discussions. In terms of the teaching certificate programme it would be the material gained from the 'literature' on teaching and learning. Embodied knowledge – 'knowing how' (Ryle 1949) or 'knowledge of acquaintance' (James 1950) – is rarely explicit and is acquired by doing. Encultured knowledge is about the process of achieving shared understandings through language. Embedded knowledge is 'knowledge that resides in systematic routines' (Blackler 1995: 1024). Encoded knowledge is to be found in handbooks, manuals and codes of practice. An example which illustrates all five of these 'images' might be the writing and marking of essays. Essays contain 'embrained' knowledge in the form of ideas and theories from the literature of a particular discipline. In marking the essays, the lecturer will deploy embodied knowledge in the way he or she scans the work, writes comments, sorts them into mark hierarchies and so on. Encultured knowledge will be used in discussions with second markers and external examiners about the characteristics of particular grades and the value of different pieces of work. Embedded knowledge relates to things such as handing-in conventions and fixed penalties for late submission or plagiarism. Encoded knowledge will be the information about essay-marking procedures to be found in the departmental handbook and in institutional codes of practice about assessment matters.

This model of types of knowledge applied to the situation of trainee lecturers in universities immediately offers insights about where potential both for conflicts of perception and of failure lies. Much knowledge about teaching is necessarily of the embodied, encultured and embedded kinds. Trowler and Knight's work on the induction of new academic staff in universities demonstrates quite clearly that learning the job successfully (not just the teaching element) relies on a complex process of sensitizing to and negotiating meanings. Induction cannot be a process that is *done* to new entrants to the profession through the simple transmission of propositional, embrained, knowledge, instead it involves organizational socialization: 'the accommodative process which takes place when new entrants to an organization engage with aspects of the cultural configurations they find there' (Trowler and Knight 1999: 178). This involves an integration of all five forms – 'knowledgeability' in Blackler's terms. Like most university courses, Lancaster's teaching certificate emphasizes embrained knowledge, requiring participants to engage with the literature on teaching in their discipline, as well as the wider literature on teaching, learning and assessment in higher education and it features in the assessment criteria. One of the areas of concern for both participants and tutors is establishing and then achieving the appropriate balance when assessing the effectiveness of the teaching in practice (embodied, encultured, embedded or encoded) and the ability to discuss theory and empirical research in relation to that practice (embrained). The following extracts from comments on assessed work reveal an emphasis on the latter:

> I agree with you that this assignment is satisfactory. I wouldn't put it any stronger, particularly if looking at it from the point of view of comparability with our MA/Diploma. If this were an MA assignment I doubt whether it achieved a pass mark . . . I wasn't at all convinced by his choice of theory . . . His writing was rather too wobbly, insufficient attention to grammar, spelling, explanation of unusual terms.
>
> (Second marker 1)

> . . . the engagement with the literature on teaching, learning and assessment is rather disappointing.
>
> (Second marker 2)

Actually, comments like these are to be expected in relation to work presented for assessment in an institution which takes pride in being 'research led', where programmes are only validated when they can satisfy the community that they are academically well-founded, that is that they are based on, and assess, embrained knowledge. However, it is easy to see how participants can experience a sense of dislocation when they are, on the one hand, working pragmatically in the 'swampy lowlands' described by Schön (1983, 1987), but being judged against a different set of disciplinary standards.

Situated identities: activity systems in universities

It can be argued that people within organizations operate within 'activity systems' and that these are the units which give validity and meaning to activities and identity to participants. The most obvious activity system for academics is their department, or research group within their department. What follows is an exploration of the concept of the activity system and its relevance to the current discussion.

Engestrom (1987) takes Vygotsky's original idea of activity theory and applies it to organizations. Activity theory basically says that all activity takes

Figure 7.1 Engestrom's diagram of an activity system (adapted)

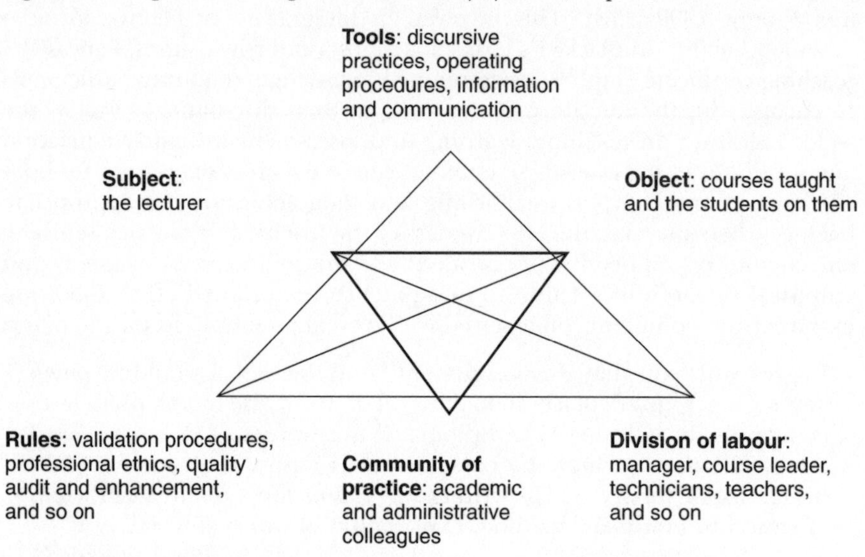

place inside coherent systems, as demonstrated in Figure 7.1. If we interpret this system first in terms of the activity system related to teaching within an academic department, we can see that the agent or subject is the member of academic staff. The object of the activity is the student, with the community element being academic and administrative colleagues. Overlaid on this triangle is a further set of elements. The community, agent and object of activity all exist within a set of concepts or a technology (way of doing things). In the case of an academic department, we might identify such things as strong disciplinary traditions (as exemplified in law in the use of Socratic debate) or the use of information and communications technology. They are governed or influenced by formal or informal rules, such as degree programmes, regulations and codes of practice. Finally, they are affected by the division of labour and knowledge. In academic departments in universities this would be the teaching of specialisms by experts as well as the apportioning of time to teaching or research through work distribution systems. The activity system has a coherence and an integrity which ties in each of the elements.

When academics join the teaching certificate programme, they immediately become participants in a rather different activity system than their departmental one, and occupy a quite different role within it (see Figure 7.2). The agent or subject is now the teaching programme leader or tutor and the lecturer has become the *object* of the activity. The community of the programme is a diverse mixture of tutors with both educational development and other specific disciplinary backgrounds. However, they share a set of concepts and technologies and the 'rules' relate to a certain set of values. Indeed, the programme at Lancaster makes quite explicit those values and

Figure 7.2 Activity system of a teaching development programme

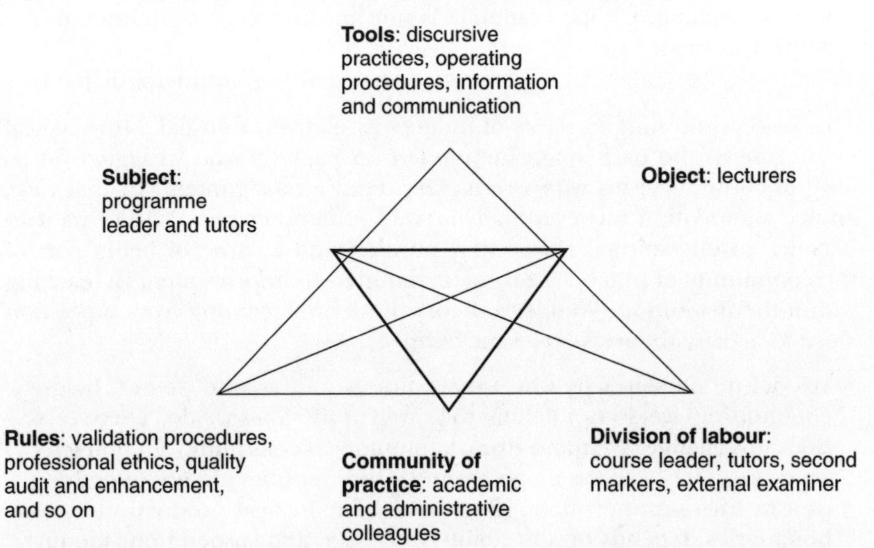

the requirement for programme participants to demonstrate them in their work.

Seen from the perspective of activity theory, it is evident why lecturers on teaching courses may well feel uncomfortable and disempowered. They are placed as 'objects' within an activity system whose rules, concepts and division of labour are quite different from their more usual activity system within the department or research group and in which they are the *subject.* Their identity is threatened.

Identity

This discussion of activity systems theory links to theories of identity and the changing culture of higher education. The traditional cultural mode of the university is that of a collegial environment, characterized by the liberal values inherent in notions of academic freedom. Individuals, units (such as academic departments) and institutions enjoy a substantial degree of autonomy. With the rise of the 'new managerialism' (Clarke and Newman 1997), the emphasis shifts towards accountability, monitoring and control with the power of the individual and the discipline declining to some extent (Becher and Trowler 2001). The training and accreditation of teachers in higher education can be seen as part of those ongoing processes of control, surveillance and redefinition of the profession of 'academic'. The need to preserve a previous identity becomes the stronger because of this invasion of alien values:

I am not now nor ever expect to be a professional teacher. If I'd

> wanted to be one I would have joined the bureaucratic nightmare that is teaching. I hope academia is not heading that way (although I suspect it might be).
>
> (Programme participant)

This bold positioning in terms of identity is relatively unusual. More typical is the case of the participant mentioned on page 89 who struggled for so long to come to terms with writing the required assignment. In that case, an accommodation was eventually arrived at between the 'I don't want to become an educational researcher' position and a sense of being part of the community of practice of those committed to improvement in teaching within the institution. Wenger's theory of identity, coming from a position close to activity theory, is relevant here:

> We define ourselves by who we are not as well as who we are, by the communities we do not belong to as well as the ones we do. These relationships change. We move from community to community. In doing so, we carry a bit of each as we go around. Our identities are not something we can turn on and off . . . [But] our ability to deal productively with boundaries depends on our ability to engage and suspend our identities . . . Our identities are the living vessels in which communities and boundaries become realized as an experience of the world.
>
> (Wenger 2000: 235)

Conclusions

So what can this discussion of participation on a teaching development programme tell us about failure and failing? The questionnaire respondents felt that participating in the programme had given them a number of insights into the experience of their own students:

> A reminder of how easy it is to miss sessions, lose concentration, feel uncooperative and settle for observing rather than taking part.
>
> I believe that it has given me more insight into the 'student condition'.
>
> It is sometimes tempting to consider students en masse and forget that they are individuals with their own personal, financial and educational concerns.
>
> The value of 'doing' for learning.

These reactions have resonances with many of the ideas discussed in this chapter. It is clear from this discussion that there are sufficient parallels between 'normal' students and participants on teaching development programmes to be able to draw some conclusions about what lecturers and support staff might do to help both the sense of failure and actual failure (in terms of withdrawal or failure in assessment) of students on university programmes.

First, staff need to be aware that joining a programme of study at university is a change in activity system. Whilst the new environment may resemble in some ways the previous activity systems they have encountered, there are significant ways in which it differs, such as the discursive practices, ethics and division of labour. These need to be negotiated and translated. This is as true of staff on teaching development programmes as it is of 'normal' students. An earlier evaluation of staff on the teaching development programme showed that those who were most successful had actively taken control over their work in the programme; they were proactive in their choice of workshops and in their decisions about subjects of their written assignments. By contrast, those who were less satisfied with the programme were far more likely to take a passive role and perceived that the programme was being done *to* them. In terms of activity theory, this second group remained as 'objects' within the teaching programme activity system. The first group had taken on the role of subject within an activity system over which they felt they had considerable control. Activity theory can thus provide a strong theoretical justification for the trend since the 1990s to encourage active learning and independent study habits.

Second, each individual student comes with his or her own identity. In a mass system this can be easily lost, as the second respondent above shows. Identity is not fixed, but it takes time to change and many adjustments need to be made by students as they negotiate the transition from school to university, and through the different stages of their university career.

Third, the nature of knowledge, knowledgeability and knowing taught and learned in universities is complex. Lecturers need to be clear about what it is that students have to learn. The emphasis is on propositional (embrained) knowledge, but there are other highly significant areas of learning that need to happen. For example students need to learn skilfulness in managing their workload and their relations with fellow students and with staff (embodied). They need to become familiar with procedures (embedded) that impinge on their daily lives and likelihood of success. Academics and support staff need to be clear about this hidden curriculum and design learning and support environments which address these areas.

Finally, it is important that academics recognize that students will have different value systems and orientations than they do. They may be far less oriented towards intrinsic satisfaction and more towards instrumental rewards. By acknowledging and valuing students' orientations when they differ from their own, academics are more likely to be able to assist students towards a reasonably successful outcome to their time at university.

Note

1. Personal details of respondents have been withheld to preserve anonymity.

8

Open as to Failure

Maggie Coats and Jo Tait

Box 8.1 Chris: a case study

Chris is a struggling Open University (OU) student, who is in danger of failing. A few months into a level three OU course, without any formal learning experiences since leaving school, Chris had no sense of the difficulty that would be involved in level three work. Someone in the regional office had sent a letter clearly saying that there is an increased risk of failure for those who begin their studies at an advanced level, but this is the *Open* University, so no-one actually closes the door. Also, the fees are being paid by a government fund and Chris presumes that this provides a sort of permission, saying, 'They wouldn't allow me to start it if they didn't think I was up to it.'

Chris is finding the work very hard, and is starting to realize that there are some tricks to writing assignments at all, let alone successfully, at level three. Already, there is a temptation to drop out – the work is taking up every spare minute of Chris's time, so family commitments and friends are all starting to suffer. It is just as well that Chris is currently unemployed, otherwise life would be impossible. Chris has told a friend that it is only the fact that the fees are being paid that keeps her going. She feels motivated by trying to prove that she is worth this investment – that their confidence in her success is justified – and by the support of the tutor who also seems to believe in her.

Tutorials are difficult to get to for geographical reasons. Chris also suffers from arthritis, so travel and stairs are problematic. But it is worth going as tutorials offer a broader picture of what the course is really about. Opportunities to talk with the other students give Chris an idea of the level – a sense of what a successful student might be doing. But even with detailed and encouraging feedback from the tutor on the first two assignments (both of which have needed an extension), Chris feels unable to actually deliver what is expected and says, 'Knowing what I should be doing isn't the same as being able to do it.'

As Chris starts to think about tackling the third assignment, behind schedule already, it feels impossible and overwhelming. The temptation to do nothing, just to stop working and fail by default, is very strong. Chris vaguely remembers reading that there are people to contact about problems, and the tutor has usually been helpful, but . . .

Introduction

The student described above is a composite, based on our experiences and conversations with students and staff of the OU. We begin in this way to engage readers in the core of the OU's mission, which is a commitment to recognizing the diversity of 140,000 undergraduate students' learning situations. An extract from the latest version of the OU mission states that it is:

- Open as to people – providing open entry higher education for a large and diverse student body, and playing a leading role in meeting lifelong learning needs . . . ;
- Open as to places – bringing learning opportunities to adults, at home and in the workplace . . . ;
- Open as to methods – using and developing distance teaching methods . . . ;
- Open as to ideas – a vibrant academic community.

(Open University Planning Office 2000: 5)

These aims have a direct bearing on how the OU's frontline staff experience and manage students' everyday learning struggles and their failures, however these are defined. While the OU is unique in the UK in terms of its dedication to 'open-ness', this chapter will be of interest to practitioners and managers across the higher education sector, as they consider performance indicators in relation to the 'access' and 'flexibility' agendas and how these affect the roles of those involved in learning support in their institutions. We draw on our experiences[1] of working and researching within the OU to illustrate how institutional and national changes can impact on the roles of those people who directly support students.

In the OU, the people who interact directly with students are over 7500 Associate Lecturers (ALs) who tutor the courses, and the guidance and advice staff based in thirteen regional centres. These interactions are described in more detail later in this chapter; the complex and changing balance between different approaches to student support in the OU forms one twist to our story.

This chapter draws on our participative research activities undertaken over the year 1999–2000, filtered through our observations. Thirty ALs provided narratives about their roles, prompted by our terms 'vulnerable students' and 'unexpected failure', and reflected how these interactions affect and inform their practice. Many of these stories present an image of the AL as central to the OU learning experience. The ALs' stories also show how guidance and management (via advisers and academics in their regional centre) link tutors to the OU with personal support and information for themselves and their students. The regional perspective for our research came from focus groups of regional staff discussing how they manage 'failing' students. There were common threads between the stories from the regional staff and those from tutors, perhaps due to the fact that many of these advisers and counsellors drew on their past and present experiences as ALs and as students.

The wider context: engaging with changing agendas

The OU is affected by the changing agenda being imposed upon all institutes of higher education in the UK. The expansion of numbers, greater accountability and transparency in the curriculum; increased student choice; the shift of emphasis from academic to vocational, from disciplinary knowledge to employability skills and from teaching to learning affect the OU's provision and its students. In the past, the OU has argued that its open access mission requires its success or failure to be judged against performance indicators other than retention or completion rates. However, as more universities offer widening participation, this argument becomes less persuasive and the pressure to comply with the central agenda increases. As distance learning becomes more 'customer driven', and centralized technology-based mediation is hailed as the economical response, our chapter focuses on the roles and relationships that are affected by these changes.

We have identified four clusters of issues, raised by participants from their perspectives on 'failing' students, illuminating these changing contexts of higher education. Table 8.1 provides an overview and suggests how they may relate to 'traditional' contexts, current changes and potential developments.

Applying the framework of Table 8.1 to organize our research findings, we discover, inevitably, that the themes interweave. For example, although we have aimed to place Chris, our composite student, at the centre of the story, she becomes overshadowed by the background complexity – in the story and in practice. The tensions of what we have called 'economics' (referring to the ways students are becoming 'customers'), the context of a dispersed community of learning support and centralized course production, and descriptions of – and participants' commentaries on – some of the working practices of the OU in dealing with students' struggles highlight

Table 8.1 Key issues raised by our research participants and questions for higher education

Research themes	*OU traditional approach*	*Changes and tensions*	*The future of higher education?*
1 Student-centred, tutor-supported learning.	Supporting diverse students' learning, responsive to circumstances.	Retention as performance indicator requires statistical success and completion measures.	Tensions between 'quality' as customer focus or standards-based performance measurement.
2 Quality, flexibility, open access, free student choice.	No selection criteria, CATS-rated courses* with compulsory Level One induction (until 1999).	Requirement for high quality induction/ guidance versus 'economy of scale' and 'marketing' approaches. Free student choice.	Competition for student recruitment balanced by individual student learning focus.
3 'Economics' – who pays and who delivers.	Self-funding (or work-subsidized) students are highly motivated, working full-time and studying part time.	Funded, unemployed students more likely to over-commit time and expectations; possibly less motivated?	Increased student/ parent payments (loans), and part-time employment changes motivations and expectations.
4 A distanced, dispersed and divided community.	Centre produces course materials; tutors support learning, managed via 13 regional centres.	Technology challenges the divide between central production, regional support roles and students.	Learning support located in 'virtual' university; independent learning in a dispersed community.

Note: *Degrees and diplomas are awarded when the student has the required number of CATS points, but these can be accumulated over any period of time, concurrently, sequentially or with considerable gaps between each course.

the issues of quality and flexibility grounded in the thread of our student's story. Any experience or any decision that results in students being unable to complete a course or an award successfully can be perceived as a 'failure' either by the students themselves, by others within the university or beyond or may be counted as 'failed' by the system. For the students, the labelling of the experience or of themselves as 'failures' reflects an individual perception related to a complex web of interacting factors in themselves, their history and their perception of the experience.

The tutor–student relationship

Tutors: supporting and supported

The OU has always recognized that an open access policy will lead to some students requiring extra support for study, and that academic needs may overlap with students' personal circumstances. Tutors have traditionally been the first point of call. Economic constraints and policy decisions are changing the structure of tutorial support, most notably by phasing out the role of 'tutor-counsellor', traditionally a student's personal point of contact from the foundation year to completion. This change in practice has complicated the system, requiring enhanced interpersonal skills from the regional guidance and advice staff and, as explained below, raising boundary dilemmas for tutors concerning appropriate amounts of time and attention for students with particular problems.

Extensive written information aims to provide guidance to tutors in their work with students who are struggling. It says that one of the most difficult decisions for a tutor to make is to judge whether a student in difficulty will actually benefit from extra help but nonetheless proposes that:

> Before you ask for a special session for a student who is academically underprepared, it is important to judge whether this will really help to make up for the lack of preparatory work. Some students who are clearly unable to cope with the level of academic work required may be best advised to withdraw (though they would need to consider the fee implications).
>
> (Open University 1999: 3.2)

OU tutor materials exemplify the self-reliant behaviour expected of students, but may create parallel problems of isolation and self-doubt.

Students: retained or released

The degree to which extra help may or may not be useful or, conversely, when withdrawal can be a measure of 'success', was addressed in some form by many of our participating tutors and advisory staff. The value judgements embedded in these stories reflect some of the difficult assumptions that may influence tutors' decisions:

> . . . a student with a severe and degenerative spinal condition [and intermittent depression]. I have been able to get for her home and telephone tutorials, home exams and so on. And the OU is now lending her a computer with internet access, etc. . . I have kept in regular contact with her, although we are not now supposed to be proactive. She is a very successful student.

The other student used by a different tutor as an example of a 'success' was in a wheelchair and suffering from ME:

> I found that by making frequent phone calls (at least once a week) I was able to gauge when she was in difficulty (in which case I would usually leave a message with her husband wishing her well) and when she was able to talk constructively about the course. She was very pleased to be pushed and prodded in this manner, and completed the course with a grade 3 pass . . . This was time well spent.

The tutors compare these positive outcomes with their negative sense of helplessness in working with students unable to benefit from support because of problems stemming from emotional or mental disease, in the following cases, diagnosed mental ill-health and a family problem:

> [The student was] unable to benefit from guidance or additional tuition sessions. Seeking only to use this time to talk to me about his plans and ambitions . . . using the OU system to gain the attention that he seemed to need . . . failed to complete his assignments and didn't sit the examination.
>
> I tried to give all the support I could . . . she never wrote anything and eventually dropped out. The learning point is perhaps a negative one. Although the OU was generous, then, with extra time, and I felt that I had done everything I could, including suggesting she contact AA, in the end I was unable to get over the domestic and personal difficulties she faced.

We recognize that tutors sometimes develop strategies to protect themselves from participating too closely in the struggles of their students. One tutor stated 'My feelings towards the student became increasingly remote: I felt that I did not want to nag her constantly about her work'. Another tutor resolved tension by detachment:

> I realized that she had all sorts of worries . . . that I was not going to be able to do anything about these. I became resigned to not receiving work except at tutorials . . . I felt that a laid-back attitude was about right.

Personal crises are generally recognized as being outside the tutor brief, although not always easy to cope with:

> A few times during my time with the OU I have rung a student to see why a missing assignment had not been submitted to find a distraught student having a life crisis. This year I rang to be told her husband had walked out leaving her with four young children. I did the right things, encouraged her to phone the counsellor on duty, but somehow it does not feel like quite enough.

However, some felt that not knowing the problems that had caused withdrawal could feel even more uncomfortable. One identified a category of student who just 'disappears' with no explanation:

> . . . despite great odds, they generally attend tutorials, and get [assignments] in on time. They typically demonstrate the desired student

progression, marks improve, confidence appears to blossom. Then just pre-exam, they disappear.

At the other end of the spectrum, is another tutor's response to withdrawal with no explanation, and frustration that the student seemed to have a positive learning relationship: 'I felt completely helpless and very frustrated. He was so nearly there!! One [assignment] to go and the final exam. *What a waste.*'

Along the continuum of withdrawal, there is a range of recognizable student behaviours with, at one end, the 'passive' withdrawal of someone who, for some reason, never really begins to study but never feels able to tell either their tutor or the region. Tutors are contracted to contact any student registered with them who does not submit a first assignment, but we heard of one tutor who contacted a silent student by letter on six occasions. Tutors need to make many complex decisions, for example how far a student could benefit from a timely intervention, and whether repeated attempts might be experienced as harassment. With a totally silent student, it can be impossible to tell.

Why might a student withdraw without contacting their tutor, or indeed not wish to contact the region either? One explanation lies in the complexity of the tutor–student relationship. Our examples show that tutors make themselves available – they may be more accessible than in other institutes of higher education – and that most students value this. On the other hand, some students might find that their tutor is too closely bound into their success and, therefore, they may prefer to contact someone with less investment. A tutor (or tutor-counsellor) described the complex relationships between student and tutor, saying, on behalf of an imagined student, 'Well, I don't feel I can easily talk to her about it because I feel I'm letting her down, and that reminds me that I'm letting myself down and . . .' A different tutor-counsellor suggests that the last person who will want to tell you about their proposed withdrawal will be: 'someone you have given a lot of help to and [are] desperately trying for them not to withdraw, they will definitely not come to you to tell you they have decided to withdraw . . . they won't face up to you and they just disappear'.

The logic of the relationship illustrated above is deeply embedded in the student-centred mission of the OU, although this complexity is not always acknowledged in its organizational structures. Before returning to Chris's options in dealing with her uncertain future, we need to look in more detail at the issues that arise from the flexibility agenda, the changing nature of the economic contract with students and the effect that distance may have on struggling students and those who support them.

Flexibility and quality in the OU

The OU's mission to be and remain 'open' affects definitions of failure, in ways that those who work in traditional higher education may find quite surprising. The open admissions policy is perhaps the most dramatic difference between the OU and higher education institutions that base intake on rigorous criteria and prior qualifications, but effects of openness extend throughout a student's association with the OU. For example, in the open structures of the OU, failure to complete any one course will almost never mean failure to complete a degree or diploma since students may keep taking the same course (as long as it is current) until they pass, or they may successfully take other courses in the future. Measuring success as progression or a completed qualification is problematic (Kember 1995: 26). It is impossible to know whether a student *intended* to complete only one course or, having taken one or more courses, they 'failed' to complete the degree they wanted. For all these reasons, any calculation of OU retention rates becomes extremely complex.

Managing open admission, self-selection and induction

All higher education institutions experience the difficult relationship between recruitment and retention, but the issues are more critical in an open admissions environment. For example, research participants particularly identified problems in their practice in connection with the following issues:

- students free to choose the course and the level of study, based on their own analysis of their needs;
- no exclusion on the basis of prior qualifications or demonstrated ability – previous educational attainment and evidence of recent study are good indicators of potential success, but absence of these does not necessarily predict failure; and
- the thin line between giving advice and 'gatekeeping' – an issue for debate since the foundation of the OU.

Personal interventions: the research story

Administrative and course-based strategies to deal with flexibility issues are held in place by the guidance and tutorial staff responding to day-to-day issues arising in students' lives. For advisers, the main problem lies in the students' expectations. Some students expect registration procedures to be based on selection and assessment processes so that students who found the course (or courses) they had chosen too onerous may be critical of the OU for 'allowing' them to enrol. Advisers told us that students say, 'But you let me do the course', 'You should have checked' and 'If I haven't got the background, you won't let me do it'. The expectations of such students may originate in their past experiences of education, in which gatekeepers either allowed them to study or told them in advance that they were unsuited. Others may have no good understanding about the demands of study in higher education or the significance of levels. In the OU, marketing materials may create unrealistic expectations in students, as this tutor found with a student:

> 'George' . . . had a totally different vision of what study part-time at a university was all about. The adverts all say . . . 'You could all study at the OU.' Yes everybody *could* study with the OU, but some people need a lot more time than others . . . And it doesn't actually give any indication of what the student has to put in, what is required of a student to make a good fist of it. George took the invitation quite literally and with his laid-back style and all his other activities and his worries about his [family] . . . It's not that George didn't have the capabilities. He didn't have the energy, as a convivial man, to spend with books. He might have prospered more in discussion groups and that type of thing, but as a lone student sitting at the kitchen table with his course notes and units, George had no chance whatsoever.

Unrealistic expectations were problematized by another tutor whose student went against advice and took on too much:

> I tried to persuade him to give up the second level course and concentrate on the first level only, but he was reluctant to do this. In the end, he only submitted half of each course (with poor marks). I did tell him that without exception amongst my previous years' students, those who score badly at the beginning on both courses but do not give up one, end up with nothing, whereas those who give up the second course have, in my experience so far, improved sufficiently to pass the first course. But I cannot make the decision for the student. I can only help him to see that reducing to one course is not a failure.

Rejection of advice, or 'not being heard', was a common adviser and tutor narrative. The frustrations of not being heeded seemed stronger in the experiences of advice staff than with tutors, although inevitably this is a common experience for both. The regional staff spoke about students who 'totally ignore whatever you say', and those who state 'I hear what you're saying but . . .' and 'The advice was there, but we didn't hear it.'

There were others who acknowledged that the responsibility for choosing remains with the student. For example, 'You can't categorize [students]. This is what makes it so complex. The student is the centre of it all so therefore we must respect students' wishes.' Another said 'These people are adults so they should know when it's time to progress in one direction or in the other . . . advising them up to that point, then it's up to them to decide . . . a very difficult boundary.'

'Economics': who pays and who delivers

A major consideration in decision making for a struggling student can be the financial implications of staying, withdrawing or progressing. National and institutional policies have affected how higher education is valued, paid for and 'delivered'. New 'access' funding sources for individual students have supplemented the Financial Assistance Fund, operated by the OU since its foundation, enabling more unemployed students to study with the OU. In our research conversations, we became aware of particular tensions between increased recruitment (supported by the extra funding) and unpredicted difficulties in supporting students whose motivations could be different from those of 'traditional' (largely self-funding) OU students.

Some advisers said that students who were not paying for their own courses were more likely to ignore advice from staff about the risks of overloading themselves, or taking on work at an unreasonably advanced level. There was heavy criticism directed at the Higher Education Funding Council for England regarding its funding for unemployed students which allowed them to study up to 120 CATS points. For *any* OU student this would be an ambitious decision particularly in their first year.

These tales were most likely to be told in the voice of a student, recollected by the adviser, yet as if quoting directly from the student, for example 'Repeatedly, I've been told "I'm not paying for the course. I don't care. If it's too much work, I'll just drop it."' Twice we heard a story in which a funded student was enrolling on a second course with no intention of studying it, they were 'just playing the system' in order to be supported by the loan of a computer. We were also told that those students who were funded by government or other sources were unlikely to be conscientious about informing administrators of their withdrawal: 'it just drags on. They never withdraw.'

As observers of these tensions, we were able to understand that, as a customer offered a product at no cost, you might not see why you should tell the provider that you no longer require it, or why it might be important actively to 'cancel' your subscription. If 'withdrawing' by just doing nothing carries no penalty, then that may seem a reasonable thing to do, especially if the student feels upset by their inability to cope and does not want to make contact with anyone in authority.

We heard comparisons between the rather passive consumers of government-funded services with the self-motivated and self-funding OU students for whom 'the last resort is to drop out . . . so reluctant to give up . . . they'll do everything they possibly can to keep going'. We also heard about enthusiastic, self-funding students whose wish to complete a qualification in the shortest possible time may have been unrealistic, who spurned advice and failed through overwork.

One region is actively researching the difference that additional financial support might make in terms of retention. Interim findings suggest that, for students on financial assistance who take up the offer of help with study costs, there may be an improvement in retention. However, it seems that the additional support offered through tutors may make no measurable difference to *overall* retention rates, as one consequence may be that early contact and support helps at least some fee-paying students make the decision to withdraw before full fees are due. Statistically, we know that students with lower previous educational qualifications are more likely to fail or withdraw, but other variables are, as always, more complex.

Our regional advice groups were clear that constantly changing regulations and parameters around funding and withdrawal meant that only they, because of their direct contact with central administrative staff, could have the up-to-date information that students would need. Which brings us to the issues and problems that abound in the OU because of its essentially dispersed structures.

A distanced, dispersed and divided community

Staff and students in a complex system

The dispersed nature of the OU was not a big topic of conversation in our 'failure' research. However, in other strands of our work, the isolation from central administration that we heard from the regions, and the way in which many tutors see themselves as peripheral to the academic community, figured quite large. We speculate that the sense of isolation contributed to tutors' willingness to identify more closely with the student perspective.

Some tutors talked about a hierarchical separation between the production of course materials, based at Walton Hall, and the mediation of the course in tutorials and by correspondence. There is some frustration about the lack of influence from tutor to course design team and, in working with students, tutors often see their job as being to compensate for shortcomings in the course.

For regional advisers, it is taken for granted that the complex workings of the OU and the amount of written materials students receive will be overwhelming; this is reflected in their forbearance. They told us that students who have not read their student handbook and asked for advice are rarely (if ever) simply referred back to the materials: '[they are] so bombarded with paperwork . . . Their understanding of what they've received [is helped by having] someone to talk it through with, [someone to] help them find their way through the maze.' Although patient with students' difficulties, some regional staff felt helpless because, they said, there was little they could do to influence the major policy decisions being taken 'at the centre', even if they felt that student learning would suffer.

For a struggling student, understanding the ways in which ALs' duties may overlap with the services of a regional adviser or counsellor adds to their difficulty when beginning to think about seeking advice. Our participants acknowledged this, particularly where changes in tutor roles have raised the profile of the regional centre as provider of general learning support that would once have been the domain of the tutor or tutor-counsellor.

Another 'layer' of potential support for students is the centrally operated telephone advice service, run in the evenings from three call centres. A review (Qualitative Consultancy 1997) suggested that many students felt indifferent to the 'loss', or happy with the evening advice line as a substitute for a personal counsellor (1997: 14), and many students commented on the convenience of being able to phone outside office hours. In dealing with potential withdrawal or failure, the report suggests that students found the advice helpful:

> I had a severe problem. I needed a lot of extensions for my essays, they were really sympathetic, gave me the advice I needed and enabled me to complete the year, as I was on the point of giving up.
>
> (1997: 8)

> When I phoned I was quite stressed . . . the tutor put me at my ease . . . he gave me very good advice that I really appreciated . . . I was ready to drop my course because I had taken on too much . . . I was given good advice on time management.
>
> (1997: 9)

These students may already have received the 'good advice' described above from either (or both) the regional advice centre and/or their tutor, but one of the complexities of this work is that the timing of the intervention can be crucial. One of the unspoken anxieties arising from the changing nature of OU student support is that these help lines may seem to do away with the need for tutors and regional advisers, in their current form. An experienced and committed regional academic described his 'worst possible scenario' as one in which all students will contact the university electronically to receive advice from a call centre where details are brought up on a screen, but where the more complex personal circumstances are unrecorded. Perhaps this is the time to return to the personal story of Chris.

Returning to Chris and the options

We have used Chris as a means of holding this chapter together – an image of a student facing a decision point. What options would be available to Chris at this point in her course?

'Passive withdrawal'

For this Chris does nothing; she does not send in the next overdue assignment or indeed any further assignments, and does not sit the exam. As a result of this, the tutor would probably write or phone offering further help or advice. Chris may be so ashamed of her inability to continue that she does not reply or make contact with the OU again. Only when she does not attend to sit her exam will she become a 'failure' and a retention statistic.

Official withdrawal

Opting out without notifying anyone is not in her character. She feels miserable because she could not meet the demands of the course and guilty that she took a 'free' place and wasted it. So Chris would be likely to write or phone the OU to say that she was formally withdrawing from the course. If she phoned, she would be offered advice and encouraged to try this or another course next year.

Struggles on

Chris might manage to submit her next assignment and all the subsequent ones, just managing a bare pass on her continuous assessment, but probably failing the exam – for which she would be offered a re-sit the following year. Even if she determined to take the exam again, given her continuous assessment score, she would probably fail.

Succeeds, despite the odds

Students like Chris do sometimes struggle on and scrape through the exam, but then face another struggle on their next course. Given that she chose initially to take a level three course, this is unlikely; the memory of her difficulties this year will probably mean she does not continue. She may surprise everyone by struggling through the year, finding a study strategy that works for her and going on to complete a degree successfully.

The best possible outcome?

Chris decides to contact her tutor. She explains her difficulties and then asks him, honestly, to tell her if he thinks she is able to pass the course. To her surprise, he says 'Yes, I'm sure you can pass, but not this year.' He goes on to explain that Chris has two very important attributes that are essential for success – she is interested in the subject and motivated to succeed. But there are problems as she is not yet ready for a level three course and just does not have the skills needed for study at that level. He advises her to apply for the relevant level one course next year and meanwhile look for a package that would help her prepare for study at university level. On his advice, she contacts the Regional Centre. Advisers there give her details of other preparatory packs and courses and she registers for a more appropriate course next year.

Conclusions

We summarize the main issues that emerged from our research and in conclusion invite readers to relate them to their own experiences of 'failure' in a higher education institution.

Redefining failure as informed choice

All students, of whatever age, have the right to make decisions about their experiences of 'failure' on any course and to redefine their withdrawal in ways that enable them to rationalize the experience so that it is as positive as possible. We argue that, as providers of educational opportunities for adults, we have a responsibility to support that process in a way that prioritizes the needs of the individual above that of the institution. The 'revolving door' (that is in then out) may endorse previous failure.

Advice and guidance rather than selection, gatekeeping or quota

This is a particular issue for the OU, where there is no 'selection'. However, as many higher education institutions become more 'open' in recruiting students, it may become a crucial issue, as it has in the further education sector. There is a tension between helping applicants make an informed decision and recruiting the full quota of students.

Open access or retention as a performance indicator

This is the opposite side of the problem. If you widen access to maximize participation there is a real risk of damaging institutional retention rates. Attempts to identify the vulnerable or 'at risk' student negates not just the ethos of openness, but also challenges notions of lifelong learning.

Flexibility requires focused information and advice

Finally, as universities offer individual students more flexible and multiple pathways through their curriculum, diversifying the nature of the learning experience, that flexibility and greater openness will lead to greater complexity. This will require the provision of more focused and relevant information in dynamic conversation with each student.

Failure as success

Finally, we return to the story of Chris, had she 'failed' her first OU course and become a retention statistic? Her tutor had a card from her at Christmas saying that she has a new job, which is going well, and that her employers are encouraging her to improve her qualifications. She has applied for a level one course next year and, if she is successful, they will fund the rest of her degree.

Note

1. The research described in this chapter is part of a 3-year project 'From Competence to Excellence: What Makes a Good Teacher?', which was based in the Vocational Qualifications Centre at the OU. The project initiates and explores activities with Associate Lecturers from all the OU regions, aiming to learn about useful ways to improve the learning experiences of students and their own development as tutors. The views expressed in the chapter are those of the authors, informed by their experience and this research, and do not represent any official OU position.

9

Developing a Positive Approach to Failure

Colin Rogers

Introduction

Failure in higher education tends to be conceptualized as primarily a matter of student retention. Retention is to do with terminal failure. Terminal failure marks the end, at least for the time being, of a student's attempt to engage with higher education. Terminal failure is clearly something to be avoided. Terminal failure, however, will be the result of a succession of events, many of which will have involved failures of a different kind, to be referred to here as interim failures, which in each case do not imply the same catastrophic consequences. Individual assignments would have been left incomplete or completed to a poor standard. The student would have failed to improve the quality of this work; they may have failed to fully appreciate that present standards were not adequate. Written material would have been left unread or misunderstood. The student would have failed to have engaged with the information and ideas imparted by the lecturers. Terminal failure is, then, the final outcome of such an accumulating series of interim failures. However, there is a further difference that will be at the heart of the approach to be adopted in this chapter. While terminal failure is to be avoided, interim failure, if it is to be dealt with successfully, needs to be understood as an unavoidable and perhaps necessary part of the learning process.

Why is failure a problem?

Intermittent failure experiences will be familiar to every reader. It is the marked accumulation of them that can lead to the less common experience of terminal failure. The position to be adopted here is that the intermittent experience of failure is an integral part of the learning process. Learning is an essentially risky business. It first requires at least the tacit acceptance of one's present ignorance. It involves the possibility that one will fail to learn what is desired, either at any point or within what would be judged to be an acceptable time period. Learning is rarely effortless or painless. Ultimate success invariably follows from a series of failures along the way – failures to understand, to meet deadlines, to accomplish tasks within the effort and energy parameters assumed and so on. Why might interim failure then be a problem, if we are to assume that it is common and largely unavoidable? First, while interim failure may be a necessary part of the learning experience, the frequency with which it is experienced will vary. Interim failures can also vary in terms of their severity. Failing to grasp one relatively small and unimportant part of a topic may be readily dealt with, while failing to grasp a point introduced as central to the whole field may not. Interim failures are also likely to have a cumulative effect. The more frequently they follow one another, the more likely it will be that they will produce a terminal failure. Attempts to map out the effects of individual interim failures and their contribution to the accumulating experience of the student would be exceedingly difficult and probably of little benefit. The range of varying situations in which such experiences will take place and the consequential range of reactions to them is simply too great to deal with sensibly.

However, it is possible to begin to spell out broad differences in the general manner in which individuals will respond to the experience of interim failure. These variations will be found to operate on both an intra- and inter-individual basis. We may expect to find that the response to interim failure by one person will vary as a function of time, place and circumstance. We may also expect to find that there are relatively stable differences between people. These differences relate to that constellation of ideas, thoughts and emotions which is generally referred to as motivation. At its crudest, an effectively motivated individual will 'bounce back' from the experience of interim failure. It will be accepted as a normal part of the learning curve, and it will demonstrate that the task at hand is one that is interesting, challenging and worthy of the investment of a significant degree of effort. Indeed, it is not a big step from here to claim that for such a motivated person the absence of interim failure could be problematic. Tasks devoid of interim failure are likely to be perceived as routine and unchallenging – in short, boring. So if interim failure can be portrayed not only as an integral part of the learning process, but also as a necessary and desirable aspect, why does it sometimes appear to be problematic?

Motivation as a response to failure

The considerable developments in motivation theory since the 1980s provide insights into the underlying causes of differing reactions to the experience of interim failure (for full accounts, see Weiner 1992; Pintrich and Schunk 1996). Three key aspects of this work will be discussed in this chapter:

- the role of attributions in motivational processes;
- the role of self-worth processes in motivation; and
- the importance of the beliefs held concerning the nature of ability and the type of goal towards which people work.

Attributions and motivation

Closely associated with the work of Weiner (1986, 2000) but explored by many others (Alderman 1999), an attribution-theory-based approach to the study of motivation makes a number of important but simple assumptions. The first assumption is that behavioural variations generally associated with motivational variables (persistence, effort expenditure, task enjoyment and sophistication in strategy use) are all linked to a person's expectations for success and the value they place on that success. Second, and most importantly, these expectations and values are heavily influenced by the ways in which that person has explained previous and related instances of success and failure. These explanations are arrived at through the process of attributing an event to a particular cause. The characteristics of this cause will determine the response to the success or failure. Thus, two people appearing to experience the same degree of failure can respond quite differently if they have arrived at different attributions for these failures. Weiner's model classifies causes of success and failure on a number of dimensions, the most important of these being locus (whether the cause is perceived as being located within the person, or without in the environment or context); stability (whether the cause will generally operate at the same level and in the same way over time and place); and controllability (whether any possible variation in the operation of the cause can be controlled or not by the individual). It is important to note that these characteristics of causes are defined in terms of how they are perceived by any one individual. As examples, Weiner and others often cite ability as a cause that will be internally located and will be seen to be both stable and uncontrollable. This is not to ascribe a set of objective and incontestable characteristics to the nature of ability. It is merely to state that this is how ability may be, and often is, seen. If it is seen in this way, certain consequences will follow. More of these in a moment. Effort, on the other hand, is often ascribed to the internal position on the locus dimension, but would be seen as unstable and controllable. Effort can vary (trying hard now does not imply that one always will) and these variations are under volitional control ('If I want to I can try as hard as anyone can').

The detail of Weiner's position involves setting out the ways in which these variations in the properties of perceived causes give rise to varying expectations and emotions. As an illustration, let us assume that I have experienced a failure and that I have attributed this to my lack of effort. As a consequence, I may feel a sense of guilt in that I assume my effort to be under my volitional control. As I clearly have not exercised this control, guilt may be an appropriate emotion. As my lack of effort is seen to be unstable, I have no reason to assume that I will fail to try hard enough next time and therefore my expectations for future success may remain fairly high. If on the other hand I had attributed the same failure to a lack of ability (and on the assumption that I see ability as internal, stable and uncontrollable), I will be unlikely to experience guilt ('I cannot help being stupid'). However, I may well feel depressed and hopeless and come to expect future failure.

It is possible to interpret Weiner's model as suggesting an essentially logical or information-processing approach to the making of attributions and the consequential impact on motivation. Regular patterns of success and failure will themselves help to determine the type of attributions made. A repeated event is more likely to be attributed to something that is itself stable. Once made, the attributions necessarily give rise to particular expectations and emotions. One cannot help but expect a greater likelihood of future success following an attribution of a current success to a stable cause. One will find it hard to avoid guilt when the cause of a failure is seen to be controllable and internal. However, Weiner and a number of his colleagues have recognized that the attributional process is not only governed by 'cold' rules of logic. There are well-documented tendencies for people to operate with an 'hedonic bias', to seek to accept credit for the good and avoid responsibility for the bad. Teachers therefore are more likely to see students as the cause of failure. They are also more likely to accept responsibility for student outcomes when these are good. Judgements of our own actions differ from those we make about others in similar circumstances (Jones et al. 1972).

Other researchers, however, have taken this further and claimed that attributions rather than simply being a determinant of motivational states are themselves also motivated.

The role of self-worth

A significant figure here is Martin Covington. Covington (1992) has argued that the processes of attribution are themselves in part determined by a desire on the part of the attributer to maximize and protect a sense of self-worth. An earlier paper of his is well known for its title 'Effort: The double-edged sword in school achievement' (Covington and Omelich 1979). Covington is suggesting that the clearly visible exertion of effort is a potentially risky business. Should failure be experienced after the clear exertion of targeted and focused effort, it is difficult to attribute that failure to a lack of effort. This increases the likelihood that the failure will be attributed to a lack of ability. In Western cultures, Covington argues, the possession of ability is highly valued. Indeed, it is often judged to be better to have ability than to be hardworking. In discussing this research with my own undergraduate students, I have taken to asking them a simple question: 'If you had to choose, would you rather be regarded as hardworking but rather limited in terms of ability, or clearly able but rather lazy?' Almost without fail, students opt for the latter. As indeed would I. This tells us something about the perceived nature of ability (the third key point to be discussed below) but also something about the value attached to ability. Of course, effort is seen as being virtuous, one would expect to be praised for trying hard. However, it is generally better to be seen to be in a position where success has come from the effortless demonstration of ability.

It is a step on from here to state that success itself has value because it serves as an indicator of the presence of ability. Failure in its turn serves as a potential indicator of the lack of ability. However, a success obtained by all is often held to be of little value. Such a success can be explained by an attribution to the ease of the task or the level and quality of support that had been given. Where the evidence available points unambiguously to such attributions, it is difficult to persuade others, but more importantly oneself, that the success clearly indicates the presence of a high level of ability. However, by the same token, other combinations of circumstances would make such a claim far easier to make and sustain. The same case can be made for failure. If the failure occurs where most others succeed, where the task is judged to be easy, where high levels of support have been provided and where it is clear that one has really tried hard, the attribution to lack of ability is hard to resist.

Again, it is the logic of the situation that leads to certain attributions. The key difference from the classic Weinerian position is that Covington assumes that we develop an understanding of the nature of these processes and that, therefore, we are able to anticipate them. Any failure presents the possible implication that one lacks ability. Some failures shriek it loudly. To avoid the implication of low ability one should avoid failure completely. This can be assured either by guaranteeing success (tricky in any situation where the task presents a challenge) or by precluding failure by not attempting anything at all (difficult if one wishes to graduate).

Covington is addressing the classic 'fear of failure' syndrome. For Covington, failure is to be feared if, and when, it implies a lack of ability. If one fails through lack of effort, there is less to be fearful of. Covington suggests therefore that people develop 'self-handicapping' strategies. The more failure is feared, because it is seen to challenge a self-belief in one's ability, the more such self-handicapping strategies will be deployed. Such strategies include the reduction of effort and procrastination. Procrastination is likely to increase the chances of failure. However, the fact of procrastination, after the event, enables the attribution for failure to 'lack of time' which in turn helps to obviate the need to attribute to ability.

Thus, the truly threatening failure is one where such an attribution to lack of ability is seen to be necessary. Those who are most concerned to protect a sense of self-worth, by maintaining a belief in their ability, are therefore the most likely to get their excuses in first. Such strategies can be regarded as mal-adaptive (Galloway et al. 1998) in that they do not assist the process of effective learning. In respect to self-worth preservation, however, they may work a treat. What someone does is a function of what they are motivated to do. We will tend to assume that students are motivated to learn and thereby to succeed. Covington suggests that many are motivated to maintain self-worth and, therefore, the adaptiveness of their actions must be judged relative to that goal.

The nature of ability and motivational goals

The analysis of Covington ends with a description of the range of defensive strategies that some students will develop. While these strategies are adaptive to the function of limiting the damage to self-worth from the experience of intermittent failure, they will not serve to reduce the chance of such failure. Indeed, they are actually likely to increase it. It is important therefore to go back to the origins of the concerns that Covington suggests govern the action of most students to some degree, and some students to a considerable degree.

Failure, it will be recalled, is seen by Covington to endanger a student's sense of self-worth via a threat to perceived ability levels. As indicated above, ability is important in Covington's approach because it carries a high value. As with other commodities, the perception of a limited supply heightens the value attached to the commodity itself. It is not surprising therefore to see a link between the view that ability is valued and a view of ability as an entity that is fixed and limited in nature.

Some fascinating work exploring the development of beliefs concerning the nature of ability has been reported by Nicholls (1989) and, more recently, by Dweck (1999). Nicholls' research focused on the developmental changes in beliefs concerning the nature of the causes of success and failure. As an outcome of these changes, young people come to differentiate ability from effort as a cause of success and failure, opening up the possibility of ability being understood as a fixed entity setting a limit on what might be achieved.

Dweck has further developed a general theory regarding the differences between people who tend to see ability (and other human characteristics) as being fixed and stable (the so-called 'entity view') and those who see these same characteristics as being amenable to change and growth (the 'incremental view').

Both Nicholls and Dweck link conceptions of ability to motivation and both do this via a consideration of motivational goals. Goal theory is now the dominant theoretical position in the study of motivational processes. Alderman (1999), Nolen (1996) and Pintrich and Schunk (1996), among others, indicate the range of the concerns of goal theorists. While terminology varies somewhat from one specific theorist to another, there is a general consensus regarding the importance of two particular goals.

Goal theory states that the purposes of action are important in determining its nature. In academic learning situations (and indeed elsewhere) an individual can adopt a learning goal or a performance goal. Many theorists argue that these goals are orthogonal to each other and that an individual may be simultaneously motivated by both. With a learning goal, an individual is primarily concerned with the degree of progress they are making in their learning. With a performance goal, the concern is primarily with the implications of current performance on perceptions (those held by the self and others) of one's ability and competence. The essential difference can be readily demonstrated by reference to student behaviour in a seminar discussion. How might a student respond during such a discussion if they do not understand a point that has been made by another participant? If the point is considered to be an important one, and the student has a dominant learning goal, then they are likely to seek clarification. If the learning goal is entirely dominant, it will not occur to the student that in asking such questions they may be 'showing themselves up' as lacking in competence. They wish to understand and so they ask for further guidance. With a performance goal, the prime objective of the student is to act in a manner that will gain positive feedback concerning levels of competence. Should that appear unlikely, the subsidiary goal is to avoid receiving negative feedback. In such circumstances, the student will be quite willing to make active contributions in the seminar when they are confident that what they have to say will generate positive feedback. However, in the above scenario asking for clarification may well be seen to invite negative feedback. If the avoidance of such feedback dominates the student's motivational strategies, the sensible thing for them to do is to keep quiet and to remain confused.

Even from the above brief and simplistic account of the motivational arguments, it will be clear that effective learning is more likely to take place when individuals work with learning goals, rather than with performance goals. A number of studies have supported this claim, showing that more effective approaches to learning, including self-directed learning, will be adopted by those with learning goals (for example Schunk and Zimmerman 1998; Elliot et al. 1999). All other things being equal, therefore, the adoption of learning goals will lead to more effective learning and, as a result, less failure.

Students working with performance goals are not, of course, unmotivated. Indeed, as Dweck has long argued (1991), performance goals can be highly effective under appropriate conditions. However, such conditions are likely to include the possession of a relatively high degree of confidence in one's ability to carry out successfully the task in hand.

The links between motivational goals and self-perceptions of ability are important in a number of ways. As just indicated, Dweck has suggested that when an individual is in pursuit of performance goals, effective motivational approaches to learning will follow when the student has confidence in their ability to perform. The desire to gain positive feedback from others, coupled with the belief that one has the ability to say and do the right things, is likely to motivate the student to engage actively in the learning tasks at hand. However, if that confidence is diminished, and the prospect of gaining positive feedback also recedes, then the secondary objective of avoiding negative feedback becomes dominant. Here the student is more likely to behave in line with Covington's self-defensive strategies. Task avoidance is a sensible strategy if one's objective is to avoid negative feedback regarding ability. Task avoidance does not aid learning (nor is it meant to).

Confidence in ability, then, is likely to be of particular importance for those who have performance goals. When learning goals dominate, confidence in ability is less important. As the whole point of the exercise is to learn and improve, the recognition that one has, perhaps, insufficient ability to complete the task now is somewhat beside the point. The student is seeking to enhance competence not to demonstrate it.

It is here that the second link with ability conceptions becomes apparent. For the student with a strong learning goal, the intermittent demonstration of relative incompetence is non-threatening as it is assumed that, through learning, competence is increased. Therefore, learning goals are linked with an incremental view of ability. Indeed, logic suggests that with an entity view of ability learning goals will very quickly have to be abandoned when difficulties are encountered. If ability determines performance, if ability is fixed and if performance levels are currently inadequate, then that fixed and inadequate level of ability will soon preclude further learning (unless there are extenuating circumstances).

The world does not readily divide into those who immediately give up and those who never do, as most individuals will hold a combination of learning and performance goals, but the fundamental distinction is of vital importance. The critical question emerges: what determines the degree to which any given individual will hold entity or incremental views of the nature of ability?

The research needed to give a definitive answer to this question is still largely waiting to be done. However, the options are fairly clear and largely predictable. One view, perhaps stemming back most clearly to the work of Nicholls, is that these differences are essentially dispositional in nature. While this still leaves open the degree to which those dispositions may themselves be a feature of experience or inheritance, the practical implication is that such differences are best understood as a function of the individual. Variations in goals (or orientations) are largely to do with the personality of the individual in question. Some people are generally disposed towards valuing learning and progress; others are more generally disposed towards concerns relating to self-worth and its defence.

The alternative view is that goals are primarily determined by the situation within which people are operating. Some learning situations will contain a powerful press towards learning goals, while others will encourage performance goals.

Both processes are probably in operation. Work completed by the present author and colleagues is indicative of an interaction between relatively stable features of the individual and more variable situationally linked change

(Galloway et al. 1998). In this work it is clear that even over a period of substantial change in the nature of the learning environment, individuals who are highly disposed to value learning tend to continue to do so. However, in terms of the motivational characteristics displayed in relation to individual tasks, variability over time and place was substantial. In other words, while there may well be identifiable and stable value systems that have some relevance to the motivational patterns displayed by students, this does not imply that all is fixed from the start of an individual's engagement with any particular task.

Tutor action to minimize bad failure experiences

No self-respecting motivational theorist would wish to argue that current understanding of motivational processes leads to a simple list of 'tips for tutors' or even to a complex list. What is probably clear is that the beliefs of tutors concerning the nature of motivational processes are themselves important as determinants of those responses in students. Eden (1993) has demonstrated how, in various contexts, the beliefs of individuals in positions of influence can affect the performance of others. These beliefs centre on conceptions of the nature of ability. In a similar vein, those concerned with the exploration of teacher self-efficacy and its effects have also demonstrated that those who see ability as being incremental in nature are more likely to be both highly self-efficacious and to encourage their students to be likewise (Bandura 1997; Tschannen-Moran et al. 1998; Zimmerman 1998).

Current trends in the general culture of higher education are possibly unhelpful here. The 'intensification' of pressures on staff in higher education to ensure 'acceptable' levels of success are likely to lead to the transmission of such concerns to students (Ryan et al. 1996), which in turn will help to encourage performance goals and entity views of ability.

It is also possible that we are entering a period in which admission to higher education is easier to achieve than ever before, while concerns about the particular institution that one can gain access to, and how well one may do once there, are increasing. Such developments can give rise to a perception of the stratification of individuals within institutions and of the institutions themselves, both of which encourage the view that it is the possession of adequate levels of ability that determines where one is and should be.

The more such a view is held, the more likely it is that any particular failure will be taken as an indication that one is not where one belongs. The role of the tutor, and of teams of tutors, is to seek to counteract the development of such a view. It is likely that student perceptions of higher education have changed recently and will continue to do so. Increasingly, students are likely to see higher education as 'tertiary schooling'. Not only students, but also their parents, will come to see higher education as a development from secondary schooling that is every bit as predictable and normal as the step from primary to secondary schooling. We already see increasing signs of parental involvement in the selection of institutions and courses. It might be assumed that such developments would reduce the pressure experienced by students as attendance at university comes to be regarded as a normal and perfectly typical part of the young adult's experience. Note, however, that it is clear that the even more typical transfer from primary to secondary school is associated with clear motivational difficulties (Rogers et al. 1994). It is unlikely that the move to university in itself still acts to confer upon the undergraduate that status of 'genius'. Instead, anxieties concerning one's ability to cope with the new regime are likely to be all the greater as the massification of higher education changes the nature of the experience.

However, any transfer carries with it the opportunity for a new start. Just as new undergraduates may doubt their ability to cope with the demands of their new courses, so their lack of familiarity with such courses leaves them open to persuasion as to the demands that those courses make and the limits of their ability to 'measure up'. The role of the tutor is not simply to try to instil confidence in levels of ability, but also to help to develop the view that ability levels can change. One of the most tempting methods of seeking to develop higher levels of confidence is to encourage a student to make favourable comparisons regarding their performance against others. Such strategies may be helpful for some, but they almost certainly ensure the development of a zero-sum game, in which every increase in confidence by one student may be marked by a corresponding loss by another. If assessment systems are intended to reveal who is doing well (and by implication who is not), as they are, then repeated references to performance as so assessed will not succeed in raising confidence levels for all. Tutors will have little control over the ways in which they assess students formally. Ongoing reviews by external agencies tend to lead to increased uniformity of practice in terms of formal systems. However, tutors can still influence the development of student attitudes in a number of significant ways.

First, a constant emphasis needs to be placed on progress. One very simple reason for the young child tending to have strong incremental views of the nature of ability is related to the constant feedback a child receives concerning how they have changed and developed. If undergraduates meanwhile receive messages concerning how they compare to others, they will be more likely to develop entity views of ability.

Similarly, regular invitations to students to engage in work which requires investigation and enquiry and which is based on the assumption that higher education is concerned with learning rather than with the demonstration of knowledge will encourage incremental views of the nature of ability. Group-based work in which students are required to engage with the difficulties that others have with the acquisition of new knowledge will also help to develop the belief that abilities are there to develop and grow. Tutors can also provide powerful role models. The most convincing argument for a link between engagement in research and effective teaching comes not from the claim that engagement in research produces tutors of the highest ability and competence. Instead, it will come from the necessary demonstration that research leads to the discovery of how little is known and how much remains to be learnt, that, in turn, research progresses through the application of skill, via learnt strategies, to problems which are only slowly unravelled.

In summary, the key to dealing with failure in higher education is to accept it as a normal and desirable part of the learning experience. Tutors' own fear of the implications of failure by their students can be the greatest obstacle to the adoption of effective strategies for dealing with it. If we hide from failure and seek to protect our students from it, they will be all the more likely to fear it themselves. Failure in itself is unlikely to harm (certainly in the case of interim failure). While it would be foolish to encourage the celebration of failure, a constructive acceptance of it is highly desirable.

10

Redesigning Success and Failure

Mike Ollerton

There's no success like failure and failure's no success at all.

(Bob Dylan)[1]

Students enter higher education with a range of preconceptions and expectations of what it will be like to study at that level. Prior experience as learners may cause trepidation and possible misconceptions. Some students will try to fulfil parental wishes; some will be driven by an interest in a chosen subject; some students will have but a vague motivation for further study and may not be sure about why they have decided to study the course on which they have embarked. Whatever these expectations and motivations, and however 'high' or realistic they are, teachers in higher education can be certain that such a range of expectations and motivations exist. A central responsibility for higher education teachers is, therefore, to acknowledge the existence of this range of differences and to work with it.

Much responsibility for 'success', which I define as completing a degree course and gaining a classification commensurate with capability and endeavour, must rest with each student; so, therefore, must 'failure'. However, institutions exist as places where learners have rights to be taught certain intended bodies of knowledge and develop necessary skills of processing and contextualizing it. Thus, institutions have responsibilities to enable students to access knowledge and develop such skills. This, in turn, has implications for tutors to pay attention to:

- course design;
- the range of teaching methods;
- types of resources; and
- modes of assessment.

How students are empowered and guided towards the possibilities of achieving success has implications for higher education teachers' beliefs and values about the nature of their subject and about how learning takes place. Empowerment is connected to ways students are helped to access their entitlement to the content of the subject, to issues of equality and to the quality of interactions between teachers and students.

To define success it is also necessary to recognize the possibility of and conditions under which failure can occur. Mathematics, in particular, is a subject about which students have strong preconceptions. For some students, failure to make sense of mathematics can be debilitating and humiliating; whilst all children are taught mathematics, some leave compulsory education with deeply ingrained feelings of failure towards the subject. For others, mathematics was a mechanistic, question-and-answer type experience, where passing tests and understanding were not necessarily mutual outcomes. Some students will have 'passed' enough tests to qualify them to embark upon a degree course with mathematics as the whole or a constituent part. In this chapter my central focus is upon the latter group of students and, in particular, upon the value of helping them redesign their conceptions of what it is to be successful as learners of mathematics. However, before developing these issues, I consider an overarching issue relating to fear of failure and, in particular, student anxiety towards mathematics.

Fear of failure and mathematical anxiety

One aspect of my work has been to support students following a primary qualified teacher status course, who requested learning support for mathematics, which included individual tutorial support. Often at the beginning of a support session students would choose to 'purge' themselves of the root cause, as they perceived it, of their anxiety towards mathematics. This involved relating events from early school days. Recognizing the emergence of common themes and statements, a research project into mathematical anxiety was constructed (Green and Ollerton 1999). The following are extracts of transcripts from interviews with two students who agreed to take part in the research:

> I feel worried and nervous and think of all the bad images that I've got. When I think of mathematics, I don't think of anything good, anything positive, I think of all my worries and all my failures and all the things I find difficult . . .

> All I remember about junior school is chanting the nine times table, I can't even remember the other times tables. I just remember . . . the absolute dread of having that finger coming to point at you.

> It was literally learning it [GCSE level] parrot-fashion, like to spill it out at the exam . . . I would just remember a page with the formula on and get through that way.

All students interviewed described how boring mathematics was, making reference to the predominance of rote learning, the use of exercises from textbooks and an absence of practical equipment. For these students, learning mathematics proved a painful, futile and mind-numbing experience.

Students such as these, who emerge from their formative years of education with a deep sense of anxiety and failure towards mathematics, have a need for confidence to be rebuilt when they enter higher education. This is not an easy task and for some may not be possible. There are other students for whom mathematics did not induce anxiety yet were still unable to gain pleasure from mathematics or perceive it as an active, creative and imaginative discipline. One aim in this chapter is to consider how this situation might be redressed.

Course design

Deciding upon the content to be learnt will obviously form the central focus when planning any course. Deciding upon the kinds of experiences students are to have whilst they learn the planned content is of equal importance. Learning is emotive and the affective aspects of learning cannot be separated from the cognitive; how students learn complements what they learn. To develop issues of course design, I draw upon a particular mathematics module taught at St Martin's College, Lancaster, which uses problem-solving as a vehicle for students to think and behave mathematically.

I provide personal reflective notes written shortly after certain sessions and draw upon extracts of students' writing taken from their coursework assignment. The assignment, assessed through coursework, was for students to produce a portfolio of work describing partial or full solutions to at least four of the problems they had met during the module. Students gave permission for extracts of their work to be used for use in this chapter.

A specific focus of the module is for students to engage explicitly with feelings of not understanding something, of becoming stuck, of recognizing 'stuckness', of being prepared for stuckness and of getting out of stuckness. In this way, stuckness is intended as a positive and potentially successful learning step rather than as a failure.

Stuckness

To gain a sense of supreme pleasure by finally understanding something we have struggled with, or to solve a problem that had earlier seemed insurmountable, usually occurs if the emotions at the other end of the spectrum, of frustration and being stuck are also experienced.

> Everyone gets stuck. It cannot be avoided, and it should not be hidden. It is an honorable and positive state, from which much can be learned. The best preparation for being stuck in the future is to recognize and

> accept being stuck now, and to reflect on the key ideas and key moments which begin new and useful activity.
>
> (Mason et al. 1982: 49)

Everybody has experienced being stuck at some time. 'Failing' to understand something, particularly when we feel others have grasped an idea, can lead to feelings of inadequacy. What we fail at, however, is not necessarily or singularly a lack of understanding about what is being taught, but a mistaken belief that we are alone in not understanding. It might be worth recalling those times when, for example, a motor mechanic has explained what is wrong with your car; how you have nodded to indicate understanding, when you actually got lost after the first sentence. In a workshop or seminar room and certainly in a lecture theatre, it can be even more daunting to demonstrate a lack of understanding. For students to feel sufficiently confident to admit this, a supportive and conducive atmosphere must exist.

Indeed, it is difficult to move out of being stuck until this state is explicitly recognized. Once stuckness is identified we can change some of the ways that led us into this state and use different approaches to try and unravel the problem. One student from my study, Student A, aptly summed this up as follows:

> Many people would view being stuck as a negative state, when in fact it is positive. This is because when you are stuck you must face it, and take steps to try and get out of it. A lot can be learned from this about how to solve problems in the future.

As stuckness is a common experience, it is important to build it into course design, to provide students with first-hand experiences of becoming stuck in order for them to seek ways of becoming unstuck. One way to approach this is to create situations explicitly intended to induce stuckness. Methodologies that use student problem-solving as an integral part of the learning process provide many opportunities for stuckness to arise. Below are extracts from my reflective notes arising from a session on stuckness. I have interspersed further retrospective comments, at various points, to explain other planning objectives.

> *Becoming stuck and getting out of stuckness* (October 1999)
> I explained my aims for the session. These were to offer the group two 'closed' problems with the intention of causing them to become stuck.

I wanted students to be less concerned about being stuck and, instead, to analyse how they felt about being stuck and what they did to try to change this state.

> I described the problems as being 'closed' in terms of there being fixed solutions both of which could be arrived at by different problem-solving approaches.

My objective here was not to indicate that the problems I offered had specific solutions, but that they could be solved using different approaches.

> The first problem was to try to dissect an obtuse-angled isosceles triangle into a finite number of pieces, all of which were triangles containing three acute angles. The second problem was to consider the mathematics behind how a card trick worked. The trick uses a full pack of cards and is carried out as follows. Turn over the top card and note its face value (J, Q, K have a value of 10).
>
> Place as many more cards, face down, as necessary so that the value of the first card and the number of extra cards make to a total of 12. Turn over the next card and repeat as before. The number of piles formed can be denoted as (p). Keep repeating this until you reach a situation where there are not enough cards remaining to make a total of 12 and place these cards in a separate remainder pile (r). Now, without looking at those cards that were turned over in each pile, it is possible to construct a formula using p and r to calculate the total (T) of the face value of these cards.

I chose to offer a spatial and an algebraic problem so that students could engage with two broad areas of mathematics.

> Students were asked to spend approximately 15 minutes on each problem. I suggested that they consider how they might wish to work – either individually, in pairs, in small groups or in a whole group. In the event, most appeared to work individually and in silence.

I am conscious of students' responses to working on problems in sessions. They usually work quietly and individually, despite my efforts to encourage discussion and to share ideas. There are issues here about how the process of working mathematically is often perceived, and the expectations students have about how they learn mathematics.

> At one point, noticing that students were working in almost silence and not communicating with each other I 'actively' left the room.

Deciding to spend a few minutes out of the room was a conscious decision to challenge students' expectations about ways of working, and to make them feel less self-conscious about discussing their work.

> As various students became stuck, I asked them to describe how they felt about being stuck and to think about the kinds of things they might do to become unstuck.

This prompted some useful discussion about affective aspects of learning and about encouraging students to stand back from what they were doing in order to try a different way of tackling the problem. This issue was noted by student A: 'I left the problem for a while then came back to it, which proved a good step. When I came back to it, I solved the problem after about 5 minutes. This made me feel extremely pleased as I did find this problem challenging and earlier on I felt very frustrated.'

> After working on both problems, several students were able to create solutions. The next issue was to decide whether to ask those who had achieved solutions to share them with those who had yet to do so.

Deciding whether to discuss solutions to problems is always a difficult decision to take. Some students may feel frustrated at not 'knowing' an answer and may give up; others may wish to continue to seek a solution without further guidance. An important consideration is the need for learners to engage with problem-solving processes and feel success by finding a solution to a problem that had earlier seemed too difficult.

> We classified the following ways of thinking used in problem-solving:
> - trial and improvement or iterative thinking;
> - starting from a non-obvious place or lateral thinking;
> - diverting away from the main path or tangential thinking; and
> - ordering and working in a step-by-step fashion or logical thinking.

I listed these ways of thinking in my notes, in part because it was my intention to share them with students. Furthermore, I wished to demonstrate that as well as asking them to write reflectively about their learning, I also engaged with these processes. As Mason states, 'To think of changing others is presumptuous; to work on changing myself may serve as a role model for others. To work on changing myself is essential if I wish to be able to help others change' (1987: 30).

Getting out of stuckness

Student A's response to stuckness was: 'Although I struggled with this problem and found it very difficult, at one point I thought to myself "problems are supposed to be difficult, they would not be called problems if they weren't."' When a problem is intentionally and explicitly offered to students to create stuckness they can, in turn, be encouraged to discuss what being stuck feels like. This leads to further discussion on ways of getting out of stuckness. As Student A explains:

> Problem solving is a very important area of mathematics. There are many different mathematical problems that can be solved and there are different processes that a problem-solver goes through to solve them. I have looked at four problems . . . Whether I succeeded or failed in finding solutions to these problems, I went through different processes each time in trying to solve them, depending on factors such as how difficult they were, how confusing they were and how frustrated they made me feel.

Using teacher–student dialogue to help students confront confusion and celebrate understanding is an essential ingredient of effective learning.

'Confessing' stuckness

When stuckness occurs in a seminar, a student may try to resolve it by asking the teacher to explain something again. Inevitably, the other students who feel stuck will be relieved that someone else has been brave enough to 'confess' this lack of understanding. However, it takes some courage to openly admit a lack of understanding.

Therefore, holding discussions about the need for honesty when one does not understand something, the relief of others in the group because one student has asked a seemingly trivial or obvious question, and the value of saying 'I do not understand', are all central to effective learning. Student B explains:

> Being stuck made me feel self-conscious . . . because I felt as though it was only me who could not do the work. I found it helpful and easier once the group had discussed being stuck and talked through the problems we were having.

Once a lack of understanding is out in the open, the teacher can try to do something about it.

> During this course, I have gone through a range of feelings. Stupidity of not seeing the obvious, thickness when I did not understand and failure when I could not reach a solution. All of these states follow 'stuckness', which is something that occurred quite often. It was reassuring to know that I was not the only one and to even [sic] find a way through the feeling of being completely stuck.
>
> (Student B)

Seeking to build students' confidence by helping them to anticipate the experience of being stuck and to seek strategies for getting out of stuckness are important aspects of course design. Underpinning the process of getting out of stuckness is asking questions. The more questions we ask, the more we can try to get to the root of understanding:

> there is only one instrument in research in order to find answers. One instrument: and that is to raise questions. To question is the instrument. And if you don't question, then don't be astonished that you don't find anything.
>
> (Gattegno in Brown et al. 1989: 14)

Other ways students need to experience learning are:

- to reflect upon what has been learnt recently and make explicit knowledge that is implicit;
- to recognize the value of working with other students and of helping each other;
- to find joy in learning in order to increase the effectiveness of their learning;

- to recognize that not all learning is pre-ordained, there can be surprises and that new ways of learning can emerge from situations;
- to know that the teacher is unlikely to have *all* the answers; and
- to encounter situations where the teacher acknowledges the students have learnt something.

Experiencing learning in such ways has implication for the types of strategies that teachers choose to develop and use.

Teaching strategies

Stating one's aims at the beginning of a session is often considered desirable; however, this is not always necessary. It is also useful to 'grab' students' attention and prevent them entering into a malaise, engendered by a predictable seminar or lecture format. By using a range of teaching strategies and resources it is possible to challenge students' expectations about how they learn; different ways of learning require different forms of teaching.

> There is now widespread support in the concept of the variation in the quality of learning approaches arising out of research and development in classrooms throughout Hong Kong, Europe, Australia, Canada and elsewhere.
>
> (Prosser and Trigwell 1999: 92)

Recently, I was invited to write a short article entitled 'How I learn'. I found the experience of analysing how I learnt in markedly different contexts, of being explicit about the implicit, fascinating and revealing. Reflecting upon ways I learn something and determining what my learning needs are, in specific contexts, has implications for the range of strategies I use in my teaching. Whilst I cannot identify accurately what individuals' learning needs are, I can anticipate that a range exists and recognize that to tap into this range I must employ a variety of the following strategies.

Furniture arrangements

Using different teaching strategies has implications for different furniture arrangements. Asking everyone to sit in a ring (without desks) can be useful for whole-group discussion – everyone can see and be seen by each member of the group and all have opportunities to contribute. To some people this arrangement can be threatening, particularly because the relative safety of sitting behind a desk has been removed. Within the discipline of mathematics there are many tasks that can be developed using a 'ring' of people. Certain tasks could be of a discursive nature, others might be more active, requiring people to move or change places in order to illustrate and bring to 'life' certain concepts. Sitting in a ring is commonplace in drama methodology; indeed, such a seating arrangement has a place in any discipline.

The issue to consider is whether students' access to intended learning outcomes is more likely to be achieved as a consequence of the furniture being arranged in particular ways.

Asking students to reflect upon their learning

Asking students to make a response verbally or in writing (or both) to a question such as 'What was all that about?', possibly towards the end of a session, can be enlightening. The intention behind such a request is for students to be explicit about what they felt they have learnt and to share some of these outcomes with the group. Of course, some students may say they have learnt nothing, however, comments such as this can provide a useful springboard for further discussion.

Discussing what learning something (or nothing) actually means, how learning can be described and how different people feel, in terms of their emotional involvement with learning, is a useful way of helping students understand the nature of learning. Indeed, these discussion points highlight important epistemological considerations that underpin learning per se.

Asking students to reflect in detail and avoid platitudinous statements such as 'I learnt about how to think' is also valuable. Closer analysis of specific learning outcomes may focus attention upon issues such as:

- deciding how to begin a problem;
- choosing whether to work alone or with others;
- the value of restating a problem;
- transferring ideas onto paper;
- keeping a note of ideas considered but not immediately pursued; and
- deciding to use a different approach to work on a problem.

Students are likely to need help to recognize that such a range of learning behaviours are possible and desirable. This requires a range of teaching strategies.

Group work

Opening up students' diverse learning potentials can be achieved in a number of ways, including group work. There must be a clear purpose for working in small groups or in pairs rather than individually. For example, discussing an idea or working co-operatively on a problem, perhaps to produce a poster or an overhead transparency as a means of feedback can be more profitable in a group than working individually. Creating situations where students work in different groups, as well as in close friendship groups, is desirable. There are many ways of forming groups, for example according to birth dates, the order in which students enter the room or by giving them each a number and asking them to form groups according to a mathematical rule or function.

Once in a group, students can be asked to discuss, disseminate, jointly solve a problem, take on different roles (such as talker, listener or observer), and make decisions about how to proceed with the task in hand. An important issue is that students are actively engaged in tasks and can take more control of outcomes, rather than passively listening to a teacher's explanations. Of course, the teacher has a significant role to play in setting up tasks that are sufficiently interesting and rich in potential inputs and outcomes.

Use of resources and active learning

It is not unusual for secondary school students to feel that working with manipulatives, such as coloured cubes, rods, pegs and pegboards, is inappropriate in terms of their movement through adolescence and their increasing maturity and self-consciousness. Offering similar manipulatives to late adolescents in higher education can be an even more risky business. However, if teachers never take risks, then opportunities for change and development might be stifled.

Asking students to volunteer to wear coloured hats, to physically act out a problem or work with equipment can produce highly desirable effects:

> If you want to learn how to ride a bicycle, you have to ride a bicycle. If you want to learn how to bake a cake, kiss a girl, understand thermodynamics, or kiss a boy, you have to do those things. Explanations from somebody who already knows can help. But no matter how good the explanation, the best way to learn is when we are actively engaged.
>
> (Sotto 1994: 22)

If students perceive that learning is something that usually occurs at 'arm's-length', or as a result of listening to the teacher telling them something, then some students are inevitably going to fail to recognize the value of personal involvement and active engagement with ideas. Using a range of resources and tasks that require student activity enhances the atmosphere of the learning environment. The role of active learning cannot be underestimated.

Modes of assessment

To complement the range of students' learning styles it is necessary to look for variety of assessment methodologies. How we assess understanding and achievement has a marked effect upon how students learn. If assessment is made on the basis of a final examination, is it likely that students will be solely interested in learning the essential knowledge required to pass the exam. However, as discussed earlier, content knowledge is only one aspect of learning. How learning occurs and how knowledge is processed are equally important. Consequently, this demands that assessment techniques must enable students to demonstrate not only *what* they have learnt but also *how* they learnt it. Student C explains:

> From doing this coursework I have discovered a lot about different approaches to problem-solving . . . I have also learnt a lot about myself . . . that I am someone who prefers pictorial representations of a problem so that I can get the problem clear in my mind. I have also discovered how much I enjoy searching through numbers looking for patterns and relationships.

To decide on the appropriate ways to assess students' understanding, we might consider how we would want ourselves to be assessed in relation to the work we do. For example, if our teaching expertise is to be assessed there are various people who might be able to do it – students, peers, a line-manager, an inspector or ourselves. Even if it were possible to devise a written assessment to evaluate our teaching, we might question the desirability of using such an approach. If we want our writing abilities to be assessed, then it would sensible to provide an assessor with some of our writing. Therefore, if I wish to find out how students solve problems, and I am interested in the process as well as the final outcome, then I can provide students with problems to solve and ask them to describe the processes they used as part of their work. In this way, students are encouraged to write about both the affective and cognitive aspects of their learning.

If I wish to assess students' abilities to solve problems under timed conditions, then an examination may be appropriate. Of course, students can be involved in the process of writing questions themselves. This produces a different dynamic both in terms of the nature of the examination and the power relationships between students and teachers. Students can be asked to write questions they believe would fully and fairly assess an aspect of their learning from the course. These questions can be collated, possibly amended, and the 'best' few chosen. Prior to the examination, the students could be encouraged to see all of the questions that have been written, but those that are finally chosen could remain unknown. Asking students to write questions can be a powerful way of engaging students with their learning.

Whatever assessment mode I use, I need to be clear that it will be the most appropriate way of gaining relevant information. I might also ask myself what students are likely to make of any information arising from the outcome of an assessment.

Seeking to assess the processes with which students have engaged whilst they have been learning the content, requires more than an examination. Such assessment can be of a written assignment or a presentation. A different medium might be used, for example during a 2-D geometric problem-solving module students produced a Motion Geometry film, which was assessed. An example of the use of a presentation occurs in a 3-D problem-solving module I teach as part of a 2-year Postgraduate Certificate of Education course in secondary mathematics. At the outset of the module, students are given the brief to set up and solve any problem that can be ascribed to the domain of mathematics in 3-D. Leading up to the presentation, students are provided with many 3-D type ideas for exploration. These ideas involve the use of manipulatives,[2] folding paper into various shapes, straws, sticks and even buckets of soapy water! The presentation is video-recorded and the outcome is both peer and tutor assessed. Prior to final presentations, students are shown videos of previous presentations and invited to assess these against given criteria.

Using such a range of equipment has implications for different teaching strategies and different classroom layouts. Therefore, the process of planning to include the assessment method is cyclical and holistic.

Seeking to cater for diversity

In seeking to accommodate a broader spectrum of students who currently study at the higher education level, I could attempt to convince myself that the range of teaching and assessment strategies I have described above will be effective for and supportive of the majority of students. However, as Brookfield suggests, seeking to be open, democratic and student-centred in the ways I teach does not suit all students: 'What we think are democratic, respectful ways of treating people can be experienced by them as oppressive and constraining' (1995: 1). Furthermore, during the 1990s 11–18 education has become market-driven, the curriculum has become more prescribed and assessment methods have narrowed and become more test-orientated. As a consequence, current and future generations of higher education students may find more open approaches to learning threatening and lacking in security.

Those students who expect the teacher or the textbook to bestow knowledge upon them, who believe that knowledge is a set of techniques accessed through repetitive exercises and consolidated by past papers, and who see learning as essentially passive and assessed by tests may 'fail'. This failure, however, will be to accommodate the flexibility associated with widely different teaching approaches, different kinds of equipment, different ways of working and different expectations. They may fail to understand the importance of taking responsibility for exploring ideas in depth, or to recognize that to struggle with a problem and come face-to-face with stuckness can be a valuable learning process.

The issues of how to accommodate students' different expectations, how to find exploratory, active learning methods that demand students take increasing responsibility, and to avoid offering passive, over-didactic teaching methods are issues I continue to struggle with and seek to work towards myself.

Conclusions

In this chapter I have considered issues of redesigning success and failure, with regard to student learning, through the beliefs I have about and the values I place upon how effective learning occurs. In considering course design, I have looked in particular at how the use of a range of teaching and assessment strategies and resources impacts upon how the subject-matter is received and, therefore, how it is learnt.

I have discussed empowerment regarding student access to the content of a subject, and student entitlement both to equality and quality of learning opportunities. Seeking to make sense of student fear of failure, specifically looking at anxiety towards mathematics, leads me to a broader consideration of some of the typical conditions that have led to the promulgation of such anxiety. I have developed affective aspects of learning, connecting this with student and tutor reflection, co-support, joy and surprises in learning. A major aspect of the chapter focuses on stuckness, looking at ways of expecting and working with notions of becoming stuck and of helping students to ask questions to seek ways of becoming unstuck.

I suggest that analysis of how one learns, specifically in terms of determining need, is a powerful vehicle for studying learning per se and, therefore, a valuable way of discerning the teaching strategies one might choose to develop. Issues referring to furniture layout, the implications for using group work, the resources I might use are all key factors in seeking to make learning more active and less passive.

Constructing a broad range of assessment methods is, I argue, a key factor in course development and, therefore, effective student learning. Finding ways of assessing achievement that take into account both process and content is integral to providing students with an holistic learning experience; deciding upon fitness for purpose is a necessary aspect of overall course design.

Finally, I discuss a 'Catch 22' problem: to define 'success' I must also consider 'failure'. By working towards a greater understanding of methods of teaching and assessment that are likely to breed greater success for more students, I must also countenance the likelihood of some students' failure. Herein lies an inescapable paradox!

Notes

1. Bob Dylan (1967) 'Love minus zero' from 'Bringing it all back home', Columbia, Sony Music.
2. A useful piece of equipment for making all the Platonic, Archimedean and many other solids are 'MATs', which are created by Adrian Pinel and produced by the Association of Teachers of Mathematics. These are the equivalent of geometrical beer mats!

Part 3

Working with Students

11

Student Counselling and Students' Failure

Shirley Brown

Introduction

In this chapter I will argue for recognition of the important role that student counselling can play in a university setting by demonstrating the links between emotional issues and academic performance. I will explain the powerful influence of failure by conceptualizing it as an internal perception, often at variance with perceptions that are external to the individual, and will also consider the important role played by failure as a catalyst for change.

While preparing this chapter, I was fascinated and perplexed by my own state of mind, which, unusually for me, was tense and unhappy, and apparently not helping the creative process. Reflecting on this, I came to realize that the subject-matter was affecting me. It seemed that it was not possible to insulate myself from the powerful negative effects of the issue in question, the issue of failure. Using the insights from my counselling work on myself, it should be possible to look at the way writing about failure made me feel, to illuminate the issues. What were my feelings? Confusion, fear of being judged, lack of self-confidence and despair were there in abundance. I was caught up in the turmoil felt by anyone confronted with a task that should be well within one's capabilities, but which suddenly and unaccountably becomes impossible. I am reminded of a number of students taking first year philosophy who I saw individually in the counselling service. Each had found themselves unable to do a compulsory essay entitled 'Whether or not you believe it to be true, is it at least intelligible to suppose that you might survive the death of your body?'. For each, the reasons for the predicament were different, but the cause of the writer's block was linked to the subject material. Writing about death was just too uncomfortable for a variety of reasons, such as grief due to a recent bereavement, or fear because they were engaged in a terrifying struggle with their own suicidal thoughts. Confronting the fear and naming the demon gave them strength and helped them to overcome it and move on. I resolved to see if the same thing would work for me.

The subject of students' failure is of immense interest to those working in higher education. Those entering higher education are, by definition, of higher ability and therefore higher expectations are placed on their progress. Whatever educational route has been taken by the student, and understanding the significance and impact of this factor on a student's self-confidence should never be under-estimated, arrival at a higher education institution inevitably presents new challenges to them. Failure to live up to those higher expectations is seen as embarrassing and expensive both to the student and to the institution, because the implications of failure are emotional and practical. The costs, whether measured in terms of self-esteem and self-confidence, or in terms of financing the student's time at university, are considerable. Student counselling is concerned with what failure means to the student and with ameliorating the suffering caused to the university by high failure levels. The current measures of institutional failure include monitoring degree classification, drop-out rates and graduate employment, and performance on these indicators has consequences for the funding of higher education institutions. The higher the expectation, the further there is to fall; the higher the stakes, the more calamitous are the results of failure.

Yet failure is a fact of higher education life. The system is based on the presumption that it is possible to measure success and in any system that measures success there will inevitably be those who do not measure up. Entry into higher education is obtained by individuals proving their worth using the measurable criteria of public examinations. Students are used to being tested and examined by academic standards, and they often perceive that their struggles with success and failure are peculiarly public – with families, friends, neighbours and teachers all knowing their exam results. Whilst these perceptions can be found in most cultures, they can be crucial for overseas students studying in Britain, particularly where the student is funded by a government or other agency, or when they come from a culture where failure is seen to reflect on the group rather than on the individual in isolation. It is interesting to note that this cultural phenomenon can endure even when families have been settled in this country for two or three generations.

In addition, there are those students who are successful in terms of external criteria, but who nevertheless have an inner sense of failure. For many, this is a failure of self-esteem. For others, the external measures may be indicating failure, but internally the student has high self-esteem and feels good about him or herself. This is because of the value that individual students put on their personal learning experiences gained while at university, and whether or not a degree is awarded is insignificant, or at least is not the most important consideration. From the university's perspective, influenced by the 'league table' mentality, opting out or leaving early are seen as failure, but this is not necessarily the case for the individual student concerned.

The role of student counselling

The vast majority of British universities now make some provision for student counselling. In most cases there is a designated 'counselling service', which works alongside centralized student support services, tutorial systems, college welfare officers, students' union activities and caring contributions from individual members of academic staff. I am aware that there are those who are of the opinion that attention to the emotional needs of students is a recent phenomenon, and an unnecessary, even unwelcome, development at that. In fact, however, a close, concerned relationship between student and teacher has been a characteristic of British higher education since the Middle Ages (Ratigan 1989: 151), which contrasts markedly with other European traditions. In many European countries there has always been, and continues to be, a much greater distance between professor and student. Many students from overseas who find their way to our counselling service at Lancaster University, express surprise and delight not only that they are able to talk individually with their lecturers about their studies, but also that there are counsellors with whom they can share their emotional crises without prejudicing their academic standing. An MA student from Europe using the counselling service during a period when his world seemed to be collapsing around him because of a number of personal crises, was completely unable to believe that it was acceptable to inform his academic department about his situation. This was despite the fact that he was missing all his deadlines and was receiving both poor marks and increasingly perplexed and angry letters from the department. Eventually, the student and counsellor together were able to compose an explanatory letter to the department, which lifted some of the tension, thus enabling the student to start working again.

It is only in the second half of the twentieth century that the tradition of pastoral care has become an area of professional concern and practice in Britain. The emergence of the profession of student counselling in Britain was spurred on by developments in North America. The first course in counsellor education was in 1911 at Harvard (Bell 1996: 13), and student 'counselors' became an established part of US universities by the middle of the century. In Britain, the 1960s and 1970s saw a rapid expansion of higher education with the arrival of many new universities and polytechnics. These new institutions reflected the philosophy of the time, which favoured self-expression, individuality and anti-elitism, and were more student centred than their older established predecessors (Bell 1996: 17). They were keen to attract students and to do this were prepared to offer a better range of facilities, including student counselling. This shift of emphasis was reflected in the agenda at conferences of the National Union of Students (NUS) at the time. Having discussed counselling at its 1969 conference, the NUS passed a resolution calling for the appointment of trained professional counsellors at its 1974 conference. The conference urged that counselling services should be set up in each institution with fully trained staff. It also said that counselling services should be seen as an integral, complementary part of the educational programme. It added that services should not merely tackle individual problems as they arose, but also look constructively at ways in which they could adapt institutions, improve learning situations and help individuals take proper advantage of the opportunities available to them, so that the typical manifestations of student problems do not occur (Thorne 1985). These proposals have proved to be amazingly optimistic and far-sighted, and the extent to which student counsellors are expected to involve themselves in matters outside the immediate confines of the counselling room is still a matter of lively debate among counsellors and between counsellors and their employing institutions. Ratigan (1989) continues this discussion and argues persuasively for a threefold division of student counselling work – one branch being remedial, involving principally one-to-one work with the client; another being preventative, which could include staff training; and the third being developmental, contributing to the wider mental health of institutions. This is quite a challenging undertaking, and enough to send many counsellors scurrying back to the relative safety of their busy waiting rooms and full diaries of clients.

The climate of support created during the 1960s and 1970s allowed student counselling to flourish. At Keele University, Audrey Newsome set up 'a comprehensive counselling service for students staffed by counsellors who see themselves primarily as educators and only secondarily as therapeutic resource persons' (Newsome et al. 1973, quoted in Bell 1996: 14). The idea that counselling in educational settings had dimensions to it other than therapeutic work with individuals was a major influence on thinking, and it was increasingly acknowledged that academic success was as dependent on students' physical and emotional wellbeing as on other factors. Thus, over time, counselling services became embedded in higher education. This is not to say that the process was without its detractors. Ratigan (1989: 152) points to the 'persistence in British society of a form of secular Calvinism which emphasizes the value of independence, and the character-building value of surmounting personal difficulties without recourse to outside, especially professional, sources of help'. Certainly, as counsellors, we often encounter clients who express extreme reluctance to ask for help. In my opinion, it is always important to acknowledge this expression of doubt. If problems can be overcome by individual contemplation and reflection, then so be it, but if they cannot, then a sensible course of action is to seek help.

Whether that help comes from a designated student counselling service, or from those who work in a variety of other roles in the university, is a matter of individual student choice (Wheeler and Birtle 1993: 122). Students choose their own point of entry into the network of support available, and this is important both for personal autonomy and for the individual's feeling of retaining control over what is happening to him or her. Although the emotional health of students is seen as important, it is not, of course, the primary focus of an educational institution. If education is about helping students to discover, release and develop potential, then the role of teacher and counsellor go hand in hand, because it is clear that there are features common to each. There is a counselling element in teaching, just as there is a learning element in counselling. Fostering co-operation and understanding between the academic and welfare aspects of university life is crucially important, both for helping individual students and for developing a supportive environment in which academic excellence can flourish.

The student experience now

It could be said that there is an even greater need for student counselling in the new millennium, than there was in the 1960s. The pressures on students are different, but no less real. Whereas in the 1960s and 1970s education was seen as a passport to independence and individual exploration, since the 1990s the pressure has more often been to conform, to aim for the security of qualifications and employment as quickly as possible (Bell 1996: 39). The 1990s saw a further and rapid expansion in higher education provision. At Lancaster University, for example, the student population doubled in 10 years – from 5000 in 1990 to 10,000 in 2000. However, during the same period the staffing did not double, and nor did the per capita funding. The result of this trend in higher education establishments throughout the country is that students often find themselves in very large institutions, with lecture halls built to house much smaller numbers, with teaching groups becoming ever larger and weekly tutorial groups a thing of the past. For many students the small, intimate learning environment has gone, and where it still exists it is often at a cost to the staff concerned who have chosen in their practice to prioritize this form of student experience. Lecturers, who frequently come into the profession because they value contact with students, now have to restrict themselves to quite limited 'office contact hours'. The times when lecturers are available to see individual students can be as little as just one hour a week, which is in stark contrast to earlier practice which allowed for greater 'open door' access. Indeed, lecturers in many institutions are encouraged to distance themselves from students by institutional pressures, which prefer prolific researchers to committed, concerned teachers. There is often a large range of courses for students to select from, but less individual guidance available about the appropriateness of courses for each student. In a more modular style of teaching, degrees are built up by a sort of academic 'pick'n'mix', and this can leave students unsure of continuity or a clear direction in their studies.

Increasingly, the preferred form of assessment is continuous assessment. With each essay or piece of coursework, even the first one written in the second year of a degree scheme, counting significantly towards the final result, this form of checking on students' progress can be felt as continuous pressure. This system works well enough when students are functioning effectively, when they are on top of their work and nothing in their personal lives is causing undue disruption. However, when they are blown off course, either by factors that they understand, such as physical illness, or those that they do not understand, such as a sudden loss of motivation, then panic can soon set in. For the individual student, not being able to work means not being able to do what he or she has always been good and successful at before. This can result in the student finding him or herself in scary, unknown territory, which can lead to a feeling of being very lost and unable to cope.

It seems that there are more uncertainties in the world that students now inhabit than there were a generation ago. Will their first degree guarantee them a job? It was more likely to in 1970. Is a first degree enough education or should they continue studying for a higher degree? Is a Masters enough, or should they consider a PhD? Is even this enough? Can they get funding, even with a first class honours degree? Can they afford to increase their debts by staying on at university? Now students no longer get grants, they can easily be more than £10,000 in debt by the time they graduate. Financial pressure is more likely to be a very real issue for students today than it was in 1970. The transition from compulsory to non-compulsory education also used to mean a transition from dependence to independence. This is now rarely the case. Students of all ages are given a very confused message when they enrol at university. Financially, they become more dependent, either on families or on student loans. The alternative of doing paid work to support themselves is one which many attempt, but which itself puts them under even greater pressure. Working five nights a week at a call centre or bar to earn the minimum hourly wage makes keeping to academic deadlines even harder.

An aspect of continued financial dependence that must not be overlooked is that this can increase a student's sense of obligation to whoever is making funds available. The expectation – whether expressed or not – of families who supply funding is that the investment will be worthwhile. Whatever parents say, most students believe that their parents want them to do well even when they say they just want them to be happy. There are also many families who wonder what the point of all their sacrifice and generosity is if not to improve the future prospects of the student. Of course, the student is not necessarily young, and for mature students the financial burden placed on partners and offspring by the mature student returning to learning can often be considerable. So the student experience, the studying part of which is often experienced as intensely lonely, is often performed to fulfil the real or imagined expectations of others, and there can be a real fear of letting people down by not doing well enough.

Helping students in the future

How best can student counselling services set about helping students in the future? The calibre of the staff in the counselling service is crucial and fundamental to a successful and effective service. Although the model that we have developed at the counselling service at Lancaster University is rather unusual, it is one that works well. The team of counsellors comes from a variety of backgrounds, including clinical psychology, 'Relate', social work, careers advice and teaching. Counsellors have also undertaken a variety of trainings both before entering the profession and since, and among our ranks are counsellors who reflect all the major theoretical approaches in counselling – person-centred, psychoanalytic, and cognitive and behavioural. I agree with Ratigan that whatever the theoretical model, much of the actual practice of counselling is eclectic and pragmatic:

> Whilst most student counsellors owe a primary affiliation to either a person-centred, psychoanalytic, or cognitive-behavioural model, and this affiliation conditions the form of the clinical work undertaken, the impression is strong that the variety of human problems facing a general purpose counsellor working in an educational institution indicates that more than a passing acquaintance with all three modalities is necessary for effective work with clients.
>
> (Ratigan 1989: 153)

Student crises need a relatively rapid response to requests for help and it is rare that these crises are beyond the competence of the professional student counsellor. A measure of theoretical flexibility is required to enable counsellors to deal not only with the range of clients but also with other counsellors and with colleagues, both from the medical and teaching professions.

All counsellors working with students, whatever their orientation, share common aims. There may be different means, but the ends are the same. These are to support students, to help them make the most of the opportunities offered by higher education, to make sense of what is happening in both their internal and external worlds, and to decide on the best action for each individual after consideration of various alternatives. Whatever the orientation, there is a growing consensus that what really makes for effective therapy is the quality of the therapeutic relationship developed between counsellor and client (Russell 1993). Not only that, but the debate about whether there is a difference between psychotherapy and counselling, which also taxes some in the profession, is increasingly coming to the conclusion that neither the length nor the therapeutic orientation of a given training has much bearing on the practitioner's effectiveness or on the client's perception of the helpfulness of what is being offered. Indeed, Dryden (1996) puts it quite succinctly when he says that the difference between a counsellor and a psychotherapist is about £8,000 a year (quoted by Thorne 1999: 229). In the counselling service at Lancaster University, we all call ourselves 'counsellors', although some could legitimately call themselves 'psychotherapists' or 'clinical psychologists'.

What counts as failure?

In the world of higher education, which is now big business, where it is expensive to take part and where the rewards are by no means certain, what counts as failure? I meet different perceptions and experiences of failure every day of my working life, and it is striking the extent to which students' own internal perceptions of failure are often at variance with external measurements of failure. The internal and external worlds do not match. It is a much-loved principle of politicians of recent years that success is measurable. League tables abound and departments and universities compete for high rankings. Whatever the rights or wrongs of this system, it is my observation that success on these criteria rarely brings happiness. Do 5-star departments enjoy their success? No, because they worry constantly about losing their ranking. Do straight-A students feel self-assured? No, because the trouble with being clever is that you can never be clever enough (Bell 1996: 33). I often hear high-achieving students report that when phoning home to tell parents that they have been given 70 per cent for an essay, they get responses like 'Just what we expected' or 'Why only 70 per cent?'

League tables make measures of success and failure seem neat and scientific, but this is not how these phenomena are actually experienced. The experience is an internal matter. The feeling of being a failure is what matters. However good something looks to the outside world, if the person feels bad inside, then that is the feeling that matters to the individual. This explains why, for example, students receiving first-class grades can also feel that they are failures. This could be perhaps because they know that even this degree of academic success will not please their family. It can also be because they do not feel confident about their abilities, always fearing that one day they will be found out (I have also heard just this fear from highly acclaimed professors). This 'impostor syndrome' is further explored by Stephen Brookfield (1995: 229–35). People's internal measurements of worth are important, and these are matters which counselling can address. Through the counselling relationship, through attentive listening and a thorough, accurate understanding of what the student is experiencing, by communicating this back to the student and by reflecting on what is actually going on, changes in perception are possible. Counselling can help people understand more about the situation in which they feel they have failed and can help them back on a path to believing in themselves.

For some students, failure, as defined by institutional criteria which might include low marks, late submission of work or absence from class might actually be considered by the student to be a successful adaptation to their particular personal circumstances. For these students, failure is not the opposite of success, it is far more complicated than that. Students' personal histories affect their responses to present problems. The role of the counsellor is to help individual students make sense of what is happening to them, to understand why they are responding in particular ways which may be destructive, and help them to find alternative responses which may be more positive and effective. What of the student who has already 'failed' during previous experiences of education, for example by failing the 11 plus examination? The failure could be for a variety of reasons, for example school might have felt like an alien environment and the young person had no desire to do well. A student's dyslexia may have remained undiagnosed, resulting in them feeling stupid, or perhaps because of bullying the student was constantly anxious and developed very low self-esteem, preventing him or her from building the self-confidence required for success. For these, and many other reasons, students feeling or fearing failure, often arrive at the counselling service presenting as depressed and lacking in motivation.

Mature students often feel that they failed during their early experiences of education. People who choose to return to learning later in life have often had negative experiences of schooling first time around. For them, not just failure, but the fear of failure has been learned long before admission to higher education. The British higher education system is highly selective and competitive and the atmosphere of competition is central and continuous throughout the student career. This has a strong influence on how students see themselves and on their capacity to study. Many mature students see education as a refuge from the world of paid work and as an opportunity to improve their lives and future prospects significantly. The reality of finding themselves constantly compared with, and judged by, others, both for their performance in seminars, where they are expected to make a major contribution, and for their written work, is often terrifying. The high anxiety levels that they experience can be disabling, and perceptions of themselves as academic failures can only be reversed over time and with considerable effort.

In the next section I use my counselling experience to illustrate issues and arguments. I would like to make it clear that none of the following case studies are about specific students with whom I have worked. Clearly, the issue of confidentiality in the counselling relationship is paramount; indeed, without it the work would not be possible. I am referring to situations which have occurred regularly over time in my practice and which I have encountered often enough to know that they are not unique to any one client.

Some examples

It might be useful at this point to consider some examples of how students present themselves at the counselling service. Let us imagine a student arriving at the counselling service as a result of an episode of self-harm. Completely unable to communicate his distress in any other way, he had taken to cutting himself. The pain and distress caused by this act had made him realize something was very wrong, and therefore he decided to seek help. It emerged that he was a bright young man, the first from his family to come to university. In fact, this was his second attempt at starting a university course, as he had previously failed to complete his first year at another university. Academically, the department was satisfied with his work, but what he could not deal with were his own feelings of lack of self-worth. It took many counselling sessions to reach a mutual understanding of what this was about, and why he felt that failing was what he deserved. In time, he was able to see that he had the right to be at university and that it was alright for him to be successful. He was then able to sit and pass his first year exams. Learning to believe in himself, understanding and adjusting his inner world, allowed him to act more appropriately in the outer world. Often the role of counselling for students who believe that they are failures, despite evidence to the contrary, is to help them rebuild self-esteem, and this can be a slow process. Failure breeds failure, and a student who feels a failure can soon find ways of justifying that feeling. The counsellor may well encourage the student initially to make small changes, so that they can begin to experience what it feels like to have some success. This is on the same principle that claims it is better to successfully climb a hill than fail to climb a mountain.

Another student who had been very successful at undergraduate level, astounded her tutors by producing late, sub-standard work for her Masters degree. This also perplexed the student, who found that for the first time in her life she could not concentrate on her work. In counselling she began to realize that she had always used the strategy of working hard to disguise a deep unhappiness in her life. Doing well to please her parents, who had always compared her unfavourably with her brother, was no longer a good enough reason to work hard. She found that she was really angry with her parents, but having discovered this and decided to do something about it, she was then able to redirect her energies into doing what she really wanted to do, which was to be a successful academic. Adjusting the view she had developed of herself as a failure allowed her to re-discover herself as a success, and this time on her own terms.

What about the student who was successful academically, but felt a failure as a person? She was always falling out with friends, male and female, and ended up feeling lonely and that she did not belong. 'People tell me I'm always miserable, so I just shrug and say, "So what, I am miserable."' She came to the counselling service saying she was depressed and wanted to leave university. It took many sessions to get behind this angry, defensive exterior to discover the hidden, frightened, hurt child inside. She had been raped as a schoolgirl but had not told anyone, fearing she would not be believed, indeed that she would be blamed, a response that had occurred before in her life when she had told her parents about a sexually abusive neighbour.

Failure as an agent for change

Failure is a very powerful force, and paradoxically because its effects can be so devastating, they can also be enabling, and act as an agent for change. Perhaps this point is best illustrated by some examples of ways in which students have used the potent weapon of failure to communicate an important message about themselves and, thus, bring about change.

- A very clear example would be when failure to complete a degree is used by a young student as a way of signalling, loud and clear, to parents to stop putting him or her under so much pressure.
- Another student might use failing her MA as the best way of telling her ambitious parents that she wants to get off the treadmill of expensive public school, excellent A levels, first class degree, then a higher degree to be followed by a career in the competitive world of commerce. She actually wants to be a social worker, but no-one would listen.
- However, failure can also be a misguided arrow, as illustrated by a student who wants to tell a demanding partner that she would like to end their relationship. Unable to find the words, she sets about failing her degree as a way of signalling 'I'm not worth knowing.' The role of counselling here would be to help the student understand herself in the relationship better, consider what she really wants and find more effective and less destructive ways of communicating.
- A student had enrolled on a fine arts course because of the enthusiastic encouragement of his father, who himself had always wanted to be an artist. When the student failed the first year, it was a shock, as it was the first time in his life that he had ever failed anything. He thought about leaving higher education and came to the counselling service to look at alternatives and to think about what he really wanted to do. He had not realized before just how much he admired, and feared disappointing, his father. Through counselling he found a way of telling him that he did not want to do art, without making his father feel rejected. Failure for this student had proved very liberating. It had stopped him in his tracks and made him confront some important issues in his life, and as a result he felt stronger.

Students arrive in higher education having already had, and to some extent been moulded by, a range of relationships and experiences. These will have a profound influence on the way they cope with the challenges presented by higher education. There is a complex relationship between effective study and personal development, and students need the opportunity to explore the issues that are important to them in order to thrive. Student counselling services can help education institutions to fulfil their primary function, which is that of education. However, education has to be understood in its widest sense, education of the whole person, a multi-dimensional experience involving learning about learning.

If we are not to fail students in higher education, we have to be aware that the issue of failure is much more than something measurable by external procedures. Failure is a more complicated concept than this implies, and internal judgements of failure are a vital part of the equation. Both external and internal perceptions matter and neither should be ignored. There are external pressures on universities and the indicators of failure that are imposed on them have to be acknowledged, as it is important for the institution to present as positive an image as possible. Student counselling services can perform a moderating and ameliorating role for the institution. The tension that can exist between students' internal and external worlds, can result in disaster if not acknowledged and managed. If universities do not have ways of handling people who have a deep sense of personal failure, then the result can be disastrous. Student counselling services have a role ministering to the internal as well as the external measures of failure affecting students, by helping individual students to negotiate their way successfully through the university experience, to the ultimate benefit of both the individual and the institution. Failure has powerful negative connotations, but we must not be scared to name it, understand it, confront and manage it. If we can do this, we can harness these same powerful negative forces to provide opportunities for positive growth.

12

The Administrator's Tale

Terry Wareham and Lesley Wareing

Introduction

In this chapter we look at the issue of failing students from the perspective of the central administration of higher education institutions. The discussion grows out of a presentation by one of the authors (Wareing) at the symposium on student failure in higher education held at Lancaster University in the summer of 1999. That presentation was a personal view based on many years' experience of working in various areas of student administration. She is currently head of the student registry, dealing with a wide range of student administration issues – admissions, registration and matriculation, course enrolments, record creation and maintenance, Higher Education Statistics Agency returns, timetabling, fees billing, progress monitoring, academic discipline, examinations, results awards and degree conferrals for those who are successful and re-sits, reviews and appeals for those who are not. In addition, she has recently taken on responsibility for Lancaster University's quality assurance mechanisms. The perspective of the other author (Wareham) is that of director of a unit responsible for educational, staff and organizational development of the institution and pastoral tutor to a group of undergraduate students. By different routes both authors are engaged in work developing the course design, learning, teaching and assessment strategies of academic departments within their institution. This range of personal experience is used as the basis for an analysis of the ways in which institutional structures and processes are encountered and negotiated by students. This leads to proposals about how higher education institutions can better understand the organizational contribution to student failure, how they might work both to minimize failure where possible and to deal constructively and creatively with failure where it becomes inevitable.

Versions of failure and the role of central institutional administrators

The average student registry has contact with hundreds of undergraduate and postgraduate students who have failed, or who have been in danger of failing, to reach the end of the course of study for which they were registered or to achieve the associated qualification. These might be 'struggling' students – they themselves may have recognized that they are getting into academic difficulties or, more commonly, their department may have identified them as being at risk. The discussions with these students usually take the form of trying to identify the problem and its causes and then exploring options for dealing with it, including work recovery plans, study counselling, other counselling, medical help, financial help, suspension of study, transfer to a different course or withdrawal from the course. Alternatively, they might be students on the struggling/failing cusp, who have fallen so far behind that their departments have recommended their exclusion from the university. The position of staff in the registry is somewhat ambiguous at this stage. Their role is partly to support the student and the department in finding ways out of the dilemmas of interim or terminal failure but, more formally, to interpret and communicate laid-down procedures for dealing with such cases. This position contains within it many of the complexities of dealing with student failure which are evident in a variety of forms across the institution. Universities have structures and cultures which support students in myriad ways to help them achieve both academic and personal fulfilment. However, they are also the upholders of standards inherent within degrees and other awards. Finding a way through this set of complexities and contradictions is the main focus of this chapter.

Most student registries, or equivalent offices, will be involved in servicing the committees which deal with academic issues, not only preparing cases for these bodies to examine, but also follow-up with both students and their departments – interceding, monitoring progress and helping students to get back on track. Unfortunately, it may also involve informing students that they have been excluded from the university and helping them to come to terms with this. Finally, the work may be to advise students who have actually failed formal assessment hurdles either at the end of the course or at one of the interim stages (for example first or second year exams) and to service the formal review and appeal panels which deal with these students.

Whilst individual academic staff may deal with the handful of students in difficulty within their department and support services (such as counselling and study advice) may deal with the individuals and specific sub-groups who make contact with them, within many universities the student registry (or similar office) staff probably encounter more instances and types of failure for a broader range of students than any other individual or department. Their work with failing students is likely to cover a very broad span, from the formally procedural to a quasi-counselling role.

Changing cultures in higher education

In theoretical terms, this range of work is enacted at the collision point between a technical-rational approach (Schön 1983, 1987) and a more humanistic, transformational one. Many higher education staff espouse the view that the process in which they are involved is a transformational one and that getting students through the assessment process is less important than sustaining and inspiring a process which changes and develops students (Trowler 1998). This attitude goes hand in hand with the traditionally collegial culture of higher education, with the student as apprentice scholar. In the days of much lower participation rates in higher education and of lower levels of monitoring and external scrutiny, staff arguably had more time to interact with students to bring about the kinds of personal and intellectual transformation they valued. However, the gradual change of culture towards the more competitive, business-oriented modes of 'new managerialism' (Clarke and Newman 1997), with higher levels of surveillance in the form of quality assurance mechanisms and requirements for strategic planning statements and the like, means that departments and institutions are being judged on their outputs, rather than on the integrity and value of their processes.

Although we are encouraged to define and describe what our students will take away with them at the end of their course of study in much broader terms than mere degree classifications, for many graduates the class of their degree is all important. In this they appear to be adopting a realistic approach to employers' actual (rather than espoused) preferences and behaviour. Brown and Duguid (2000) describe higher education as 'warranting' students for employment – the classification of degree and, increasingly in the UK, the institution from which it was obtained are the main factors in accrediting the student for certain types of work rather than the substance of the degree. At the same time, we are being asked to be much more explicit about inputs and outcomes and we have to think about process measurement, control and minimizing variation in an attempt to ensure equality of opportunity and consistency of treatment. There is a nagging tension in these two positions – richness, variety, relevance of experience and responding to individuals are required by one set of pressures, while on the other hand there is the drive towards performativity (Barnett 1990, 1994):

> The measurable performance of core activities, or the appearance of such performativity in the form of measurable products of research, student learning outcomes and student and quality inspector assessments of teaching, is becoming increasingly centre-stage in higher education in the United Kingdom.
>
> (Deem 1998: 53)

Deem argues for the notion of performativity specifically in relation to the work of academics in UK universities, but Barnett tracks this growing trend within society as a whole. Students have to perform and demonstrate skills and capabilities in a system of close scrutiny. It is no longer sufficient for lecturers and students alike to know implicitly what constitutes a 'good' degree. Lecturers now have to work with benchmarks, qualifications frameworks and programme specifications. Students have to produce personal profiles, records of achievement and other detailed documentation about themselves and their achievements.

The current assessment system is predicated upon the belief that a student's academic ability and performance can be measured objectively against clearly defined standards through a fair and transparent process of discriminating between those who achieve the standard and those who do not. This sounds simple and logical, if rather brutal, and is another example of the technical-rational approach. Students who fail to achieve the standard and who face exclusion from their course are subject to the review and appeal procedures which apply in these circumstances. These set out in a very logical and precise way the grounds for appeal and the courses of action open to the review and appeal panels. In theory this is all clear and neat, but in practice things can be extremely messy. As Peelo points out in Chapter 13 of this book, transactions which surround these processes are complex and difficult.

Working with students

First, as is evident from other contributions to this book, there are degrees of failure. Some people define failure in terms of those students who fail to get the qualification for which they were aiming, but this applies to only a very small number of students. More telling, and more problematic from a student registry perspective, are those students who, for whatever reason, fail to realize their perceived potential. At the end of each academic year, institutions are faced with dozens of students pleading that their 2:2 should be upgraded to a 2:1, that their 2:1 should be upgraded to a first or, in extreme cases, that their first class degree should consist of even higher marks.

A second feature is that students seem increasingly inclined to question the judgement of their examiners. As we are encouraging students to become independent learners and critical thinkers, we should not be surprised at this. Many lecturers build self- and peer-assessment into their courses either to aid reflection and learning (formative) or as part of the formal, summative assessment process, precisely to allow students to learn to evaluate their progress and performance. The growth in personal development profiling and records of achievement at both school and higher education levels also encourages students to reflect on and take ownership of their development. The move from an 'elite' to a 'mass' higher education system (Trow 1972) also means that students do not all come from backgrounds where the values and standards of a university education are implicitly understood and accepted. This makes it much more likely that they will question and require justification for courses of action taken by their teachers. Indeed, the disjunction between the norms of the institution and the students' understanding may be so overwhelming that the student may never comprehend or believe the standards that are being required of them. One of the stated reasons for the introduction of the complex web of quality assurance mechanisms by the Quality Assurance Agency, which require the articulation of standards, processes and mechanisms, some would say to an excessive degree (Bassnett 2001) is that all stakeholders – students, parents and employers – should have a clear understanding of the degree programmes being offered and the standards that are being maintained. In addition, the trend to question traditional 'authorities' is noticeable across public life. Numerous recent examples of poor or perverse judgement in the areas of medicine, the law and education have given rise to understandable scepticism about the ability of those in authority to set valid and reliable standards. We can hardly expect our students to accept meekly the judgements made about them any more.

Since the tacit understandings about university processes which might have characterized the experience of earlier generations of students may now be problematic, it follows that certain features need greater clarification. Many people do not find the assessment process to be fair and transparent. There is often confusion about what is required, for example the relationship between input and output. Many students find it difficult to accept that the work assessed is not of the right standard when they have put a lot of effort into producing it. The authors detect an increasing tendency for students to think that because they have attended all the relevant lectures and seminars, read all the recommended books, spent hours revising/preparing and have submitted pages and pages of writing, their 2:1 is assured. The academic notion that a product of study (such as the essay, project report and exam answer) is to be judged in its own right and that the judgement is divorced from the individual's circumstances is difficult to accept when students have invested so much of their physical, cognitive and emotional energy in it.

Feedback on performance is another area where misunderstandings arise regularly, sometimes because it is not given in a clear and explicit way and sometimes because students hear only what they want to hear. Tutors may try to support students by avoiding being too negative and cushion their criticisms with encouraging remarks. This can easily lead to students getting unclear messages and latching on to the positive when in fact there is an urgent need to address the negative.

The worst situation for students, their tutors and central registry staff is when a student actually fails a degree. It suggests that the system in place to monitor, encourage and correct failure at an early stage has failed. By this point, it is usually too late to salvage anything very much as the options are fairly limited. Most higher education institutions allow students one or maybe two opportunities to recoup failures, but if the student cannot do so, they face exclusion. At this point, the review and appeal panels come into play.

For those in the central university administration and for the students involved, the rules of the game now change. Whereas, at earlier stages of the process, students could use a range of mitigating circumstances to gain extensions of hand-in dates and other forms of dispensation, their options now become not only more limited, but also qualitatively different. At the same time, the role of the administrator begins to change and the emphasis shifts from helper to gatekeeper and overseer of standards. Grounds for appeal are usually limited and the options open to formal panels and committees are few. Admissable grounds for appeal in most higher education institutions usually relate entirely to the validity and proper conduct of the assessment process. However, in our experience, students rarely cite these grounds for appeal. The reasons for this are obscure, since the procedure is made clear in the documentation the student receives and, certainly at the authors' institution, there is a raft of experienced support available to students through the college tutorial system and the students union advice centre. Just occasionally a student may cite examination procedures that have not been followed correctly or examiners' being prejudiced, in the sense that they were unsympathetic to a theoretical position or a methodological approach being adopted by the student. However, the student is in a curious position. Despite the fact that the processes involved in review and appeal bear many resemblances to legal processes of trial and appeal, there are significant differences. As Cawkwell and Pilkington (1994) point out, a person appealing in a court of law against a judgement will have been present at the original judgement and will have heard all the arguments being made against and for them. This is not so in a university appeals procedure, where the initial judgement on their work will have been made in private. Although second marking and examination board procedures will have given weight to the judgement, there is evidence (Partington 1995) that complex processes come into play which involve tacit and unexamined assumptions and prejudices.

More often students are likely to resort to citing the problems they have confronted as an explanation of why they have failed. These problems may be truly appalling and increasingly include financial difficulties, mental health and domestic difficulties, but, whilst review panels can appreciate the difficulties with which the student has been wrestling, they cannot award a degree where the standard has not been met. Even when the review panel is sympathetic, the most the student can hope for is a further resit opportunity and it may well be that the reasons the student did not perform well in the original assessment prevent her or him from succeeding in the resit, so little is achieved other than prolonged anguish for all concerned. Does the student really want the panel to say, 'We agree with the examiners that the thesis is not of a standard to merit the award of a PhD, but we feel so sorry for you that we are going to give you one anyway'? A version of this form of sympathy may well have happened numerous times for a failing student and it is quite possible that students are not aware of the point at which support switches swiftly and inexorably to discipline.

Whilst university assessment, review and appeal procedures may ostensibly be based on rational principles, students who have failed are often not particularly rational. They are frequently extremely emotional, feeling humiliated, disappointed, angry with themselves or with the system which they see as having failed them. In addition, there may be anxiety about loss of face. For most students there are several additional stakeholders in their degree success – family, friends, previous teachers, sponsors and home governments. It is not unknown for students to beg on their knees to be allowed to remain in the university. Most student registries will be able to quote many examples of student behaviour which demonstrates the catastrophic effect that failure can have on an individual's self-esteem and their relations with others.

People who are facing failure get upset and behave in ways which are difficult to cope with no matter how sympathetic one may feel towards them. Failure is difficult for students; it is also difficult for staff. Having to inform a student that they have failed provokes a range of powerful emotions – shame, guilt, fear and embarrassment. Staff have to develop coping strategies to deal with this, which may include officiousness, cynicism and scepticism and there is a need to be aware of this danger and to guard against it (Peelo and Wareham 1999). Whilst failure may be a set of procedures and statistics for an institution, for each individual involved it is a personal and unique experience and this needs to be recognized. Review and appeal panels tend to operate at one remove from the student, protected by a degree of anonymity and formality. This remoteness is arguably essential to allow their members to take a detached and objective view of the case. However, someone, often a member of central administration staff, must break the bad news to the student. Panels are likely to be much tougher in their judgements when they know that they will not have the messy job of dealing with the student in question. Again, in a court of law it is the judge in person who hands down the verdict. In terms both of openness of process and of giving support to central staff, there may be an argument for the panel as a whole to inform the student.

Conclusions

Universities are uncomfortable with the notion of failure. There is a common view that higher education is a public good in itself and often people will go to inordinate lengths to find ways of enabling students to remain in the system by giving them another chance. Sometimes this is not in the students' best interests. Why do we find it so difficult to accept that failure is a natural part of the system and that leaving the university is sometimes a better course of action for some individuals than prolonging the agony and increasing their eventual sense of failure? To become a 'serial failer' at university sets up (or perhaps confirms) a self-image that could be damaging for life. For some students, it comes as a huge relief to be given permission to stop their studies and take a different route. It is difficult to know how to prepare students for the possibility of failure. Students need to learn the 'game' of higher education, that is how to achieve the rewards, how to collect money as they pass 'Go' and how to get out of jail. Clearly it is impossible, politically, to discuss failure in recruitment information or during students' induction into the institution, but we need to find some way of preparing students for the possibility of failure and ensure as far as we possibly can that they understand how to work the system to protect themselves from dangers of this kind.

From the perspective of a central student registry, there seem to be two main areas where institutions may be failing students – the ways in which we educate student expectations and the ways in which we manage failure. Many of the problems arise from failure of communication, others are the effect of institutional cultures. Our examination of the issues suggests the following areas for action by institutions.

- We need to be transparent, honest and precise about what students will have to do in order to succeed, namely to clear certain hurdles and jump through various hoops. Some of this can be done by improving information sources. Other elements of this process may not be so susceptible to being publicly and officially stated. There is a tension between different philosophies within universities. On the one hand, we want to promote deep learning, self-expression, independence and creativity; but, on the other, we need to advise students to be strategic (Entwistle 1984) if they wish to succeed and get the bit of paper – their 'warrant'.
- Whilst acknowledging that no assessment system is perfect, institutions must endeavour to have in place assessment strategies which are sufficiently transparent, reliable and negotiated for staff and students to have confidence in them.
- We need to ensure that students receive clear and unambiguous feedback about their progress and performance on both individual courses or modules and more widely on programmes. Feedback can only be clear and unambiguous if the institution and the student are speaking the same language – if they share certain understandings. For this to happen, a process of careful acculturation needs to be in place.
- It needs to be clear what the limitations of the review and appeal processes are and what can be done to redeem failure once it has happened. Since these processes offer little hope to the student in terms of redeeming a situation of terminal failure, we must ensure that the bulk of institutional effort is focused on preventing students reaching this point.
- For those who do fail, we need to provide constructive support and advice (such as careers advice) about what they can do next. This should help them to understand what has happened, how they can explain it to themselves and others, and why it will help them move forward and perhaps learn from the experience.
- At an institutional level, we must ensure that the measures in place to assure the quality of programmes and teaching are not simply a mechanical

response to external demands but instead are principled and allow the institution to identify areas where students are more likely to be at risk of failure and to address these.

The emphasis in much literature on student drop-out and failure is on the internal processes and circumstances of the student or perhaps on the perceived inadequacies of individual lecturers or courses. From the authors' perspective of central administration and services, it is evident that the issue is far wider. As Blythman and Orr argue in Chapter 4 of this book, the outcome of any student's experience of university is the result of a complex and shifting web of understandings and actions involving peers, academic staff, tutors, learning support staff and many others. The regulatory and support structures of the institution bring together central administration and departmental processes and cultures. We would argue that this nexus is the key starting point to address issues of both interim and terminal failure.

13

Struggling to Learn

Moira Peelo

Introduction

My response to failing students has grown out of the experience of developing and maintaining a learning support practice within a university. This is mostly one-to-one and group work which, while it supports students as they solve study problems, is also shaped by a belief in the benefits of encouraging all students' potential and independence as learners. In this chapter, I describe the themes which emerge from my learning support work with struggling students and I explore how practice can be developed as a result of working with students who experience failure or who define themselves as failing in some way.

There are, in reality, countless ways of experiencing academic failure. Some students may perceive themselves to be in danger of failing, while others fail courses or choose to withdraw from study. Students can fall below their own standards, although they are doing fine according to everyone else. The belief that anything below a 2:1 is not worth getting is currently commonplace. In my learning support practice I usually meet students who are struggling to complete *specific*, individual pieces of assessed coursework on time and to the required standard, rather than facing total failure. Their experience of academic work, nonetheless, is to live permanently with the spectre of potential failure, whatever the final outcome; and failing, in this context, is invariably experienced as problematic or unpleasant.

The reasons why students fail, withdraw from university, drop out or do not progress are often expected to lie within the individual student. Even when researchers hunt for wider explanations, patterns are sought in possible commonality linking individual students' decisions. However, in my experience of learning support work, what shapes the outcome of a period of struggle will be a complex set of relationships. The decision to continue at university or to leave will be influenced by relationships between students and institutions; students, their courses and teachers; and between students and a sense of how their lives might be. There is, most importantly, a relationship between the current setting – amalgamating all these other relationships and focused on specific academic tasks – and the student's prior academic, emotional and social experiences. Not all students who struggle while at university will show up as failing by any of the usual definitions. It is not clear *while* working with struggling students what the eventual outcome will be – completion or non-completion of their degree courses.

Mostly, students do not undergo a sudden-death failure, more usually they find a way through or decide to withdraw from study. For some, university just never comes to feel like the right option. For others, the possibility of successfully completing a degree fades over time. Maybe good marks have never been achieved, or some crisis has occurred which has interrupted progress and a student may never again fully pick up the strands. Coursework assessment, in particular, underlines the slow pace of failure. There are students for whom multiple and accumulating deadlines become paralysing. It can mean that some students live in the shadow of possible failure throughout large parts of their time at university. Not all students who struggle academically fail overall or decide to withdraw; and not all those who withdraw from a course necessarily struggle academically. Yet it may not seem worth the effort of continuing to struggle academically if a range of other matters make life at university uncomfortable.

A student who is struggling academically (for whatever reasons) may well be referred to a learning support agency or worker for additional help. Before continuing to describe the key themes which I have extracted from my work with struggling students, the context of 'learning support' needs to be described and explained more fully.

Learning support work

'Learning support' or 'study support' is one of the most recent arrivals in the provision of student support services. It is not, as yet, a settled or established occupation, even though it can be seen to have been practised, in various forms, in tertiary education for some years. Its practice is derived from study skills teaching, but, for the most part, has moved beyond the remedial or deficit model implied by a study skills approach. Its practitioners may be influenced by various models of learning and development, including language teaching, dyslexia or counselling, and have developed their practices in a range of adult educational institutions. Study support work has developed according to local conditions and needs (Peelo 1994; Wolfendale and Corbett 1996; Blythman and Orr forthcoming). Its staff may be found in specialist centres, as sessional workers, or attached to other student support agencies.

Learning support work can be described as 'reactive' or 'proactive' and usually operates at three levels – with individual students, direct teaching of groups of students and by working with staff. As a perspective and an activity, it is an integral part of all academic-related work in libraries, information systems or staff development activities. Hence, learning support workers' activities (in both proactive and reactive forms) cut across administrative boundaries in universities – as an information service for staff and students; as part of welfare provision by providing ongoing study counselling and group support for individuals; as teachers, of staff and students alike, about learning at university; and as researchers, informing and developing practice and contributing to a wider debate.

The work is most obviously reactive when responding to particular students' learning and work-related problems or crises. However, it is also reactive when responding to individual students' needs which may arise out of a physical disability, dyslexia or some other ongoing state of being which need not (automatically) hamper intellectual development. Instead, impairment can be more or less disabling according to the barriers thrown up within an institution, which the Quality Assurance Agency argues can be in facilities, attitudes or styles of teaching (1999: 3, para. 9). This touches on constant tensions underpinning access to reactive learning support work within a system of mass higher education, namely should such support only be available when there is a problem and does a situation always need to be problematized (by students as well as staff and institutions) before individual need can be addressed? Blythman and Orr (forthcoming) describe well how their own study support team is based on 'the discourse of learning potential' rather than on a deficit model of weakness and remediation. The team is available to 'an ever-changing group of students who may use the study support services available', some of whom are receiving low marks and others who may wish to gain high marks.

Study support staff often struggle to leave behind assumptions of a mechanistic approach to specific academic tasks, which can encourage limited solutions (Peelo 2000a). So, for example, Blythman and Orr (forthcoming) describe their team and their wider study support strategies as encompassing a range of responses which, amongst other factors, 'allow for different conceptions of writing development'. Individual differences between learning support workers in teaching or counselling styles reflect varied views of what learning is about. Study support staff, then, do not necessarily share a common body of knowledge or agreed methods of working. This is so, even where learning support is part of the activities of a particular profession, such as counselling. Bell (1996: 93–8), for example, outlines the variety of approaches to learning support work which can arise from differing counselling dimensions, and describes the different study and study skills' solutions implied by behavioural–cognitive, person-centred and psychodynamic approaches to counselling.

However, individual differences in support style are positioned – sometimes wedged – between institutional and political factors. Although notions of personal, intellectual development guide many study support staff, the 'study skills' and deficit-model history has left behind an expectation that study advice can provide a commonsensical means of tackling academic performance. What are often called study skills can appear to provide an unemotional, clear-cut means of responding either to those in academic crisis or to those with recognized and specified needs. However the reality of the work is more complex, reflecting struggling students' myriad relationships – academic and non-academic – with their pasts and futures, as well as within the current academic environment.

Working with struggling students

'Failing' describes a current situation, allowing the outcome to remain open and the student–institution dialogue to continue, whereas 'non-completion' is, by comparison, a retrospective category. Yorke's (1999b: 39) study identified factors influencing non-completion, which included (for full-time and sandwich students) poor quality of student experience, inability to cope with programme demands, social unhappiness, the wrong choice of course(s), financial need and dissatisfaction with the university's provision. All of these may be found in the lives of academically struggling students, but the relative balance and importance of individual items is not clear while students still see successful completion as an option. Hence, echoes of Yorke's factors are discernible in the themes that run through my day-to-day work, but without the clarity inherent in retrospective accounts.

Learning support work commonly concentrates on students' problems with academic writing, reading and examinations (these are not the only tasks, but they are frequently of major importance in a student's life). I have selected three common, recurring themes which have emerged as important during my work on these academic tasks with struggling students – time, students' responses to change and challenge, and the social context for study. These themes reflect the complex interplay of relationships underpinning students' academic endeavour, both with the institution and with their own academic and emotional histories.

Time

It is rarely clear which of the students I work with will actually formally complete their degrees. There are students who cannot finish coursework unless they are right up against the most painful of deadlines. Some pull amazing feats out of the hat, while others fall at relatively small (albeit final) hurdles. A successful student must be highly organized and able to work with absolute regularity. The remorselessness of coursework assessment deadlines means that it is not wise to gather too much overdue work. Modular courses set a stern pace, making it difficult for uncertain students to digest new material. The speed of the British degree system allows little room for manoeuvre if things go wrong, and leniency today sometimes builds up worse problems for tomorrow.

Struggling students can be in a state of chaos. Often there are layers of confusion and anxiety which take some time to unwrap. Not all matters that become crystal clear later are clear at first; indeed, the process of meeting and talking is part of what helps to identify the issues. However, time ticks away on degree courses and such clarification can seem painfully slow on occasions. At a later point, students may decide to take time out, work flat out to complete a degree, to start again elsewhere or leave altogether. Those later decisions are not obvious at first, and trying to find a way to help the student forward with their work can be intertwined with what turn out to be major life decisions about, for example, course completion or future career choices.

A personal crisis can exaggerate difficulties a student has juggling multiple deadlines, and existing learning problems can be compounded by the number of assignments to be completed. A part of my role is to help people complete tasks one at a time – not as easy as it sounds when there are a range of additional assignments waiting to be done. In spite of the constraints of time, it helps if students can learn to be more analytical and specific both about their strengths in the situation and about what is hampering progress. So, for example, being a slow academic reader holds up a variety of other work, from preparing essays and laboratory reports to additional reading for tests. As long ago as 1966 a marked difference was found in reading scores between successful and unsuccessful students, and Small commented on the impact of problems with academic reading:

> So much abstract material has to be studied at the university and absorbed in a limited time that deficiencies in reading ability often lead both to tedium in private study and to a superficial or erroneous understanding of what has been read.
>
> (Small 1966: 16)

In my experience, lack of speed is not the only or main problem, instead it is a whole approach to study shaped by expectations of success or difficulties with reading. I refer to 'slow reading' as a whole reading style which usually focuses on one reading task (for example translation of the meaning of individual words or coverage of material) to the exclusion of other essential reading tasks, such as critical evaluation of the text. Working on reading, then, may make completing writing tasks more manageable.

Many students (but not all) who find academic reading difficult are dyslexic. 'Dyslexia' is used as a blanket term, yet students with dyslexia differ greatly, with varying strengths and weaknesses which Gilroy and Miles (1996: 1) have described as 'a distinctive balance of skills'. These variations interact with subjects differently, depending on the demands of the course of study. At first glance, juggling multiple tasks can appear to be just a time management issue. However, for those students with dyslexia, who experience pronounced difficulties with organization of material in essays, the pressure of preparing a number of essays simultaneously may feel overwhelming. This will be particularly so if additional pressures arise – whether personal or academic.

Students' responses to change and challenge

University life for staff has known patterns of academic tasks and cycles of assessment. For students, university is a series of transitions between different worlds and different stages in life – starting and finishing university, moving between years, accommodation, friends, time out, time abroad and work experience. 'Transition' is challenging too for those arriving by routes other than schools, such as mature students and overseas students, and for graduates moving into Masters or doctoral work. Time pressures require students to make maximum use of the early stages of their degree, yet in reality these are often used as 'settling-in' periods. Adjustment problems must depend, in part, on the level of match between prior courses and university work.

Even within university courses, changes in standards between years can be challenging, especially if a new course does not make immediate sense. The design of a student's whole year (across all the courses they are taking) may not foster slow, steady growth of understanding. So those who fall behind on modular courses, for example, may find it difficult to catch up as they constantly stop and start new, short modules. Learning to grapple with difficult assignments is an essential educational experience for students, however individual tasks take on undue importance when they occupy too much time and trigger a problematic backlog.

Change is exciting and challenging, partly because it is destabilizing. Rickinson has commented that academic stimulus at university challenges students, hence successful students 'need to be able to tolerate the temporary loss of balance necessary as one level of understanding is relinquished and a new one created' (1998: 99). Lack of confidence and self-esteem make students especially vulnerable at times of transition. For those who learnt early that academic success belonged to others, a setback at university can resonate with earlier failure. If you have learnt that an academic challenge is proof of lack of ability, then it is difficult to find the spirit as well as the strategies to overcome the problem. This means that all life's failures are felt again with each unwritten essay, failed examination or missed deadline.

If the student's struggle becomes defined as dyslexia, then additional changes need to be assimilated. Identification of dyslexia at university, especially for mature students, can be a curious experience – whereas before students have thought of themselves as stupid, there are, instead, a new set of interpretations to consider. For some, identification comes as a relief, for others it is a worrying and troublesome label, hence Gilroy and Miles' advice that providing a diagnosis without proper discussion could be experienced as undermining (1996: 2). In addition, late identification does not give immediate relief to the work crisis which gave rise to initial testing – the academic challenge remains to be tackled while students are reassessing their capabilities, the demands of academic tasks and their own intellectual histories.

One reason for choosing a particular university course is the anticipation of work following graduation. Courses which are directly relevant to work after graduation, such as social work or nursing, require commitment to those careers. Other courses may have been selected because they are perceived to be useful in the job stakes, such as law or engineering. Course selection for many is a matter of compromise between abilities and preferences, the offer of a place and the future prospects or life choices. For a few students, a commitment to specific subjects (often dance, drama, music or art) is so deeply rooted that no amount of commonsense advice from friends and relatives about their future job prospects makes other, more obviously applicable courses worth the effort involved to complete. Where the challenge of academic work is bound up closely with important life choices, profound personal changes may have to take place before courses can be completed.

The social context for study

Working with struggling students is a reminder of the social context in which learning takes place. There is a network of friends, tutors, families, embassies, grant-awarding bodies and employers who can all, to some extent or another, have a legitimate interest in a student's performance. However anonymous universities may seem, a student will carry the concerns of their particular networks. In this sense, failure is highly public – whether across the board or task specific.

Occasionally, patterns of ineffective working or, in some cases, ceasing to work at all, may have become so well established that crises are looming with departments that until then had been kind and supportive. Students go through complicated processes of appealing for leniency on the basis of a special need – perhaps due to personal circumstances or illness. A struggling student will have talked to staff more often than other students do, to ask for extensions, to discuss low marks or uncompleted work – all of which put students in the embarrassing role of supplicant. Additionally, students face the daunting task of explaining themselves to people they may not otherwise meet, such as staff in administrative roles or in support services as well as those in academic departments. Those most attuned to the social codes prevailing in universities must be best able to manage these interactions successfully, whereas those least attuned will find that these social tasks add another layer of complication.

Hence, students are occasionally referred for study support work when they are behaving in what is seen as a difficult manner. In the muddle of heightened emotions which accompanies the experience of 'slow failure', misunderstanding arises on both sides. A seemingly difficult student and a hurried or accidental meeting in a corridor leaves room for thoughtless comments or misheard words. Failing people start to become embarrassments – they do not always go easily or quietly, and start to object to what they experience as poor or shoddy treatment. Unsurprisingly, a sense of humiliation leads people to behave in ways they may regret later (then again, they may not regret harsh words or outrageous actions at all). Students become alarming by stepping outside assumed codes of behaviour. Indeed, a part of their failing behaviour may arise out of an inability to decode the unspoken assumptions surrounding university work.

Decoding what used to be called 'the hidden curriculum' (see Snyder 1971) is a part of performing academic tasks successfully. So, Miller and Parlett's (1974) classic study described how students differ in their cue-consciousness in assessment procedures. They described groups of students in their study as 'cue-seekers', 'cue-conscious' and 'cue-deaf' in relation to information derived from lecturers about assessment tasks and criteria (Miller and Parlett 1974: 49–52). The final degree results of the members of this group reflected their response to cues, with cue-seekers being represented among the firsts and the cue-conscious tending to be among the 2:1s. While there were some notable exceptions, Miller and Parlett commented that 'the marks of the cue-deaf are significantly lower than those of both the cue-conscious and cue-seekers' (1974: 55), illustrating the complexity and importance of the student–institution dialogue for the achievement of academic tasks. Similarly, this long-standing research tradition which assumes a student–institution dialogue as its starting point is typified by Becker et al.'s publication *Making the Grade* (1968). This study, moreover, conceptualizes the student–institution dialogue as filtered through students' social networks and constructions, which are different to those of an authoritative department, faculty or administration (Becker et al. 1968: Chapter 1, especially 1–14). Such an approach to research allows one to explore the complex social and cultural construction of academic tasks, as well as the cognitive aspects of learning.

Questioning practice

Where does learning support work fit into this and how, as a practitioner, can I evaluate and develop my practice with regard to failing students? Study support practice with individuals takes its departure from the student's reference point; but this is an intense focus which can leave the activity vulnerable to becoming a collection of received and unquestioned techniques. Hence, it is important to review the work and to add new knowledge to one's repertoire in the light of experience in order to avoid practice becoming self-referential and limited. I believe that developing the work means learning to question my practice constructively:

- through reflection and self-monitoring;
- by examining relevant research and theory to make practice more informed; and
- by considering how learning support work fits in systemically, within the wider setting of a whole university and the higher education system.

Reflection and self-monitoring

It is commonplace in universities to engage in monitoring other people's opinion of your work, particularly through use of feedback questionnaires. There is a danger that such feedback is seen as sufficient, squeezing out constructive reflection and deeper self-evaluation. The aim of reflection and self-evaluation is to use the year's experience, to hold onto what is good practice and to enrich it with new knowledge so that group and individual work can be strengthened. Educationalists need notions of effectiveness which are not dependent solely on how others see us or, indeed, how much they like us. Setting up a version of the counselling model of supervision is one strategy which might be considered as a means to encourage depth and honesty. Honesty is particularly difficult if questioning whether more could have been done for particular students or perhaps if one feels in some way concerned when desired outcomes are not achieved. It requires a careful choice of supervisor, and, as Mearns has commented, the sense of ease required to make it useful means 'line-managers make poor supervisors' (1990: 92).

As a form of teaching, study support reflects Atkinson and Claxton's description that teaching as a professional practice is 'characterized by complexity, is dynamic and interactive and happens in a very specific and constantly changing context' (2000: 6). Although not all students who approach learning support services are in crisis, there are those for whom the work crisis has become acute. The closeness of final failure or withdrawal is such that the work is both complex and pressured. An effective response to students' academic crises requires the component parts of what Claxton has described as intuition – expertise, implicit learning, judgement, sensitivity, creativity and rumination (2000: 41). All these ways of knowing are expressed in the act of responsiveness to a specific study support problem, and, *in the moment*, rarely operate at a conscious or deliberate level. Nonetheless, they do require both development and depth in appraisal. Hence, an overly rational or purely monitoring approach alone is unlikely to make constructive use of experience at the depth required to change future practice. Instead, such a narrow approach, in Atkinson and Claxton's thesis, mistakes rational articulation of understanding for the whole of that which constitutes reflection.

Making practice more informed

Mearns suggests that counsellors should respond to failure within therapeutic relationships by attempting to work out what they do correctly as well as what has gone wrong, and this advice is also relevant to learning support work. The literature is one obvious place to turn to for help in enriching understanding, and also for ideas to help sift through what are strengths and what are weaknesses in practice.

Work with individual students needs to be informed by research – one's own and other people's. Research is not necessarily carrying out large-scale, expensively funded surveys, but is a part of the process of self-reflection. It starts by stepping back from day-to-day work and asking questions which arise from practice – about patterns and oddnesses, repetitions and omissions. A part of study support work includes offering an informed 'sounding board' to help students reconceptualize their view of the situation or to consider adopting new learning strategies. Knowledge of a wider world of research alerts me, as a practitioner, to listen more closely to strands I might otherwise miss or discount; to notice changes in the wider world, where I might otherwise stay comfortably with what I have learnt so far; and to be able to offer more alternatives in approaches to learning.

However, there is no one obvious, unified corpus of knowledge on which study support is built, and so awareness of alternative choices and preferences in practice needs to be constructed out of careful examination of what is written. Additionally, as Yorke (1999b) has commented, there is little research into what he calls 'student non-completion'. What constitutes relevant knowledge depends on the situation and the problems to be addressed and the generalized nature of much work about student learning will not necessarily help the practitioner when faced with specific individuals. My world view is constantly challenged by what I hear from students and each student's experience is, in addition, quite different from mine, from other students' experience and from the broad generalities of research. In order for theory and research findings to be useful to the practitioner, they need to go through a process of interpretation, adaptation and integration. The intention is to find theory or research which can expand understanding – informing practice and going beyond one's own personal experience, thereby making possible more creative responses to the particular situations met in practice.

This approach has obvious implications for the organization of effective study support work, especially when working with struggling students who are at or approaching a crisis point. Organizationally, the main issue ceases to be one of fitting in as many meetings as possible with individual students. Instead, an effective service provides learning support staff with opportunities for reflection, supervision, further training, attendance at conferences and interaction with a wider world of practice and research.

How does learning support work fit in?

This chapter has explored the notion of student failure as it has emerged in my experience and in relation to developing effective professional practice as a learning support worker, particularly in one-to-one work. This does not mean, however, that failing in higher education should be conceptualized purely as an individual student issue, even though it is a formative and powerful experience in individual lives. Indeed, the relationship between the institutional setting and the student – including all of his or her prior academic, emotional and social experiences – is the central one which succeeds or fails when individuals engage in degree-level work.

Moreover, the type of study support described in this chapter follows the 'safety net' model. Educational problems in an era of mass higher education cannot be resolved by employing more and more learning support workers to provide individual support. Instead, curriculum and course design, resources and materials available, and course delivery across the whole institution are the major means by which students' educational needs are addressed. Acceptance of the limitations of the traditional 'study skills' approach informs recent innovative attempts to use course and curriculum design as a means to enable students to reflect on, and potentially improve, how they learn (see, for example, Rust and Gibbs 1997). Taking a step back to reflect on individual and group practice includes questioning how the sort of study work described in this chapter relates to the teaching and learning strategies supported and promoted in the wider institution. This could be in highly specific ways, by questioning the extent to which learning support work has been embedded into curricula and into course delivery. It could also be in the wider sense of questioning how central student learning issues are to teaching styles and strategies.

Conclusions

It is not my wish to eliminate struggle or occasional failure, both of which are important and formative experiences in education. However, I do wish to avoid escalation leading to inevitable crisis, obliging the student to fail or to withdraw without experiencing the situation as one in which there are choices. Choices come with knowledge that academic challenges can be met. True learning engages the whole person (socially, cognitively and emotionally) and so does failing. As well as outright failure, students decide to withdraw, take time out or to start again on different courses elsewhere. Such decisions, at a personal level, can represent a successful and constructive outcome to a personal dilemma even when interpreted as 'failure' by outsiders. From a developmental point of view, course completion can be viewed as a failure to decide to call a halt, to do something else. Alternatively, completion can be viewed as a victory for emotional stamina and persistence.

In this chapter, I have discussed themes from my work and have explored how study support practice can be developed in the light of working with students who experience themselves as struggling or failing in some way. Yet other, less obvious failures occur in the midst of apparent success. How successful is it if a student continues to pass courses, but without growing in academic confidence? Success, in an institutional sense, is more than the sum total of non-failures, and also lies in the quality of the education and the quality of the educational experience. Examining course design and teaching styles does more than provide earlier intervention for struggling students, it also represents a development in university education to match the intellectual needs of students educated in a much-expanded system. In retrospect, how would this year's graduates describe their experiences? Perhaps there a need, post hoc, for accounts that make sense of major decisions for those who complete degrees as well as those who do not. The important question for study support work, as for all academic provision, is 'How does this work contribute to the quality of students' educational experience, both for struggling students and for universities in general?'

14

Failing to Assess or Assessing Failure?

Karen Hinett

Introduction

Believing that you have failed hurts. In an interview with an undergraduate student, she confided to me, 'I'd die if I got a bad mark.' Failure is an uncomfortable, often humiliating experience and is generally something we try to avoid. To fail is to be insufficient, unsuccessful and is synonymous with rejection and shame. We may consider ourselves to have failed if we do not meet our own expectations or have been dubbed a failure by others who consider our performance wanting. Traditionally, it has been accepted that there are those individuals who pass and those who fail. Judgements are made about competence and ability and these are justified by reference to standards and the need to perform reliable assessment. As Cullingford neatly states:

> When we first look at the service industry that assessment has become it is easy to assume it is necessary. Assessment has become an academic way of life. We constantly make judgements and build theories against which to make them. We can be forgiven if we sometimes lose sight of the consequences.
>
> (Cullingford 1997: 265)

In this chapter I will explore whether assessment, or at least assessment that invokes a feeling of failure in individuals, is necessary and whether there are less damaging alternatives. By differentiating between those who can and those who cannot, we make explicit and potentially harmful judgements. In our zeal to measure, count and produce league tables, we neglect to question the functions that failure serves and to consider the effects of judgement upon intellectual and personal development. Here I problematize the notion of failure and explore how and why assessment results in some students being considered unworthy.

Four sections make up this chapter. First, consideration is given to the role of failure within the context of higher education. To what end do we judge and measure and does this mirror our aspirations for graduates? The second section draws on the literature of educational psychology in articulating a theory of failure against which the findings of research into student learning are examined. Underpinning this exploration are notions of power, authority and identity. The third section considers how assessment invokes 'power'-full feelings in students and how these impact on their perceptions of ability and self-efficacy. Finally, I examine plagiarism and the effects of failure on pedagogy, development and a willingness to contribute to society.

The function and context of failure

The recognition by governments that higher education is big business explains much of the new-found enthusiasm for learning and teaching. Knowledge is traded as a commodity and degrees are the global currency. Politicians and students alike are aware of the value, both educational and commercial, of their investment in higher education.

That assessment serves different purposes has been highlighted as a problem in much of the literature, begging the question of how assessment systems can provide evidence of accountability at institutional level *and* enhance the personal qualities of individual knowledge. Astin (1993) outlines what he describes as two competing functions – 'resource and reputation' and 'talent development'. The first refers to the grades, league tables and statistics compiled by institutions and government to extend and maintain reputations as providers of quality education. These are used as evidence of accountability and comprise an 'assessment discourse' employed primarily to communicate standards to stakeholders. By contrast, 'talent development' relates to the formative comments, feedback and guidance offered to individuals to help them achieve and improve their learning.

Many other researchers have also differentiated between the functions of assessment (see Knight 1995; Biggs 1996; Hagar and Butler 1996). There is not space here to elaborate on each, but all make a significant contribution to the debate. Interestingly, the common feature of all these works is an acknowledgement of the dichotomy between assessment for accountability and assessment for development.

Quite clearly, different systems are required to serve two different functions – accountability and talent development. However, higher education is not arranged in a way that easily accommodates both. Stakeholders require different kinds of assessment information. League tables are constructed from quantitative information that relies on the differentiation and stratification of students' abilities. This leads to a dependency on scientific, measurable, largely cognitive-driven assessment strategies, as these methods produce the neat, quantifiable data required. Therefore, failure and a narrow view of achievement can be seen as a necessary part of this system.

The pace of technological development and the globalization of higher education mean that accountability will undoubtedly increase. In relation to the discussion of failure, this means that, if unchecked, the transparency of assessment systems is likely to take precedence over what they were designed to assess. As Eisner highlighted, it is one thing to ask 'Did the student learn what was intended?' and quite another to ask 'What did the student learn?' (in Rowntree 1987: 65). There is a danger that academics will become so preoccupied with justifying their practice in the name of standards that the people whom it affects most will be forgotten. As Brown and Glasner point out, 'Too often we assess when it is convenient for our systems rather than when it is helpful to students' further development' (1999: 11).

However, it is not only that assessment serves several functions and multiple audiences that creates problems for learners. It is that woven into the fabric of assessment are values and conceptions of what constitutes success and failure. Biggs suggests that assessment is such a controversial topic precisely because it serves institutional maintenance and 'taps into belief systems about what learning is and what education is for' (1996: 5). What we assess says a lot about what we think is important. Our assessment systems indicate to students and to the outside world what constitutes a quality learning experience. It is this tension between transparency and what we value that makes assessment such a controversial issue. In the context of the information society, we need to know what, how and the extent to which a student can apply knowledge. Increased access and participation in higher education could promote a shift in what we assess. As Birenbaum and Dochy suggest, 'Successful functioning in this era demands an adaptable, thinking, autonomous person, who is a self-regulated learner, capable of communicating and co-operating with others' (1996: 4).

In this climate, assessment needs to be much more sophisticated than it was previously. We need to ascertain the extent to which the learner has competence in several domains to include cognitive competencies (knowledge, analysis, communication and critical thought), meta-cognitive competencies (planning, monitoring and self-regulation) and social competencies (leading discussions, persuading, working in groups and affective dispositions, such as perseverance, internal motivation, responsibility and independence). Traditional assessment systems are adept at measuring the cognitive, and significant steps have been made in recent years in assessing the social and meta-cognitive skills such as self-assessment (Stefani 1994; Boud 1995; Hinett and Thomas 1999). However, in the UK at least, we are still conservative about evaluating affective qualities. Examples of practice in the United States (Mentowski and Associates 2000) and Australia (Sadler 1989; Boud 1995) offer guidelines, but the UK has yet to embrace them wholeheartedly.

We accept that assessment serves both exhibition (transparency) and erudition (development of the individual). Within this context, failure also serves a purpose – it differentiates between those who can and those who cannot and, therefore, contributes towards selection, recruitment and potential to advance. In sociological terms, it is a mechanism for stratification which enables the 'best' qualified to be recruited to the most valued positions in society. What is less often acknowledged is that failure also impacts upon the affective zone, signifying defeat and stigmatizing individuals as less valuable. The next section asks how the perception and conceptionalization of oneself as a failure impacts on learning.

Towards a theory of failure

The literature on assessment documents a history of students the world over who 'play the game' (Becker et al. 1968), 'learn the assessment culture' (Miller and Parlett 1974) and adopt approaches to assessment based on their perceptions of what is required (Frannson 1977; Entwistle 1981; Hinett 1997; McDowell and Sambell 1998; James 2000). We know that the way in which a student anticipates the assessment task affects the response he or she gives. It is likely that this action is prompted in part by a desire to avoid 'failure'. Educational psychology offers some useful theories for understanding how failure is conceptualized. I make no attempt to explore the literature in full, but use it as a framework for understanding the impact of failure upon learning and development.

In her compilation of work on 'self-theories', Carol Dweck (2000) outlines a number of research studies attempting to understand how people organize their world and give meaning to experiences. It also neatly explains the differentiation in academic performance. She maintains that all learners subscribe to either an 'entity' or 'incremental' theory of intelligence. Entity theory holds that intelligence is fixed and final. By contrast, incremental intelligence is something that can be cultivated through learning and increased with effort. Building on the nature/nurture debate, Dweck reveals through her research that learners who subscribe to an entity theory are more likely to favour performance goals (measuring and validating ability), whereas those with an incremental view of intelligence favour learning goals (increasing competence and mastering new tasks). Dweck differentiates between students who want to 'look smart' and those who have a 'desire to get smarter'.

Entity theory is characterized by commitment to statements such as 'Although I hate to admit it, I sometimes would rather do well in a class than learn a lot.' Incremental theorists are more likely to commit to the statement of 'It's much more important for me to learn things in my classes than it is to get the best grades' (Dweck 2000: 22). What is interesting is the effect that such a belief has on students' emotional responses to assessment. Students favouring performance goals do so in order to gain 'positive judgements of competence and avoid negative ones'. If failure is experienced, these students are likely to adopt what Dweck calls a 'helpless' response, which means that they denigrate intelligence, lose faith in their ability and are likely to become depressed and withdraw from the learning situation. By contrast, students holding an incremental view and favouring learning goals adopt a 'mastery-oriented' response, which means that they do not attribute lack of ability or any other blame for failure. These students see learning as a challenge, as something to be tackled.

Two important issues arise from this work. First, the research suggests that it is possible to identify a student's theory of intelligence and, second, this is likely to correlate to the kind of learning goal to which the student aspires. The personal commitment an individual makes to a theory of intelligence is indicative of their self-perception. Students who subscribe to an entity theory believe that failure is the final point, the outcome of their achievements. They need 'a diet of easy successes' (Dweck 2000: 15) to confirm their ability and are fearful of learning goals as this involves an element of risk and potential failure. Assessment for these students is an all-encompassing activity that defines them as people. If they fail at the task, they *are* failures. Challenges are a threat to self-esteem as it is through being seen to be successful that these students define themselves. Furthermore, as they believe that intelligence is fixed, they carry with them the belief that having failed at a task there is no point in trying at subsequent tasks. Their commitment to entity theory is debilitating therefore not only in the present but also for any future success.

Perhaps predictably, those students who believe that intelligence is incremental have little or no fear of failure. A typical response from such a student is 'The harder it gets, the harder I need to try.' These students do not see failure as an indictment of themselves and separate their self-image from their academic achievement. When faced with a challenge, these students are more likely to continue in the face of adversity because they have nothing to prove. For such individuals, 'the goal is to learn, not to prove they're smart' (Dweck 2000: 17).

Dweck's research offers a novel interpretation of failure; students who believe that learning is limitless chose challenge. The link from theory to practice is easy – assessment should offer these students opportunities to build on their experience. However, the research revealed that at school and college level there was roughly a 50:50 split between students adopting an entity theory and those adopting an incremental theory. How then can the entity students best be provided for? The answer lies in helping students to appreciate challenge and to shake off the fear of failure. It involves identifying how conceptions of academic failure can be separated from ego. The work of Weiner (1982) offers a way forward.

Attribution theory attempts to explain the ways in which individuals seek understanding in discovering why an event has occurred. In the context of this chapter, it helps to identify how students make sense of failure. Weiner identifies three dimensions of causality – locus, stability and controllability. Against these dimensions, intelligence and ability are seen as internal, stable and uncontrollable. By contrast, effort, whilst still a factor internal to the individual, is seen to be *unstable and controllable*. External factors include the ease (or difficulty) of an assessment task and quality of teaching. These are seen to be unstable *and* uncontrollable. So, for Weiner, intelligence is an internal, stable, uncontrollable factor. This would seem to be in line with the perceptions held by Dweck's entity theorists, who deride effort as associated with low intelligence. For these students, having to work hard at something means you are no good at it. If you were good (that is intelligent), you would not need to expend effort (Dweck 2000: 40).

Effort for Weiner is unstable and controllable. Incremental theorists appear to embrace this perspective, viewing effort as 'something that, far from determining your ability, allows you to fully realize your potential' (Dweck 2000: 40). These theories suggest that the extent to which students feel they have control over the assessment task correlate with their image of themselves as failures. The more perceived control the student has, the more they are likely to view learning as an incremental activity. The corollary being that the less perceived control, the more the student is likely to disengage. If you are not in control, you are not responsible or accountable to yourself or anyone else.

Weiner claims that 'in achievement-related contexts the perception that an individual has failed because of a lack of effort gives rise to greater punishment than failure attributed to low ability' (1982: 187). In other words, as effort can be controlled, the student feels justified in self-flagellation because lack of achievement is their fault. Blaming oneself for failure indicates an incremental theory of intelligence. Students believe they could have done something to avoid failure and will try harder next time. In his seminal work on student perceptions of assessment, Becker argues that students believe that they control their academic fate by the amount of effort they put in: 'Thus they attribute variations in student performance to an unwillingness to give sufficient time and effort to academic work or to a deliberate decision to put one's major effort elsewhere' (Becker et al. 1968: 39). Recent research by McDowell and Sambell (1995) confirms this, suggesting that the move toward more student-centred assessment has not had a significant impact on students' perceptions.

Extrapolating from the two theories, it could be suggested that students who believe that intelligence is fixed are more likely to cite external factors such as the difficulty of the assessment task or poor quality teaching as an explanation for their failure. If they feel they have no control over the situation, it is easier to blame someone who does and, in the case of higher education, this is likely to be the tutor. Attributing blame to someone else is a coping mechanism to protect the ego. Exploring academic ability, Eshel and Kurman posit that students maintain 'favourable self-concept by using selective perception, interpretation and memory of feedback' (1991: 194). In other words, students choose how they interpret feedback and failure so as to lessen the emotional damage. Students deny the validity of teacher, peer and professional judgement if it disagrees with their own self-concept. Eshel and Kurman argue that this occurs most often when students are faced with a traumatic experience such as academic failure 'on which they have practically no control' (1991: 194). They explain that 'illusory self-esteem is more likely to be associated with failure to cope with the demands of school [or university] than with enhanced effort to live up to required academic standards' (1991: 194–5). In common with Dweck, Eshel and Kurman found a correlation between self-concept and achievement in both bright and less able students. Being confident about success involves taking risks. Students face looking foolish in front of peers if grades are not as high as expected and feeling embarrassed if they do not live up to their own expectations. Consequently, 'It stands to reason that pupils who are unwilling to take these risks, or those whose self-confidence is somewhat lacking, will prefer to lower their expectations and present themselves less presumptuously' (1991: 195).

What these theories reveal is that failure is largely felt or experienced as a result of a personal construct rather than a judgement imposed by others. Failure may be *attributed* on the basis of poor performance, but it is likely to be *felt* as a result of the constructs and personal interpretations the individual makes of the world.

In the light of the theories of intelligence, I now consider the extent to which assessment systems provide or deny opportunities for students to 'take control' over their learning.

Assessment, power and emotion

The tension between assessment for learning and assessment for accountability is responsible for many of the problems that students face. Despite a shift towards student-centredness in terms of learning and teaching methods, assessment is still largely an area where traditional authority remains unchallenged and, as Falchikov argues, 'Through its emphasis on external rewards and punishments generates the wrong set of motivation in students' (1986: 152). Universities and individual tutors may well endorse the idea of developing the kind of societal competences outlined at the beginning of this chapter, but much of current assessment practice negates this (Boud 1995; Heron 1998). Traditional tutor-led assessment perpetuates a power differential whereby the learner is reduced to a position of 'assessee' – someone about whom judgements are made rather than an independent, motivated learner. As Brew succinctly expresses, 'To assess is to have power over a person' (1999b: 161). Of course, being a novice and therefore not knowing inevitably places the learner in a position of relative subordination, but it is the way in which students perceive themselves within this relationship that is likely to affect their self-image. The extent to which academic staff acknowledge this power differential and provide scaffolding for challenging assessment is also likely to impact on students' willingness to engage.

These arguments are well rehearsed in other literature (Sadler 1989; Boud 1995; Heron 1998). From a humanistic perspective, it is interesting to note the extent to which lack of control over assessment contributes to a sense of personal failure. In his work with mature students in higher education, James explores the connection between self-confidence and assessment. His interviews with students reveal strong feelings: 'I'm so dependent on other people's assessment of my work for my own feelings, which is crazy and I hate that I should be so dependent on other people, because they're only assessing a piece of paper, not me' (James 2000: 153).

My own research with undergraduates produced similar expressions from students who felt the emotional impact of assessment: 'I'm tough on myself. I wouldn't say I was happy with work when I get it back. I always want something more and if I get less than I thought I would it bothers me, really knocks my ego' (Hinett 1997: 128).

It is impossible to determine whether these students, had they been part of Dweck's studies, would have favoured an entity or incremental theory of intelligence, but the quotations suggest that the judgements placed upon them are both hurtful and likely to affect motivation for future tasks. Dweck offers a detailed analysis of the way that students internalize beliefs about their own capabilities, but provides a fairly cursory account of the effects of other people's judgement upon the affective domain. Offering a more detailed explanation on the role of motivation on learning, Pintrich and Garcia (1996) have created a 'Motivated Strategies for Learning Questionnaire'.[1] This is a self-report instrument designed to assess college students' motivational orientation and learning strategies. The results reveal that:

> Students who approached their course with an intrinsic goal for learning, who believed that the material was interesting and important, who have high self-efficacy beliefs for accomplishing the task, and who rated themselves as *in control of their learning* were more likely to do well in terms of course grade. At the same time, students who reported being anxious about tests overall were less likely to do well in the course.
>
> (Pintrich and Garcia 1996: 332; emphasis added)

This confirms the view that perceived control over assessment is a major contributing factor to students believing they can accomplish a task. Furthermore, it emphasizes the relationship between ability and self-concept. Dweck noted that students with an entity theory were more likely to adopt a 'helpless' approach and admit defeat. In research testing drive and emotion, Spielberger and Sarason found more than 20 per cent of high-anxiety students were classified as academic failures and did not complete their college education compared with 6 per cent of low anxiety students. Interestingly, even those in the lowest ability groups did better than those of supposed higher ability and with higher anxiety levels (Spielberger and Sarason 1975: 128). These findings may beg questions about methodology and the effects of being labelled, but the research does indicate a correlation between students who perceive assessment as threatening to their ego and poor academic performance.

The implication of this for learning is that assessment practices should be designed with individuals in mind. When judgements are made, it is very difficult to differentiate between what is related to the task and what is related to the individual. Black and Wiliam (1998) suggests that in designing assessments care should be given to indicate what is 'task' and 'ego' involving. Ideally, students should be able to separate critical comments on their work from a criticism of them as people. Rowntree argues that:

> It should be possible for a student who has 'failed' at one learning task to compensate by his success on another task. Unfortunately, the ethos of competitive assessment often leads the student who has failed on a few tasks (e.g. learned more slowly than other people) to feel that he has failed *as a person.*
>
> (Rowntree 1987: 42; emphasis added)

Dweck would argue that having already failed, students with an entity view cease to try to succeed because for them they are bound by the limits of their intelligence. The idea that students rely on a fixed notion of ability as an emotional crutch has resonance with much of university teaching. Assessment systems operate on the assumption that students need both certification of ability and personal validation of their worth. The creation of an illusory self-concept and subscription to particular pedagogic or personal values are subconscious coping mechanisms put in place to deal with failure. This is the case for high achievers who risk falling from intellectual grace and low achievers who risk the stigma of failure.

Turning attention briefly to academic staff, it would appear that they too indulge in certain patterns of behaviour around assessment. The traditional power relationship between staff and student is perpetuated though the judgements made about work and the feedback given to students (Sadler 1989; Higgins 2000). Traditional assessment means that students rely on staff to make judgements about their work. By contrast, the talent-development view of assessment raises the status of the student to assessor. The rise in competency-based systems and the use of reflective statements and peer assessment dilutes the authority of the staff member by placing responsibility for assessment in the hands of students. For some staff this is threatening. Part of the traditional remit of the academic member of staff is to provide feedback and judgement about the quality of student work. Passing judgement is a status activity, it is associated with authority, arbitration, the ability to referee and to be an accepted expert. If they believe they have lost control over this function, they too are likely to perceive this as a personal slight.

Tradition is one reason for maintaining the belief that lecturers are the only people able to make judgements about the quality of student work. Accountability and a focus on standards is another. Whilst assessment is such an important business, it is unlikely that staff will feel comfortable about relinquishing power. If standards fall, they are to blame, the tables are turned and they become the failures of the assessment system.

Another point to bear in mind in the climate of accountability is that academic staff have considerably less control over assessment systems than previously. As James states 'In many courses, assessment practices reflect the traditions, regulations, wishes and even creativity of institutions, professional bodies, employers and other interests as well' (2000: 157). At the same time that control is reduced, staff are obliged to show evidence of the use of a range of learning, teaching and assessment practices. A fear of being perceived to have failed to support or facilitate these new pedagogic practices is also likely to weigh on the minds of staff. In the UK, Subject Review by the Quality Assurance Agency means that staff are increasingly accountable for displaying a range of learning, teaching and assessment opportunities. The self-image of staff also appears to be closely linked to the perception staff have of themselves as successful and as having *control* over assessment. It seems that both giving and receiving judgement is a personal and emotional activity.

The next section looks briefly at the role of plagiarism and examines whether students' propensity to cheat is related in any way to maintaining ego.

Plagiarism and self-efficacy

It has been argued that students are adopting surface and strategic approaches to assessment tasks because the system allows it (Kneale 1996). Indeed, there is some sympathy to be had for the argument that says that having laid open the requirements and stated what the learner will be able to do at the end of the programme, we are hostage to our own transparent fortune. The rhetoric suggests that students are by-passing process, taking short-cuts on deep learning and, excuse the metaphor, taking the slip road via the super-highway to outcome avenue.

However, this is an easy and unsubstantiated argument to make. Before we accuse students of cheating, we should be clear about what we mean. Stefani (1999) defines four types of what I shall refer to as 'problem activities':

- 'copying', reproducing or imitating a specimen answer;
- 'collaboration', working in association with another;
- 'plagiarism', stealing the thoughts or writing of others and passing it off as their own; and
- 'collusion', an agreement to deceive.

In an article in the *Times Higher Education Supplement* (1999) Jenny Moon calls this deliberate attempt to deceive a third party simply 'cheating'. These are useful distinctions to make when discussing the potential for students to cut corners. It emphasizes the difference between lack of consideration or adherence to the rules and a deliberate exercise of will to defeat the assessment system. The reasons cited for cheating can be loosely considered in three categories. In rank order, these are 'stress and the pressure for good grades' (Franklyn-Stokes and Newstead 1995: 160); inadequate assessment that 'encourages students to cheat' (ibid: 170); and a genuine confusion about what constitutes cheating (Ashworth et al. 1997: 196).

These findings suggest that reaction to failure and attempts to avoid subsequent failure are likely to take students down the path of deception. Dweck found that when faced with failure, students with an entity view of intelligence were 'significantly more likely to say that they would try to cheat on the next test' (2000: 35). Students also cited cheating as the 'last resort' when they felt that all avenues, presumably such as effort and study, had been exhausted. Researchers into student perceptions of assessment speak of alienation (McDowell 1995) and feelings of not being part of the assessment process (Hinett 1997). This sense of separatism is also likely to contribute to a student giving up and resorting to deceitful tactics.

The research by Becker et al. (1968), Miller and Parlett (1974) and Glasner (1999) indicates that assessment is perceived as a game to be played. Distrust of more informal assessment techniques is understandable given this context. Course work and new techniques of assessment, such as peer assessment, are more likely to result in questions being asked about individual effort and the extent to which students have 'pulled their weight' in a team effort. For entity students, this is threatening because it opens up discussion about areas of development. The boundaries of success and failure are widened and it is less clear who is 'smart'. By comparison, examinations, whilst derided by students and staff alike as failing to test what is valued, are considered controllable. It is also easier to depict who has succeeded and who has failed and, ironically, this is comforting for students who rely on immediate feedback on their self-efficacy.

Conclusions

In the light of this discussion, what can we do to diminish the negative effects of failure and maximize learning? The psychological literature illustrates the potential for assessment systems to induce negative emotional responses to tasks that debilitate development. We know that changing assessment systems alone will not invoke a deep approach to learning (Marton and Saljo 1976). We need to focus on helping students to differentiate between ego and task, such that academic failure does not infringe upon personal self-efficacy.

The literature suggests that respect for assessment as a genuine test of ability and effort is likely to invoke commitment in students so that they are less likely to resort to underhand methods to seek success. Engaged in genuinely stimulating assessment tasks within a supportive, non-competitive environment students are less likely to fear not looking 'smart'. This means increasing the opportunities to engage in problem-solving, real-life simulations and the process of judgement.

Self-evaluation, reflection and an active dialogue with staff and peers about assessment criteria have all proven to be successful ways of increasing students' motivation (Boud 1995; Brew 1999b). Clearly, dialogue also needs to encompass academic and student values regarding cheating. Increasing a sense of moral integrity and commitment to personal goals rather than those of the institution and external stakeholders may also help to reduce the need for students to see evidence of their success. As Berger and Luckman point out, 'The self is a reflected entity, reflecting the attitudes first taken by significant others towards it; the individual becomes what he is assessed as' (1966: 152). First, students must be helped to appreciate and understand academic values. However, perhaps the main task is to help them to conceptualize their own values such that succeeding becomes a welcome challenge. Viewed in this light, combating difficulty and the concept of failure become part of the process of bettering oneself rather than the outcome. Achieving in the face of adversity becomes a positive reflection of the self. If this becomes possible, students embrace failure, and the overcoming of it, as an indication of their achievement. It is helping students to see the world as a set of tasks to be dealt with rather than a succession of ego-restricting experiences.

Acknowledging that assessment systems often fail to assess that which we claim to value is the first step towards creating a system where students feel in control of their own learning. The second is to make use of developmental tasks that require cognitive ability *and* sustained effort. The third modest proposal is simply to do less assessing. As Cullingford wisely points out, 'The more tests there are, set against standard criteria, the more opportunities there are for some to fail' (1997: 271). At the very least, we could take time to stop and consider whether it is really necessary.

Note

1. There are six sub-categories in the motivational scales: 1 intrinsic goal orientation; 2 extrinsic goal orientation; 3 self-efficacy, which encompasses both expectancy for success and judgement of one's ability to accomplish a task; 4 value components (why students engage in one task over another); 5 task value beliefs (how interesting and useful course content is); and 6 control beliefs (belief that outcomes are contingent upon their own effort rather than external factors).

References

Alderman, M.K. (1999) *Motivation for Achievement: Possibilities for Teaching and Learning.* Mahwah, NJ: L. Erlbaum Associates.

Ashworth, P., Bannister, P. and Thorne, P. (1997) Guilty in whose eyes? University students' perceptions of cheating and plagiarism in academic work and assessment, *Studies in Higher Education,* 22(2): 187–203.

Association of University Teachers (AUT) (January 1996) *Professional Accreditation of University Teachers,* discussion paper. London: AUT.

Astin, A. (1993) *Assessment for Excellence – The Philosophy and Practice of Assessment and Evaluation in Higher Education,* American Council on Education Series. Phoenix, AZ: Oryx Press.

Atkinson, T. and Claxton, G. (2000) *The Intuitive Practitioner: On the Value of Not Always Knowing What One is Doing.* Buckingham: Open University Press.

Audit Commission and Ofsted (1993) *Unfinished Business: Full-time Educational Courses for 16–19-year-olds.* London: HMSO.

Ball, S.J. (1991) Power, conflict, micropolitics and all that!, in G. Walford (ed.) *Doing Educational Research.* London: Routledge.

Ball, S.J. and Goodson, I.F. (1985) *Teachers' Lives and Careers.* Lewes: Falmer Press.

Ball, S.J. and Rowe, R. (1991) Micropolitics of radical change, in J. Blase (ed.) *The Politics of Life in Schools: Power, Conflict, and Cooperation.* London: Sage.

Bandura, A. (1997) *Self-efficacy: The Exercise of Control.* New York: Freeman.

Barnett, R. (1988) Entry and exit performance indicators for higher education: some policy and research issues, *Assessment and Evaluation in Higher Education,* 13(1): 16–30.

Barnett, R. (1990) *The Idea of Higher Education.* Buckingham: SRHE and Open University Press.

Barnett, R. (1994) *The Limits of Competence.* Buckingham: SRHE and Open University Press.

Bascia, N. and Hargreaves, A. (2000) (eds) *The Sharp Edge of Educational Change.* London: Routledge/Falmer.

Basic Skills Agency (1997) *Staying the Course.* London: Basic Skills Agency.

Bassnett, S. (2001) Comment, *Independent,* 8 February.

Beard, R. and Hartley, J. (1984) *Teaching and Learning in Higher Education.* London: Harper & Row.

Becher, T. (1989) *Academic Tribes and Territories: Intellectual Enquiry and the Cultures of Development.* Milton Keynes: SRHE and Open University Press.

Becher, T. and Trowler, P. (2001) *Academic Tribes and Territories*, 2nd edn. Buckingham: Open University Press.
Becker, H. ([1952] 1995) The career of the Chicago public school teacher, in R.G. Burgess (ed.) *Howard Becker on Education*. Buckingham: Open University Press.
Becker, H., Geer, B. and Hughes, E.C. (1968) *Making the Grade: The Academic Side of College Life*. New York: John Wiley.
Bell, E. (1996) *Counselling in Further and Higher Education*. Buckingham: Open University Press.
Berger, P. and Luckman, T. (1966) *The Social Construction of Reality*. London: Penguin.
Bergner, R.M. (1995) *Pathological Self-Criticism: Assessment and Treatment*. New York: Plenum.
Biggs, J. (1996) Assessing learning quality: reconciling institutional, staff and educational demands, *Assessment and Evaluation in Higher Education*, 21(1): 5–15.
Birenbaum, M. and Dochy, F. (eds) (1996) Assessment 2000: towards a pluralistic approach to assessment, *Alternatives in Assessment and Achievements, Learning Processes and Prior Knowledge*. Boston, MA: Kluwer Academic Publishers.
Black, P. and Wiliam, D. (1998) Assessment and classroom learning, *Assessment in Education: Policy, Principles and Practice*, 5(1): 7–74.
Blackler, F. (1995) Knowledge, knowledge work and organizations: an overview and interpretation, *Organisation Studies*, 16(6): 1021–46.
Blase, J. (1991) The micropolitical perspective, in J. Blase (ed.) *The Politics of Life in Schools: Power, Conflict, and Cooperation*. London: Sage.
Bligh, D. (1998) *What's the Use of Lectures?*, 5th edn. Exeter: Intellect.
Blythman, M. and Orr, S. (forthcoming) Joined-Up policy: a strategic approach to improving retention in the UK context, *Journal of College Student Retention*.
Boud, D. (1995) *Enhancing Learning Through Self-Assessment*. London: Kogan Page.
Bourdieu, P. (1997) The forms of capital, in A.H. Halsey, J. Floud and C.A. Anderson (eds) *Education: Culture, Economy and Society*. Oxford: Oxford University Press.
Bourner, T., with Reynolds, A., Hamed, M. and Barnett, R. (1991) *Part-time Students and their Experience of Higher Education*. Buckingham: SRHE and Open University Press.
Braxton, J.M. (2000) *Reworking the Student Departure Puzzle*. Nashville, TN: Vanderbilt University Press.
Brew, A. (1999a) Research and teaching: changing relationships in a changing context, *Studies in Higher Education*, 24(3): 291–301.
Brew, A. (1999b) Towards autonomous assessment: using self-assessment and peer-assessment, in S. Brown and A. Glasner (eds) *Assessment Matters in Higher Education: Choosing and Using Diverse Approaches*. Buckingham: SRHE.
Brookfield, S.D. (1995) *Becoming a Critically Reflective Teacher*. San Francisco: Jossey-Bass.
Brown, J.S. and Duguid, P. (2000) *The Social Life of Information*. Cambridge, MA: Harvard University Press.
Brown, L., Hewitt, D. and Tahta, D. (eds) (1989) *A Gattegno Anthology*. Derby: ATM.
Brown, R. and Kulik, J. (1977) Flashbulb memories, *Cognition*, 5: 73–99.
Brown, S. and Glasner, A. (1999) *Assessment Matters in Higher Education*. Buckingham: SRHE and Open University Press.
Burt, C. ([1937] 1961) *The Backward Child*. London: University of London Press.
Callender, C. (2000) *Changing Student Finances: Income, Expenditure and the Take-up of Student Loans Among Full-time and Part-time Higher Education Students in 1998/9*. London: DfEE.

Cave, M., Hanney, S. and Kogan, M. (1991) *The Use of Performance Indicators in Higher Education: A Critical Analysis of Developing Practice.* London: Jessica Kingsley.
Cawkwell, J. and Pilkington, P. (1994) Rights and representation, in S. Haselgrove (ed.) *The Student Experience.* Buckingham: Open University Press.
Chaiklin, S. and Lave, J. (1993) *Understanding Practice.* Cambridge: Cambridge University Press.
Clarke, J. and Newman, J. (1997) *The Managerial State: Power, Politics and Ideology in the Remaking of Social Welfare.* London: Sage.
Claxton, G. (2000) The anatomy of intuition, in T. Atkinson and G. Claxton (eds) *The Intuitive Practitioner: On the Value of Not Always Knowing What One is Doing.* Buckingham: Open University Press.
Committee of Enquiry into the Academic Validation of Degree Courses in Public Sector Higher Education (1985) *Academic Validation in Public Sector Higher Education,* Cm 9501. London: HMSO.
Committee of Vice-Chancellors and Principals (1985) *Report of the Steering Committee for Efficiency Studies in Universities.* London: CVCP.
Committee on Higher Education (1963) *Higher Education. Report of the Committee appointed by the Prime Minister under the Chairmanship of Lord Robbins 1961–63,* Cm 2154. London: HMSO.
Costa Jr, P.T. and McCrae, R.R. (1991) *NEO-PI-R Professional Manual.* Odessa, F.L.: Psychological Assessment Resources.
Council for National Academic Awards and the Polytechnics and Colleges Funding Council (1990) *The Measurement of Value Added in Higher Education.* London: CNAA and PCFC.
Covington, M.V. (1992) *Making the Grade: a Self-worth Perspective on Motivation and School Reform.* Cambridge: Cambridge University Press.
Covington, M.V. and Omelich, C.L. (1979) Effort: the double-edged sword in school achievement, *Journal of Educational Psychology,* 71(2): 169–82.
Cowan, J. (1998) *On Becoming an Innovative University Teacher: Reflection in Action.* Buckingham: SRHE and Open University Press.
Creme, P. and Lea, M.R. (1999) Student writing: challenging the myths, in P. Thompson (ed.) *Academic Writing Development in Higher Education: Perspectives, Explorations and Approaches.* Reading: Centre for Applied Language Studies, University of Reading.
Cullingford, C. (1997) *Assessment Versus Evaluation.* London: Cassell.
Deem, R. (1998) 'New managerialism' and higher education: the management of performance and cultures in universities in the United Kingdom, *International Studies in Sociology of Education,* 8(1): 47–70.
De Gues, A.P. (1988) Planning as learning, *Harvard Business Review,* March/April: 70–4.
Department for Education and Employment (1997) *Higher Education for the 21st Century: Response to the Dearing Report.* London: DfEE.
Department for Education and Employment (1999) *Learning to Succeed: a New Framework for Post-16 Learning.* London: DfEE.
Department for Education and Employment (2000a) *The Excellence Challenge.* London: DfEE.
Department for Education and Employment (2000b) *Changing Student Finances: Income, Expenditure and the Take-up of Student Loans among Full-time and Part-time Higher Education Students in 1998–99,* research report 33, by Claire Callender and Martin Kemp. London: DfEE.

Department for Education and Employment and Office for Standards in Education (1997) *Departmental Report*, Cm 3610. London: DfEE.
Department of Education and Science (1983) *Degree Courses in the Public Sector of Higher Education: An HMI Commentary*. London: HMSO.
Department of Education and Science (1985) *The Development of Higher Education into the 1990s*, Cm 9524. London: HMSO.
Department of Education and Science (1987) *Higher Education: Meeting the Challenge*, Cm 114. London: HMSO.
Department of Education and Science (1991) *Higher Education: A New Framework*, Cm 1541. London: HMSO.
Donovan, C. (ed.) (2000) *The relationship between research and teaching in higher education: present realities, future possibilities*, report of a seminar jointly organized by Southampton Institute and the Higher Education Funding Council for England, Chilworth Manor, Southampton, 19–20 January. Southampton: Southampton Institute.
Dryden, W. (1996) A rose by any other name: a personal view on the differences among professional titles, *Self and Society*, 24(5): 15–17.
Dweck, C.S. (1991) Self-theories and goals: their role in motivation, personality and development, *Nebraska Symposium on Motivation*, 38, 199–235.
Dweck, C.S. (1999) *Self-theories: Their Role in Motivation, Personality and Development*. Philadelphia, PA: Psychology Press.
Dweck, C.S. (2000) *Self-theories: Their Role in Motivation, Personality and Development*. Lillington, NC: Taylor and Francis.
Ecclestone, K. (1995) *Can N/SVQs be used as a Framework for Academic Staff Development?*, UCoSDA Briefing Paper 22. Sheffield: Universities and Colleges Staff Development Agency.
Eden, D. (1993) Interpersonal expectations in organisations, in P.D. Blanck (ed.) *Interpersonal Expectations: Theory, Research and Applications*. Paris: Cambridge University Press.
Eisner, E.W. (1972) *Educating Artistic Vision*. New York: Macmillan.
Elliot, A.J., McGregor, H.A. and Gable, S. (1999) Achievement goals, study strategies, and exam performance: a mediational analysis, *Journal of Educational Psychology*, 91(3): 549.
Engestrom, Y. (1987) *Learning by Expanding: An Activity Theoretical Approach to Developmental Research*. Helsinki: Orienta-Konsultit.
Entwistle, N. (1981) *Styles of Learning and Teaching – An Integrated Outline of Educational Psychology*. London: John Wiley and Sons.
Entwistle, N. (1984) Contrasting perspectives on learning, in F. Marton, D. Hounsell and N. Entwistle (eds) *The Experience of Learning*. Edinburgh: Scottish Academic Press.
Entwistle, N. (1988) Motivational factors in students' approaches to learning, in R.R. Schmeck (ed.) *Learning Strategies and Learning Styles*. New York: Plenum.
Entwistle, N. (1997) Contrasting perspectives on learning, in F. Marton, D. Hounsell and N. Entwistle (eds) *The Experience of Learning: Implications for Teaching and Studying in Higher Education*, 2nd edn. Edinburgh: Scottish Academic Press.
Echel, Y. and Kurman, J. (1991) Academic self-concept, accuracy of perceived ability and academic attainment, *British Journal of Educational Psychology*, 61(2): 187–96.
Falchikov, N. (1986) Product comparisons and process benefit of collaborative peer group and self-assessments, *Assessment and Evaluation in Higher Education*, 11(2): 146–66.

Fisk, S.T. and Taylor, S.E. (1984). *Social Cognition.* Reading, MA: Addison-Wesley.
Fitzcharles, N. (2001) A report on factors influencing the retention of students in further education, in Scottish Further Education Unit (ed.) *Policy and Practice: Studies in Further Education,* Vol. 3. Edinburgh: SFEU.
Floud, J. and Halsey, A.H. (1957) Intelligence tests, social class and selection for secondary schools, *British Journal of Sociology,* 3(3): 33–9.
Franklyn-Stokes, A. and Newstead, S. (1995) Undergraduate cheating: who does what and why?, *Studies in Higher Education,* 20(2):159–72.
Frannson, A. (1977) On qualitative differences in Learning. IV – Effects of motivation and test anxiety on process and outcome, *British Journal of Educational Psychology,* 47: 244–57.
Freire, P. ([1972] 1996) *Pedagogy of the Oppressed.* London: Penguin.
Fulton, O. (1977) Drop-outs in Great Britain, *Paedagogica Europaea,* xii(3): 13–30.
Further Education Funding Council (1994) *Funding Learning.* Coventry: FEFC.
Further Education Funding Council (1996) *Vocational Higher Education in the Further Education Sector, National Survey Report.* Coventry: FEFC.
Further Education Funding Council (1997) *Learning Works* (Kennedy Report). Coventry: FEFC.
Galloway, D., Rogers, C.G., Armstrong, D. and Leo, E. (1998) *Motivating the Difficult to Teach.* London: Longman.
Geertz, C. (1973) Thick description: towards an interpretive theory of culture, in C. Geertz (ed.) *The Interpretation of Cultures.* New York: Basic Books.
Gibbs, G. (1992) *Teaching More Students,* Developing Teaching Series. Oxford: Polytechnics and Colleges Funding Council Oxford Centre for Staff Development.
Gibbs, P. (2001) Higher education as a market: a problem or solution?, *Studies in Higher Education,* 26(1): 85–94.
Giddens, A. (1979) *Central Problems in Sociological Theory: Action, Structure and Contradiction in Social Analysis.* London: MacMillan.
Gilroy, D. and Miles, T. (1996) *Dyslexia at College,* 2nd edn. London: Routledge.
Glasner, A. (1999) in S. Brown and A. Glasner (eds) Innovations in student assessment: a system-wide perspective, *Assessment Matters in Higher Education.* Buckingham: Society for Research into Higher Education and Open University Press.
Goleman, D. (1996) *Emotional Intelligence.* London: Bloomsbury.
Green, S. and Ollerton, M. (1999) *Mathematical Anxiety amongst Primary QTS Students,* British Society for Research into Learning Mathematics day conference proceedings, June, ISSN no. 1463–6840.
Gronn, P. (1986) Politics, power and the management of schools, in E. Hoyle (ed.) *The World Yearbook of Education 1986: The Management of Schools.* London: Kogan Page.
Hadow Report (1926) *The Education of the Adolescent.* London: HMSO.
Hagar, P. and Butler, J. (1996) Two models of educational assessment, *Assessment and Evaluation in Higher Education,* 21(4): 367–78.
Hargreaves, A. (1994) *Changing Teachers; Changing Times.* London: Cassell.
Harris, R. and Thorp, D. (1999) Language, culture and learning: some missing dimensions to EAP, in H. Bool and P. Lyford (eds) *Academic Standards and Expectations: The Role of EAP.* Nottingham: Nottingham University Press.
Hennessy, P. (1992) *Never Again: Britain 1945–1951.* London: Vintage.
Heron, J. (1998) Assessment revisited, in D. Boud (ed.) *Developing Student Autonomy in Learning,* 2nd edn. London: Kogan Page.

Higgins, R. (2000) 'Be more critical!': rethinking assessment feedback. Paper presented to the British Education Research Association Annual Conference, Cardiff, 7–10 September.

Higher Education Funding Council for England (1996) *Widening Access to Higher Education*, Report 96/9. Bristol: HEFCE.

Higher Education Funding Council for England (1997) *Undergraduate Non-completion in Higher Education in England*, Report 97/29. Bristol: HEFCE.

Higher Education Funding Council for England (1998) *Widening Participation in Higher Education: Funding Proposals*, Report 98/39. Bristol: HEFCE.

Higher Education Funding Council for England (1999a) *Widening Participation in Higher Education, Funding Decisions*, Report 99/24. Bristol: HEFCE.

Higher Education Funding Council for England (1999b) *Learning and Teaching: Strategy and Funding*, Report 99/26. Bristol: Higher Education Funding Council for England.

Higher Education Funding Council for England (1999c) *Performance Indicators in Higher Education, 1996–97, 1997–98*. Bristol: Higher Education Funding Council for England.

Higher Education Funding Council for England (2000) *Performance Indicators in Higher Education in the UK, 1997–98, 1998–99*, Report 00/40. Bristol: HEFCE.

Hinett, K. (1997) Towards meaningful learning: a theory for improved assessment in higher education. Unpublished PhD thesis, University of Central Lancashire.

Hinett, K. and Thomas, J. (eds) (1999) *Staff Guide to Self- and Peer-Assessment*. Oxford: Oxford Centre for Staff and Learning Development.

Hollis, P. (1997) *Jennie Lee: A Life*. Oxford: Oxford University Press.

Holt, J. (1974) *How Children Fail*. Harmondsworth, Middlesex: Penguin Books.

Ilott, I. and Murphy, R. (1999) *Success and Failure in Professional Education: Assessing the Evidence*. London: Whurr Publications.

Independent Committee of Inquiry into Student Finance (1999) *Student Finance: Fairness for the Future*. Edinburgh: ICISF.

Institute for Learning and Teaching Planning Group (1998) *Implementing the Vision*. London: CVCP.

Institute for Learning and Teaching Planning Group (1999) *The National Framework for Higher Education Teaching*. London: CVCP.

Ivanic, R. (1998) *Writing and Identity: The Discoursal Construction of Identity in Academic Writing*. Amsterdam: John Benjamins.

Jackson, B. and Marsden, D. (1966) *Education and the Working Class*. London: Pelican.

James, D. (1995) Mature studentship in higher education. Unpublished Ph D thesis, University of the West of England.

James, D. (2000) Making the graduate: perspectives on student experience of assessment in higher education, in A. Filer (ed.) *Assessment: Social Practice and Social Product*. London: Routledge/Falmer.

James, W. (1950) *The Principles of Psychology*. New York: Dover.

Jones, E.E., Kanouse, D.E., Kelley, H.H. et al. (1972) *Attribution: Perceiving the Causes of Behaviour*. Morristown, NJ: General Learning Press.

Kelly, G. (1955) *The Psychology of Personal Constructs*, Vols I and II. New York: Norton.

Kember, D. (1995) *Open Learning Courses for Adults: A Model of Student Progress*. Englewood Cliffs, NJ: Educational Technology Publications.

Kemmis, S. (1993) Action research, in M. Hammersley (ed.) *Educational Research: Current Issues*. London: Chapman.

Kenwright, H. (1996) *Developing Retention Strategies: Did they Fall or Were they Pushed?* York: York College of Further and Higher Education.

Kilhstrom, J. (1995) Exhumed memory, in S.J. Lynn (ed.) *Truth in Memory*. New York: Guildford Press.

Kneale, P. (1996) Informal presentation at the Motivation Conundrum Conference, University of Central Lancashire.

Knight, P. (1995) *Assessment for Learning in Higher Education*. London: Kogan Page and the Staff and Education Development Association.

Knight, P. and Trowler, P. (2000) Departmental-level cultures and the improvement of learning and teaching, *Studies in Higher Education*, 25(1): 69–83.

Lazarus, R.S. (1983) *The Costs and Benefits of Denial*. Monogram. New York: International Universities Press.

Lillis, T. (1997) New voices in academia? The regulative nature of academic writing conventions, *Language in Education*, 11(3).

McDowell, L. (1995) The impact of innovative assessment on student learning, *Journal of Innovations in Education and Training International*, 32(3): 302–13.

McDowell, L. and Sambell, K. (1998) The construction of the hidden curriculum: messages and meaning in the assessment of student learning, *Assessment and Evaluation in Higher Education*, 23(4): 391–402.

McDowell, L. and Sambell, K. (1999) Fitness for purpose in the assessment of student learning: students as stakeholders, *Quality in Higher Education*, 5(2): 107–23.

McGivney, V. (1996) *Staying or Leaving the Course. Non-Completion and Retention of Mature Students in Further and Higher Education*. Leicester: NIACE.

McInnis, C. and James, R., with McNaught, C. (1995) *First Year on Campus: Diversity in the Initial Experiences of Australian Undergraduates*. Melbourne: Centre for the Study of Higher Education, University of Melbourne.

Mallenson, N. (1972) Student wastage in the UK, in H.J. Butcher and E. Rudd (eds) *Contemporary Problems in Higher Education: An Account of Research*. Maidenhead: McGraw Hill.

Mann, S. (2001) Alternative perspectives on the student experience: alienation and engagement, *Studies in Higher Education*, 26(1): 7–19.

Martinez, P. (1995) *Student Retention in Further and Adult Education: The Evidence*. Blagdon: FEDA.

Martinez, P. (1996) *Student Retention: Case Studies of Strategies that Work*. Blagdon: FEDA.

Martinez, P. (1997) *Improving Student Retention: A Guide to Successful Strategies*. Blagdon: FEDA.

Martinez, P. and Munday, F. (1998) *9000 Voices: Student Persistence and Drop-out in Further Education*. Blagdon: FEDA.

Marton, F., Hounsell, D. and Entwistle, N. (1984) *The Experience of Learning: Implications for Teaching and Studying in Higher Education*. Edinburgh: Scottish Academic Press.

Marton, F., Hounsell, D. and Entwistle, N. (1997) *The Experience of Learning: Implications for Teaching and Studying in Higher Education* (2nd edn). Edinburgh: Scottish Academic Press.

Marton, F. and Saljo, R. (1976) On qualitative differences in learning – II Outcome as function of the learner's conception of the task, *The British Journal of Educational Psychology*, 46: 115–27.

Mason, J. (1987) *Only awareness is educable, Mathematics Teaching*, 120, Journal of the Association of Teachers of Mathematics.

Mason, J., with Burton, L. and Stacey, K. (1982) *Thinking Mathematically.* Reading, MA: Addison Wesley.

Mearns, D. (1990) The counsellor's experience of failure, in D. Mearns and W. Dryden (eds) *Experiences of Counselling in Action.* London: Sage.

Mentowski, M. and Associates (2000) *Learning that Lasts: Integrating Learning, Development, and Performance in College and Beyond.* San Francisco, C.A.: Jossey-Bass.

Miller, C.M.L. and Parlett, M. (1974) *Up to the Mark: A Study of the Examinations Game.* Monograph 21. London: Society for Research into Higher Education.

Miller, G.W. (1970) *Success, Failure and Wastage in Higher Education.* London: George G. Harrap.

Ministry of Education (1966) *A Plan for Polytechnics and Other Colleges.* London: HMSO.

Modood, T. and Acland, T. (1998) *Race and Higher Education.* London: Policy Studies Institute.

Moon, J. (1999) How to stop students from cheating, *The Times Higher Education Supplement,* September.

Morley, L. (2000) Quality and equality in lifelong learning: intersections and collisions, in A. Hodgson (ed.) *Policies, Politics and the Future of Lifelong Learning.* London: Kogan Page.

National Committee of Inquiry into Higher Education (1997a) *Higher Education in the Learning Society, Main Report.* London: NCIHE.

National Committee of Inquiry into Higher Education (1997b) *Higher Education in the Learning Society, Report of the Scottish Committee.* London: NCIHE.

Newsome, A., Thorne, B. and Wyld, K. (1973) *Student Counselling in Practice.* London: University of London Press.

Nias, J. (1993) Primary teachers talking: a reflexive account of longitudinal research, in M. Hammersley (ed.) *Educational Research: Current Issues.* London: Chapman.

Nicholls, J.G. (1989) *The Competitive Ethos and Democratic Education.* London: Harvard University Press.

Nolen, S. (1996) Why study – how reasons for learning influence strategy selection, *Educational Psychology Review,* 8(4): 335–55.

Norwood Report (1943) *Curriculum and Examinations in Secondary Schools.* Report of the Committee of the Secondary School Examinations Council. London: HMSO.

Oakes, J., Wells, A.M., Yonezawa, S. and Ray, K. (2000) Change agentry and the quest for equity: lessons from detracking schools, in N. Bascia and A. Hargreaves (eds) *The Sharp Edge of Educational Change.* London: Routledge/Falmer.

Open University (1999) *Supporting Open Learners Pack.* Milton Keynes: The Open University.

Open University Planning Office (2000) *Plans for Change: The University's Strategic and Development Plans, 2000–2010.* Milton Keynes: The Open University.

Orr, S. (2000) Lecturers' conceptions of literacy in post-sixteen education, *College Research,* 3(3).

Orr, S. and Blythman, M. (2000) *Have you got ten minutes? Can you just sort my dissertation?* Proceedings of the 6th Annual Writing Development in Higher Education Annual Conference 1999. Leicester: WDHE.

Parry, G. (1999) Education research and policy making in higher education: the case of Dearing, *Journal of Education Policy,* 14(3): 225–41.

Partington, J. (1995) *Assessment Processes and Personal Judgement in Higher Education – A Discussion Paper.* Sheffield: CVCP.

Peelo, M. (1977) Problems of Transition from School to University. Unpublished MPhil thesis, University of Edinburgh.

Peelo, M. (1994) *Helping Students With Study Problems.* Buckingham: Open University Press.

Peelo, M. (2000a) Learning reality: inner and outer journeys, *Changes,* Summer, 18(2): 118–27.

Peelo, M. (2000b) Learning support: counselling or teaching?, *Association of University & College Counsellors Journal & Newsletter,* November, 4: 8–10.

Peelo, M. and Wareham, T. (1999) How to help students who fail exams, *Times Higher Education Supplement,* 9 July.

Phillips, D.C. (1993) Subjectivity and objectivity: an objective inquiry, in M. Hammersley (ed.) *Educational Research: Current Issues.* London: Chapman.

Pillemer, D.B., Rinehart, E.D. and White, S.H. (1986) Memories of life transitional: the first year in college, *Human Learning,* 5: 109–23.

Pintrich, P. and Garcia, T. (1996) Assessing students' motivation and learning strategies in the classroom context: the motivated strategies for learning questionnaire, in M. Birenbaum and J. Dochy (eds) *Alternatives in Assessment of Achievements, Learning Processes and Prior Knowledge.* Boston, MA: Kluwer Academic Publishers.

Pintrich, P.R. and Schunk, D.H. (1996) *Motivation in Education: Theory, Research and Application.* Columbus, OH: Prentice Hall.

Prosser, M. and Trigwell, K. (1999) *Understanding Learning and Teaching: The Experience in Higher Education.* Buckingham: SRHE and Open University Press.

Qualitative Consultancy (1997) *Evening Advice Line Research: Final Report.* Milton Keynes: The Open University.

Quality Assurance Agency for Higher Education (1999) *Students with Disabilities.* Code of Practice for the assurance of academic quality and standards in higher education, Section 3. Gloucester: QAA.

Ramsden, P. (1991) A performance indicator of teaching quality in higher education: the course experience questionnaire, *Studies in Higher Education,* Vol. 16, 2(91): 129–50.

Ramsden, P. (1992) *Learning to Teach in Higher Education.* London: Routledge.

Ramsden, P. (1997) The context of learning in academic departments, in F. Marton, D. Hounsell and N. Entwistle (eds) *The Experience of Learning,* 2nd edn. Edinburgh: Scottish Academic Press.

Randall, J. (1997) Progress on the Dearing quality agenda, *Higher Quality,* 2. www.qaa.ac.uk.

Ratigan, B. (1989) Counselling in higher education, in W. Dryden, D. Charles-Edwards and R. Woolfe (eds) *Handbook of Individual Therapy.* London: Tavistock/ Routledge.

Rickinson, B. (1998) The relationship between undergraduate student counselling and successful degree completion, *Studies in Higher Education,* 23(1): 95–102.

Roberts, G.L. and Webb, W. (1980) Factors affecting drop-out, *Adult Education,* 53(2).

Robinson, J.A. (1980) Affect and retrieval of personal memories, *Motivation and Emotion,* 4, 149–74.

Rogers, C. (1983) *Freedom to learn for the 80s.* Columbus, OH: Bell and Howell.

Rogers, C.G., Galloway, D., Armstrong, D., Jackson, C. and Leo, E. (1994) Changes in motivational style over the transfer from primary to secondary school: subject and dispositional effects, *Educational and Child Psychology,* 11(2): 26–38.

Rowntree, D. (1987) *Assessing Students: How Shall we Know Them?,* London: Kogan Page.

Russell, R. (1993) *Report on Effective Psychotherapy: Legislative Testimony.* Lake Placid, NY: Hilgarth Press.

Rust, C. and Gibbs, G. (1997) *Improving Student Learning through Course Design.* Oxford: Oxford Centre for Learning and Staff Development.

Ryan, R.M., Sheldon, K.M., Kasser, T. and Deci, E.L. (1996) All goals are not created equal: an organismic perspective on the nature of goals and their regulation, in P.M. Gollwitzer and J.A. Bargh (eds) *The Psychology of Action: Linking Cognition and Motivation to Behaviour.* New York: Guilford Press.

Ryle, A. (1969) *Student Casualties.* London: Pelican.

Ryle, G. (1949) *The Concept of Mind.* London: Hutchinson.

Sadler, R. (1989) Formative assessment and the design of instructional systems, *Instructional Science,* 18: 119–44.

Schön, D.A. (1983) *The Reflective Practitioner.* New York: Basic Books.

Schön, D.A. (1987) *Educating the Reflective Practitioner.* San Francisco: Jossey-Bass.

Schunk, D.H. and Zimmerman, B.J. (eds) (1998) *Self-regulated Learning: From Teaching to Self-reflective Practice.* London: Guilford Press.

Scottish Office (1998) *Higher Education for the 21st Century, Response to the Garrick Report.* Edinburgh: SOEID.

Secretary of State for Education and Employment (2000) Funding Letter to the Higher Education Funding Council for England, 29 November.

Select Committee on Education and Employment (2001a) *Higher Education: Student Retention,* Sixth Report. London: House of Commons.

Select Committee on Education and Employment (2001b) *Higher Education: Access,* Fourth Report. London: House of Commons.

Seymour, E. and Hewitt, N.M. (1997) *Talking about Leaving: Why Undergraduates Leave the Sciences.* Oxford: Westview Press.

Skidmore, D. (1999) The discourse of learning difficulties and the condition of school development, *Educational Review,* 51(1).

Small, J.J. (1966) *Achievement and Adjustment in the First Year at University.* New Zealand Council for Educational Wellington Research: New Zealand.

Smith, D.M. and Saunders, M.R. (1991) *Other Routes: Part-time Higher Education Policy.* Buckingham: SRHE and Open University Press.

Snyder, B.R. (1971) *The Hidden Curriculum.* New York: Knopf.

Sotto, E. (1994) *When Teaching becomes Learning: A Theory and Practice of Teaching.* London: Cassell.

Spens Report (1938) *Report of the Consultative Committee to the Board of Education on Secondary Education.* London: HMSO.

Spielberger, C. and Sarason, I. (eds) (1975) *Stress and Anxiety,* Vol. 1. Washington, DC: Hemisphere Publishing Corporation.

Sporing, M. (2001) Benefits for all, *AUTLOOK,* January.

Stefani, L. (1994) Peer, self and tutor assessment: relative reliabilities, *Studies in Higher Education,* 19(1): 69–75.

Stefani, L. (1999) Pragmatism, Plagiarism and Pedagogy. Paper presented at the Institute for Learning and Teaching seminar on assessment, Bristol, 15 November.

Stephenson, J. and Yorke, M. (1998) Creating the conditions for the development of capability, *Capability and Quality in Higher Education,* pp. 193–225. London: Kogan Page.

Thorne, B. (1985) Guidance and counselling in further and higher education, *British Journal of Counselling,* 3(1): 22–34.

Thorne, B. (1999) Psychotherapy and counselling are indistinguishable, in C. Feltham (ed.) *Controversies in Psychotherapy and Counselling*. London: Sage.
Tight, M. (1991) *Higher Education: A Part-time Perspective*. Buckingham: SRHE and Open University Press.
Tinto, V. (1993) *Leaving College: Rethinking the Causes and Cures of Student Attrition*, 2nd edn. Chicago, IL: University of Chicago Press.
Tinto, V. (1997) Classrooms as communities: exploring the educational character of student persistence, *Journal of Higher Education*, 68: 599–623.
Trigwell, K. and Prosser, M. (1991) Relating approaches to study and the quality of learning outcomes at the course level, *British Journal of Educational Psychology*, 61.
Trow, M. (1972) *The Expansion and Transformation of Higher Education*. Berkeley: General Learning Corporation.
Trowler, P. (1998) *Academics Responding to Change: New Higher Education Frameworks and Academic Cultures*. Buckingham: SRHE and Open University Press.
Trowler, P. and Knight, P. (1999) Organizational socialization and induction in universities: reconceptualizing theory and practice, *Higher Education*, 37: 177–95.
Trowler, P.R. and Knight, P.T. (2000) 'Coming to know' in higher education: theorising faculty entry to new work contexts, *Higher Education Research and Development*, 19(1): 27–42.
Tschannen-Moran, M., Woolfolk Hoy, A. and Hoy, W.K. (1998) Teacher efficacy: its meaning and measure, *Review of Educational Research*, 68(2): 202–48.
Turner, J. (1999) Academic writing development in higher education: changing the discourse, in P. Thompson (ed.) *Academic Writing Development in Higher Education: Perspectives, Explorations and Approaches*. Reading: Centre for Applied Language Studies, University of Reading.
Tversky, A. and Kahneman, D. (1981) The framing of decisions and the psychology of choice, *Science*, 211, 145–58.
Universities UK (2001) *New Directions for Higher Education*, the final report of the funding options review group. London: Universities UK.
University Grants Committee (1968) *Enquiry into Student Progress*. London: HMSO.
Wankowski, J. (1991) Success and failure at university, in K. Raaheim, J. Wankowski and J. Radford (eds) *Helping Students to Learn: Teaching, Counselling, Research*. Buckingham: SRHE and Open University Press.
Watson, D. and Taylor, R. (1998) *Lifelong Learning and the University: A Post-Dearing Agenda*. London: Falmer.
Weiner, B. (1982) in M. Clarke and S. Fiske (eds) The emotional consequences of causal attributions, *Affect and Cognition: The Seventeenth Annual Carnegie Symposium on Cognition*, 185–209. Hillsdale, NJ: Lawrence Erlbaum Associates.
Weiner, B. (1986) *An Attributional Theory of Motivation and Emotion*. New York: Springer-Verlag.
Weiner, B. (1992) *Human Motivation: Metaphors, Theories and Research*. London: Sage.
Weiner, B. (2000) Intrapersonal and interpersonal theories of motivation from an attributional perspective, *Educational Psychology Review*, 12(1), 1.
Wenger, E. (2000) Communities of practice and social learning systems, *Organization*, 7(2): 225–46.
Wheeler, S. and Birtle, J. (1993) *A Handbook for Personal Tutors*. Milton Keynes: SRHE and Open University Press.
Wilson, H. (1971) *The Labour Government 1964–70: A Personal Record*. London: Penguin.
Wolfendale, S. and Corbett, J. (1996) *Opening Doors: Learning Support in Higher Education*. London: Cassell.

Yorke, M. (1999a) *Getting it Right First Time.* Cheltenham: Universities and Colleges Admissions Service.

Yorke, M. (1999b) *Leaving Early: Undergraduate Non-completion in Higher Education.* London: Falmer Press.

Yorke, M. (2000) A cloistered virtue? Pedagogical research and policy in UK higher education, *Higher Education Quarterly,* 54(2): 106–26.

Yorke, M. (2001) Telling it as it is? Massification, performance indicators and the press, *Tertiary Education and Management,* 7(1): 57–68.

Yorke, M., with Bell, R., Dove, A. et al. (1997) *Undergraduate Non-completion in England,* Report 1, in *Undergraduate Non-completion in Higher Education in England,* Research Report 97/29. Bristol: Higher Education Funding Council for England.

Zimmerman, B.J. (1998) Developing self-fulfilling cycles of academic regulation: an analysis of exemplary instructional models, in D.H. Schunk and B.J. Zimmerman (eds) *Self-regulated Learning: From Teaching to Self-reflective Practice.* London: Guilford Press.

Index

The Society for Research into Higher Education

The Society for Research into Higher Education (SRHE) exists to stimulate and coordinate research into all aspects of higher education. It aims to improve the quality of higher education through the encouragement of debate and publication on issues of policy, on the organization and management of higher education institutions, and on the curriculum, teaching and learning methods.

The Society is entirely independent and receives no subsidies, although individual events often receive sponsorship from business or industry. The Society is financed through corporate and individual subscriptions and has members from many parts of the world.

Under the imprint *SRHE & Open University Press*, the Society is a specialist publisher of research, having over 80 titles in print. In addition to *SRHE News*, the Society's newsletter, the Society publishes three journals: *Studies in Higher Education* (three issues a year), *Higher Education Quarterly* and *Research into Higher Education Abstracts* (three issues a year).

The Society runs frequent conferences, consultations, seminars and other events. The annual conference in December is organized at and with a higher education institution. There are a growing number of networks which focus on particular areas of interest, including:

Access
Assessment
Consultants
Curriculum Development
Eastern European
Educational Development Research
FE/HE
Funding
Graduate Employment
Learning Environment
Legal Education
Managing Innovation
New Technology for Learning
Postgraduate Issues
Quantitative Studies
Student Development
Vocation at Qualification

Benefits to members

Individual

- The opportunity to participate in the Society's networks
- Reduced rates for the annual conferences

- Free copies of *Research into Higher Education Abstracts*
- Reduced rates for *Studies in Higher Education*
- Reduced rates for *Higher Education Quarterly*
- Free copy of *Register of Members' Research Interests* – includes valuable reference material on research being pursued by the Society's members
- Free copy of occasional in-house publications, e.g. *The Thirtieth Anniversary Seminars Presented by the Vice-Presidents*
- Free copies of *SRHE News* which informs members of the Society's activities and provides a calendar of events, with additional material provided in regular mailings
- A 35 per cent discount on all SRHE/Open University Press books
- Access to HESA statistics for student members
- The opportunity for you to apply for the annual research grants
- Inclusion of your research in the *Register of Members' Research Interests*

Corporate

- Reduced rates for the annual conferences
- The opportunity for members of the Institution to attend SRHE's network events at reduced rates
- Free copies of *Research into Higher Education Abstracts*
- Free copies of *Studies in Higher Education*
- Free copies of *Register of Members' Research Interests* – includes valuable reference material on research being pursued by the Society's members
- Free copy of occasional in-house publications
- Free copies of *SRHE News*
- A 35 per cent discount on all SRHE/Open University Press books
- Access to HESA statistics for research for students of the Institution
- The opportunity for members of the Institution to submit applications for the Society's research grants
- The opportunity to work with the Society and co-host conferences
- The opportunity to include in the *Register of Members' Research Interests* your Institution's research into aspects of higher education

Membership details: SRHE, 3 Devonshire Street, London W1N 2BA, UK Tel: 020 7637 2766. Fax: 020 7637 2781.
email: srhe@mailbox.ulcc.ac.uk
world wide web: http//www.srhe.ac.uk./srhe/
Catalogue: SRHE & Open University Press, Celtic Court, 22 Ballmoor, Buckingham MK18 1XW. Tel: 01280 823388. Fax: 01280 823233. email: enquiries@openup.co.uk